The NFL Off-Camera

The NFL Off-Camera

An **A–Z Guide** to the League's Most Memorable Players and Personalities

Bob Angelo

Foreword by Ray Didinger

TEMPLE UNIVERSITY PRESS
Philadelphia • Rome • Tokyo

TEMPLE UNIVERSITY PRESS
Philadelphia, Pennsylvania 19122
tupress.temple.edu

Published 2023

Library of Congress Cataloging-in-Publication Data

Names: Angelo, Bob, 1953– author. | Didinger, Ray, writer of foreword.
Title: The NFL off-camera : an a-z guide to the league's most memorable players and personalities / Bob Angelo ; foreword by Ray Didinger.
Description: Philadelphia : Temple University Press, 2023. | Summary: "In this book, the author shares stories from his 40 years working for NFL Films to reveal new insights into the players, coaches, owners, and media members he met. Stories are organized into alphabetical entries by the name of the person who serves as the story's subject"— Provided by publisher.
Identifiers: LCCN 2022040343 (print) | LCCN 2022040344 (ebook) | ISBN 9781439923672 (cloth) | ISBN 9781439923696 (pdf)
Subjects: LCSH: Angelo, Bob, 1953—Anecdotes. | NFL Films—Anecdotes. | National Football League—Anecdotes. | Football—United States—Anecdotes. | Football players—United States—Anecdotes. | Sportscasters—United States—Anecdotes. | LCGFT: Anecdotes.
Classification: LCC GV950.5 .A64 2023 (print) | LCC GV950.5 (ebook) | DDC 796.332/6406—dc23/eng/20230110
LC record available at https://lccn.loc.gov/2022040343
LC ebook record available at https://lccn.loc.gov/2022040344

♾ The paper used in this publication meets the requirements of the American National Standard for Information Sciences—Permanence of Paper for Printed Library Materials, ANSI Z39.48–1992

Printed in the United States of America

9 8 7 6 5 4 3 2 1

Table of Contents

Pro Football Hall of Famer

Super Bowl Champion

Pete Rozelle Radio-Television Award winner

C

D

E

F

G

H

P

Q

R

S

T

U

V

W

X

Y

Z

Foreword

Ray Didinger

Football coaches have a term for it—triple threat.

It means a player who can win games by running with the football, passing the football, and kicking the football. Washington's Sammy Baugh was a triple threat in the 1940s. Doak Walker was a triple threat for Detroit in the 1950s. Paul Hornung was that player for Vince Lombardi's Green Bay Packers.

Bob Angelo was a triple threat for NFL Films, the cinematic juggernaut created by Ed and Steve Sabol, the film studio that changed sports television forever and helped make pro football America's game. Bob was there for forty-three years and collected enough Emmys to fill a warehouse, but it is the memories he cherishes most.

That's what this book is about—those memories. The games, the players, the coaches, the reflections across four decades spent filming, interviewing, and profiling the likes of Tom Brady, Peyton Manning, John Elway, and Jim Brown. Bob was up close and personal with all of them.

He was close enough to hear Brett Favre groaning in pain on the bench. He was close enough to see the tears of joy in Lyle Alzado's eyes when he celebrated his first Super Bowl victory. He was close enough to hear the chilly exchange between coach Chuck Noll and quarterback Terry Bradshaw when Noll snapped, "What play was that?" and Bradshaw shot back, "Touchdown."

Bob lived inside the game for all those years, a camera perched on his shoulder, capturing that emotion. When he traveled with his NFL Films gear, people in airports and hotel lobbies often asked what it was like to be on the sidelines, to be that close to the action. In this book, he takes you there.

It is not all smiles and hearty handshakes. Pro football is like any other business—it has its bullies and bad actors, and Bob encountered his share. He brings those stories to the book as well. When he talks about a sneering Norm Van Brocklin asking, "Did you ever play football?" it has the ring of truth. Our heroes aren't always what they seem.

I was a newspaper columnist before I joined NFL Films as a producer in 1996. Bob was one of the first people I met on the job. I had seen his name in the credits of countless NFL Films productions. He welcomed me and said, "If I can ever help you out, just let me know." I knocked on his door on many occasions.

Bob was one of Team Sabol's most valuable players. He was both a cameraman and a senior producer. He shot games on Sunday and then flew home and was back in the office Monday, hunched over an editing machine, cutting a show, writing a script, going to meetings, and doing all the things producers do.

In the cafeteria, some producers sat around discussing movies and TV shows—this was a film company, after all. Bob was all football. He grew up in western Pennsylvania, playing on the same dusty fields that produced Joe Namath, Joe Montana, and Dan Marino. Bob loved the Steelers, he loved Penn State (he once took a phys-ed class with Franco Harris), but most of all, he loved the game.

There was never a more perfect marriage than Bob Angelo and NFL Films. This book—warm, insightful, funny, and heartfelt—makes that clear.

Bob was a high school quarterback, so he knew the game from the inside. He was the perfect sideline cameraman because he anticipated where the good sound would be. He would see a player come off the field, see the look on his face, and know immediately, "I'm following this guy to the bench." That's how he captured classic moments like Denver's Shannon Sharpe grabbing the sideline telephone and shouting, "We need the National Guard. We need as many men as you can spare because we're killing the Patriots."

He hung up the phone and announced, "They're coming. Help is on the way."

If there is a sound bite Hall of Fame, Sharpe is in it, thanks to Bob.

When NFL Films launched the *Hard Knocks* series on HBO in 2001, Steve Sabol wisely put Bob in charge. It was the first sports-based reality show, a video diary of an NFL training camp, which meant a delicate balancing act between the team—the defending Super Bowl champion Baltimore Ravens—and the film crew who would be recording every practice, every meeting, every minute of a long, hot summer. How can you make that work?

Bob found a way, coming to an understanding with coach Brian Billick about where the cameras could go, what was fair game, and what was off limits. As it turned out, very little was off limits—at one point, Billick actually lobbied for *more* profanity. The result was a highly-acclaimed debut for a television series that still appears annually in various incarnations on HBO.

Bob retired in 2018 after more than eight hundred games and countless miles of priceless footage. I was frankly surprised that at the next Super Bowl, just before kickoff, the referee didn't look around and say, "Hey, where's Angelo?" He was that much a part of the scene.

When Bob finally had a chance to step away and consider his career, he realized what appeared on the screen all those years was only part of the story. He felt a need to tell the rest, so he sat down and wrote this book. Now, he can tell us about asking Johnny Unitas for his autograph, getting teary-eyed when his Steelers lost in Super Bowl XXX (30), and smiling when George Halas, the legendary "Papa Bear," told him, "You don't look Italian."

Steve Sabol once famously said, "Life is great; football is better."

When you read Bob's book, you'll understand.

The NFL Off-Camera

Introduction

Bob Angelo *(born 1953)*

Producer, Director, Writer, Editor, Cameraman, Football Fan

I spent my entire professional career at NFL Films. I did thousands of interviews with players, coaches, owners, and team executives. Over forty-three football seasons, I worked with just about every NFL broadcaster or commentator of note. I shot more than 850 NFL games and forty Super Bowls. I've heard things that most people haven't, been places most people aren't allowed to go, and experienced things most people will never see. Needless to say, I have stories!

My favorites are in this book.

On June 6, 1975, at 1:35 P.M., Ed Sabol, the founder and executive producer of NFL Films—based on his son Steve Sabol's recommendation—offered me a production job. I accepted it on the spot. By the time the NFL season began, I was editing and writing segments for NFL Films's weekly highlight shows. Soon, I was added to the field production roster, which meant working with network TV commentators on nationally televised pregame and halftime pieces (in particular, CBS's *The NFL Today* and NBC's *GrandStand*). By my third season, 1977, I started shooting a hand-held film camera on the sidelines of NFL games. And so it went for the next four-plus decades.

Along the way, I produced enough quality work to collect twenty-one Emmy Awards and create some enduring legacies. One particular project I pioneered lives on: *Hard Knocks* on HBO Sports. I retired on February 16, 2018—just four months shy of forty-four full years in the business.

I abandoned this book more than once. I told myself that nobody truly cared about an NFL Films producer's *memoirs*. The word itself sounded pretentious. And who the hell was I anyway? Then, one night during COVID-19 hibernation, a friend of the family said, "Robert, these stories have *value*!" Suddenly, I had a brand-new outlook and the resolute determination to finish what I'd started.

This book is designed to be read in short installments. No story exceeds three pages, and all can be read in a few minutes. Even if you suffer from a short attention span, you will learn things that will amuse or inspire or anger you about pro football people from someone who sat in their presence and questioned them, who worked among them in games, at practices, and in their homes for more than four decades. My objective is to reveal, in a quick read, new and unseen aspects of familiar NFL names. My "Random Access" Table of Contents takes you to your favorites. You can read a story before bed. Or during a commercial break. Or while you're taking care of business in the bathroom—before the *paperwork*.

I have written only about people with whom I had *personal* interactions. When I could quote a subject directly, I did. Where I paraphrased from memory, I did my best and indicated that in the text. *Nothing* in this book is made up to embellish a story. I depict my subjects just as I remember them: some good, many amusing or complicated or problematic, and a handful—pretty damned despicable. Football players and coaches, at the end of the day, although exceptional by their occupation, are *still* people. Some are decent, and some struggle to be. All make their mark. Cameras can only capture so much. This book is my attempt to reveal more.

So, take this book to your bathroom and get started.

Jared Allen *(born 1982)*

Defensive End

- Kansas City Chiefs (2004-07) ▪ Minnesota Vikings (2008-13)
- Chicago Bears (2014-15) ▪ Carolina Panthers (2015)

After four-plus decades of observing, filming, and studying great NFL pass rushers, I've reached the following conclusion:

The greatest pass rushers are *not* created in weight rooms. They are *not* created on practice fields. Strength and technique can only accomplish so much. How about height, weight, and wingspan? How about not! Hall of Famer John Randle and future Hall of Famer Aaron Donald are both just six feet one inch tall with relatively short arms. Larger men either can't get to the QB regularly or simply run out of gas along the way. I acknowledge some exceptions, but here's my bottom line:

Great pass rushers are born that way! "Want to" and "Will do" coarse through their veins. They smell blood in the water. My long-time acquaintance Jared Allen was such a guy.

At less than 260 pounds, Allen was much smaller than the tackles he lined up against. He once remarked to me, "Your arms are bigger than mine!" He was exaggerating, but I appreciated the notice. He looked more like a small forward on a college basketball team. Cleveland offensive tackle and future Hall of Famer Joe Thomas said about him, "At the top of the pocket, when he started to turn the corner, all of a sudden you would lose him. You thought you had your hands on him . . . and then you didn't. . . . He was a little unorthodox . . . and he was slippery."

The Kansas City Chiefs selected Allen in the fourth round (126th overall) of the 2004 NFL Draft. In his senior year at Idaho State (a 1-AA college in the Big Sky Conference), he recorded 17.5 sacks and led his team to an 8–4 finish, the first time the school ever posted back-to-back eight-win seasons. In Kansas City, Allen earned the league minimum salary in each of his first three seasons. In 2007, his 15.5 sacks led the NFL and earned him All-Pro honors. It prompted the Chiefs to place a franchise tag on him, which elevated his 2008 base salary to $8.8 million.

That's when Minnesota entered the picture. The Vikings sent KC a basket full of draft picks, then signed Allen to a multi-million-dollar six-year contract, the largest ever for a defensive player at the time. Over those half dozen seasons, Allen recorded 85.5 sacks, including 22 in 2011, just a half sack shy of Michael Strahan and T. J. Watt's single-season record of 22.5.

I got to know Jared by sticking my wide-angle lens in his face during pregame warm-ups. Before the 2008 postseason, he declared, "Playoff football, man. . . . You gotta have a mullet and a Fu Manchu." He fluffed the hair hanging out of his helmet, then got on with his business. In a later interview, Allen remarked, "The mullet isn't just a hairdo, it's a lifestyle. . . . I might cut it at some point . . . when I die!"

Yet for all his bravado, Allen didn't mangle quarterbacks. He wrangled them down, then immediately transitioned into his signature "Rope a Steer" celebration. At one-per-sack, he performed at least 136 of them over his twelve-year career, making him twelfth on the all-time sack-leader board. He also forced 36 fumbles, recorded 4 safeties, and scored 4 touchdowns—2 as a receiver and 2 more on defensive turnovers. Rumor has it, he also could have made an NFL roster as a long-snapper.

We cemented our relationship in London. The Vikings (0–3) were scheduled to play the Steelers (0–3) at Wembley Stadium on September 29, 2013. The Discovery Channel had contracted NFL Films to produce a ninety-minute, behind-the-scenes special called *NFL in Season.* Two full production teams were dispatched: one to Pittsburgh, and the other to the Grove Hotel/Resort in the historic old town of Watford, England. That's where the Vikings stayed. I drew the overseas assignment.

On our first day there, Allen joined Vikings quarterback Matt Cassel on the golf course. Cassel birdied the second hole. Allen played in flip-flops and struck his ball much farther than Cassel, but more often. Later that evening, my Minnesota-based soundman Paul Dahlseid and I walked to the complex's pub and sat down for a few glasses of ale. Allen showed up with a pair of teammates, acknowledged our presence, then sat at an adjacent table. When his peeps departed early, Jared politely asked, "OK if I hang out with you guys?"

Soon, we were discussing ultimate matters. I learned that Allen was a practicing Christian who believed that Earth was created by God about six thousand years ago. He learned that I had a philosophy degree and was writing a book on human subjectivity (self-published in 2014). We agreed to disagree on the whole Adam and Eve, Garden of Eden thing.

Eventually, our conversation turned to Sunday's game against the Steelers, at which time, Allen offered this prediction: "Their left tackle can't handle me. . . . I'm gonna have a day." This man was a born pass rusher, so I believed him. At precisely three minutes before midnight, Allen drained his final drink, then walked down the lane toward his dorm, just in time to make curfew.

As foretold, on Sunday, Allen recorded four quarterback hits and recorded 2.5 sacks against Big Ben Roethlisberger. On Pittsburgh's final possession, with his team clinging to a 7-point lead, Allen forced Big Ben to fumble, which the Vikes recovered just 11 yards shy of a game-tying touchdown. Game over. Final score: Vikings 34–Steelers 27. Allen wanted to—and so he did.

At season's end, Allen and the Vikings parted company. In Chicago in 2014, pneumonia ended Allen's consecutive game streak that dated back to September 2007. It also affected Allen's God-given pass-rushing skills. In 2015, the Bears switched to a 3–4 defense and converted Allen to an outside linebacker. He played there just three weeks before Chicago traded him to the Carolina Panthers. As luck would have it, the Panthers won the NFC Championship, and Allen's last NFL game would be Super Bowl 50.

When I spotted Allen in a stadium corridor, I asked, "Why not you today, Jared?" He understood. His heart-felt reply as we shook hands: "You're right, man. Why not?" Allen didn't get a Super Bowl ring that day: Denver won, 24–10. But he rode off into the sunset tied for a pair of NFL all-time pass-rushing records, two years leading the league in sacks, and the most career safeties (4). His eleven consecutive games with a sack from 2011–12 remain the standard by which all future generations of "naturally born" quarterback-wrangling pass rushers will be judged.

Marcus Allen *(born 1960)*

Running Back

- Los Angeles Raiders (1982-92) - Kansas City Chiefs (1993-97)

Over the phone, Marcus Allen dictated very specific directions to his Brentwood, California, home. I asked about mileages and road markers along the way. I made him repeat specifics as I wrote everything down. This was the early 1990s: MapQuest wasn't reliable, GPS wasn't yet an option, and I didn't want to arrive at the wrong address in a strange part of Los Angeles with my tail between my legs. When I was certain I knew where we'd be driving and how to get there, I thanked Allen profusely, reconfirmed the call time, then hung up. I still had my doubts.

On interview day, we piled our equipment into rental vans outside the LAX Marriott, then headed north toward Brentwood, one of LA's poshest communities. I navigated while a crew member drove the lead vehicle. We arrived long before our scheduled early-afternoon call time, then checked the multiple mailboxes in front of the building to which we'd been directed. The name on the mailbox that matched Allen's address read SCHWARTZ. Hmm . . . ?

So, we waited. An hour passed. Our call time came and went. My crew grew restless. We played whiffle ball to pass the time. We consumed cold beers from our Styrofoam cooler. A second hour passed. Mutiny swelled in the ranks. I assured everybody that my directions came from the man's own mouth and that we were parked outside the exact style of building he had described over the phone. But nobody answered the doorbell, and there was no sign of life within. So, we waited.

Finally, as we began repacking our gear, a sleek sports car with tinted windows approached. Mr. "Schwartz"—aka Marcus Allen—powered down the driver's side window.

He smiled that mischievous smile of his, then said, "Man, you guys were *serious*!"

We took our good old time lighting Allen's well-appointed sitting room. His tardiness aside, this guy already had a Hall of Fame NFL résumé. But one particular thing he said during my interview stood out: "You know what I'd really like to do someday? Be MVP of the Pro Bowl." When I asked him why, he responded simply, "It's one of the only awards I haven't won yet."

In 1981, at the University of Southern California, Allen was a first-team All-American. He won the Heisman Trophy, the Maxwell Award, the Walter Camp Award, and Pac 10 Player of the Year honors. He was the second person ever to rush for 2,000 or more yards in a season, and he led the nation in scoring. As an LA Raider, he was the NFL Rookie of the Year (1982), the Super Bowl MVP (1983), and the league's Most Valuable Player (1985), the year he also won the NFL rushing title. In 1993, as a Kansas City Chief, he won the NFL Comeback Player of the Year award.

As you can plainly see, his résumé was not complete.

Allen possessed one of the most complete skill sets of any running back I've ever seen. He played quarterback and defensive back in high school, then began his college career as the blocking back for Heisman Trophy–winning tailback Charles White. In the pros, his receiving ability plus his red-zone elusiveness resulted in 145 total touchdowns, the highest total of all time in 1997. (As of 2022, he ranks sixth.) Anybody who witnessed his 74-yard reverse-field TD run in Super XVIII (18) will never forget it. I watched it from behind Washington's bench. As it unfolded, I could feel the "agony of defeat" settling in for Washington.

But "Marcus Magic" was not contagious. Raiders owner Al Davis pioneered the "vertical passing game," meaning that the more Allen handled the football, the fewer times it was being thrown. And Big Al certainly didn't like Allen's reminder that "as 60 percent of the Raiders' offense, I want[] to be paid accordingly" or the remark "We need to run the ball more." Again, hmm . . .?

By 1987, Marcus was sharing running-back duties with Bo Jackson. Allen became the Raiders' fullback, blocking for the younger, bigger, faster man. Yet Allen still scored 26 touchdowns to Jackson's 16 during Jackson's four-year Raiders tenure. In 1991, Davis brought in former 49ers star Roger Craig to share the rushing load. The next year, it was Eric Dickerson. Eventually, Davis labeled Allen "a cancer to the team." During a halftime interview with ABC's Al Michaels that aired on *Monday Night Football* on December 14, 1992, Allen described his relationship with Davis thusly: "Acrimonious at best. . . . What do you think of a guy that has attempted to ruin your career? . . . If you don't like me, let me go play football someplace else."

So, in 1993, Allen joined the Kansas City Chiefs. I shot sound in Kansas City the day the Raiders came to town (October 3, 1993). I knew what was at stake. In pregame, Allen told me, "I don't say much, I'm one of those quiet guys." In the second quarter, Allen scored a touchdown, the 100th of his NFL career. As he approached the Chiefs' sideline, head coach Marty Schottenheimer told him, "That couldn't happen to a better guy in a better situation." On the bench, Allen read the Jumbotron, then told a teammate, "That's a whole lot of touchdowns." Finally, in the Chiefs' postgame locker room, as he pulled off his game jersey, Marcus addressed my camera: "Poetic justice, that's all it is. I don't question fate, I just appreciate it. It's in my favor, that's all."

Over his career, in ten games against the division-rival Raiders, Allen's new team beat his old team nine times.

At some point near the end of Allen's career, I produced and directed a commercial for the Pro Football Hall of Fame. Marcus was the talent. As we walked through the hall's exhibits, lit our backgrounds, and made our shots, Allen confided, "I really hope I get in here someday."

I reminded him that at one point in Kansas City, he had been the active career rushing leader in NFL history. On the day of our shoot, no running back in history had scored more touchdowns.

In 2005, eight years after he left football, Allen was elected to the Hall of Fame. His body of work rivals anybody who's ever played the position. After his enshrinement, I sent a note to his Brentwood, California, address, not even sure whether he still owned the place. My note read, "Dear Schwartz, congratulations. But you never did get that Pro Bowl MVP." I never heard back.

Lyle Alzado *(1949–92)*

Defensive End and Tackle

- Denver Broncos (1971-78) · Cleveland Browns (1979-81)
- Los Angeles Raiders (1982-85, 1990)

Over his shortened lifespan, gentle giant Lyle Alzado offered many ways to remember him, each intentional to whom he wanted or *needed* to be at that moment.

I first met him in the early 1980s at the original Gold's Gym in Venice, California.

On a late spring morning, he strolled off the boardwalk, asked me what my film crew needed to capture, then loaded more than seven hundred pounds on a leg press.

"Ready when you are," he said. Without so much as a stretch or a toe touch, he performed three dozen deep-squat reps before asking, "You guys got enough?"

I should have known then what the entire world would learn a decade later from *Sports Illustrated*: Alzado was juicing—big time! In that now-famous tell-all exposé titled "I Lied," dated July 8, 1991, he admits that he'd been using anabolic steroids since 1969 and claims that 90 percent of the athletes he knew were using them. When he was diagnosed with lymphoma of the brain, he attributed his advancing infirmity and abbreviated life expectancy to their use and abuse.

He died in 1992 at age forty-three.

Yes, I knew the same Lyle Alzado whom family and friends, players and coaches had observed for most of his brief life: a great big cuddly bear when speaking with sick children in a hospital room, as he did for the segment I was producing that day; a fire-breathing, man-eating beast when pissed off on a Sunday afternoon, once quoted as saying, "Anybody who tells me they go out there to have fun playing football . . . they're a liar. This game is a war!"

One of my all-time favorite NFL Films images features Alzado (as a Bronco) pointing his index finger at and threatening the worldly existence of Raiders guard Gene Upshaw. The future Hall of Famer wisely took refuge in the Raiders huddle.

"I've never been afraid of any man in my life," Alzado brags in that infamous *SI* article.

Born in Brooklyn and raised in Long Island, Alzado played his final two years of college football at a tiny National Association of Intercollegiate Athletics (NAIA) school in South Dakota called Yankton College, which no longer exists. As the legend goes, a Broncos scout discovered Alzado by accident while studying film of Yankton playing Montana Tech. Denver selected Alzado in the fourth round of the 1971 NFL Draft.

Steve Sabol took an immediate liking to him. An early NFL Films segment shows Alzado back home in New York, helping his mother arrange flowers, a visual testament to his softer side. It also shows him breaking a two-man blocking sled, then fiddling with the mangled parts, as if trying to put the thing back together. It's comical to watch. I never did hear the full story behind that one.

In 1977, Alzado rounded into All-Pro form. Not coincidentally, that's also the year Denver went 12–2, made the postseason for the first time in franchise history, then beat the Raiders in the AFC Championship Game, 20–17. But in Super Bowl XII (12), Dallas dismantled Denver, 27–10. Following a stellar 1978 season, when the Broncos wouldn't meet Alzado's contract demands, he announced that he was retiring to become a heavyweight boxer and that his first fight would take place in Denver's Mile High Stadium in July 1979—an exhibition against Muhammad Ali.

In February 1978, Ali lost his world title to Leon Spinks in a fifteen-round split decision. Later that year, he regained that title in a rematch victory over Spinks. Soon thereafter, "The Greatest" retired.

During his collegiate years, Alzado had boxed as an amateur. Records show that he won 44 of his 45 bouts. In 1969, at a Midwestern Golden Gloves tournament in Omaha, Nebraska, Alzado pounded his way to the semifinals. Presumably, that was the last time he had boxed, so why was he willing to risk life and limb against a three-time world champion just days prior to the start of Denver's training camp? I genuinely believe that Alzado thought that he could win the fight.

Alzado said, "I grew up in Brooklyn . . . and I don't particularly think there's a person in this world who can kick my ass." With indomitable courage and steroids on his side, how could he lose?

Alzado reportedly mortgaged his home to help make this cross-sport, pseudo–super event happen. Ali agreed to the "exhibition," but he insisted that the contest be an eight-round event, a situation favoring his experience and savvy. Alzado said yes. He trained like Rocky Balboa. Ali made a few promotional stops in Denver and barely lifted a glove. Ali weighed in at 235 pounds, a good thirteen pounds more than he carried when he defeated Spinks in his world championship rematch. Of course, Ali had also beaten Joe Frazier twice and George Foreman once, not to mention every other world-class heavyweight of his generation.

When I later asked Alzado about the July 14, 1978, event, his remarks were telling. He remembered going after Ali early, hoping to use his weight advantage and strength to corner the champ so he could land "one big shot." He remembered landing several body blows and sensing early on that Ali was not in peak condition.

He also recalled a quick Ali flurry—"a bunch of punches that I never saw"—followed by a clinch that Ali initiated so he could whisper in Alzado's ear, "We can do this any way you want."

This candid recollection sent a chill up my spine. Bravado aside, I can imagine how Alzado must have felt. After eight rounds, the fight ended in an unscored "no decision."

In January 1984, Alzado, now with the Oakland Raiders, ran Washington off the field, 38–9, in Super Bowl XVIII (18). Late in the game, one of our cameras captured an image of Alzado clenching his fist toward adoring Raiders fans. I witnessed the moment. His triumphant expression was truly priceless. That's how I choose to remember this gentle giant of a man who feared nothing in this world, perhaps contributing to his own early demise.

Morten Andersen *(born 1960)*

Placekicker

- New Orleans Saints (1982-94) · Atlanta Falcons (1995-2000, 2006-07)
- New York Giants (2001) · Kansas City Chiefs (2002-03)
- Minnesota Vikings (2004)

Placekicking takes a rare confidence. The possibility and memory of failures are ever present. A placekicker must commit to the moment and approach each new attempt without trepidation. The number of kickers who can stand unthreatened in the shadow of the uprights is very small—much smaller than the number of roster spots in the NFL. The most mentally tough kickers are in great demand year after year after year. Understandably, many put together long careers.

Hall of Fame placekicker Morten Andersen (aka the Great Dane) hails from a small town in Denmark. He migrated to America as an exchange student, kicked an American football for the first time at Ben Davis High School in Indianapolis, then earned All-American honors while kicking at Michigan State (1981).

New Orleans selected him with their fourth pick (eighty-sixth overall) in the 1982 NFL Draft. For thirteen seasons, Andersen piled up points for the Saints, earning six Pro Bowl trips along the way. When New Orleans dumped him due to salary-cap concerns, he joined the Atlanta Falcons. In a 1995 game against the Saints, he became the first kicker to hit three 50-yard field goals in a single contest. He scored seven points in Atlanta's 34–19 defeat in Super Bowl XXXIII (33).

In 2006, Andersen passed Gary Anderson to become the NFL's all-time leading scorer. He retired officially in 2008 with 382 games played, also the most of all time. Not until 2018 did Adam Vinatieri pass Andersen to become the game's most prolific placekicker. Only Hall of Famer George Blanda (age 48 years, 109 days) was older than Andersen (age 47+) while still active.

Even before his retirement, Andersen was developing his broadcasting and communication skills. Several NFL Films Super Bowl productions show Andersen doing Danish radio broadcasts. His résumé includes motivational speaking, keynote addresses, TV appearances, and much more. So, imagine my surprise when he showed up in my life one night in London, England.

In 2009, Films sent me to London to shoot the Patriots–Buccaneers game at Wembley Stadium. My wife, Barbara, accompanied me. On our first night, we visited a popular local pub where lots of NFL Films folks had gathered. Many pints of ale later, the entire team was pretty toasted. In these spirited situations, my wife—normally a nonsmoker—sometimes craves a cigarette. So, she spent a few euros on a pack and then headed outside with a friend to indulge. Sometime later, she returned with Andersen in tow. He'd been bumming Barb's cigarettes.

"Morten, what are you doing here?" I asked, followed by "I see you've met my wife."

For the next few hours, Andersen sat with all of us and drank. We talked about the NFL and lots of other things, none of which I remember. When the pub closed, Andersen tagged along with us back to our hotel. There, in a huge, deserted lobby, a group of us continued the conversation. I lingered after Barb went to bed. So, it wasn't until the next morning that Barb disclosed that the NFL's all-time scoring leader had invited her to go to a party with him. Not *us*, just Barb.

In 2017, I was happy to learn that Andersen would be inducted into the Pro Football Hall of Fame. But when it comes to the Great Dane, I derive even more satisfaction from this: If his overtures toward my wife constituted a tactful but intentionally crafted "scoring attempt," his mighty kick sailed wide right. But I'm sure he'll shake it off and bum his next cigarette with the exact same confidence.

The Bahr Brothers

Chris Bahr *(born 1953)* 🏆

Placekicker

- Cincinnati Bengals (1976–79) · Oakland/Los Angeles Raiders (1980–88)
- San Diego Chargers (1989)

Matt Bahr *(born 1956)* 🏆

Placekicker

- Pittsburgh Steelers (1979–80) · San Francisco 49ers (1981)
- Cleveland Browns (1981–89) · New York Giants (1990–92)
- Philadelphia Eagles (1993) · New England Patriots (1993–95)

In college, my dorm buddies all knew about a Philadelphia high school soccer phenom enrolled at Penn State named Chris Bahr, aka Thunder Foot. They dragged me out to watch him. Although I didn't understand or appreciate the sport, I could see that Bahr boasted a "big leg." Chris earned All-American honors three times as a soccer player and once as the Nittany Lions placekicker (1974). He signed a pro soccer contract with the Philadelphia Atoms in 1975, then became the North American Soccer League's Rookie of the Year. In 1976, he transitioned to the Cincinnati Bengals in the NFL.

Chris Bahr's younger brother Matt followed exactly the same career path. After a brief 1978 stint in the North American Soccer League, Matt was selected in round six of the 1979 NFL Draft by the Pittsburgh Steelers. I first encountered him at a preseason game that summer. Steelers Hall of Fame receiver John Stallworth noticed me shooting Matt while the rookie kicker stood quietly in the bench area. Stallworth walked over and lifted one of Matt's arms in the air, as if to say, "I'm a Steeler now, so I'm going to be a winner." His youthful expression radiated innocence.

Placekickers often encounter a tough workplace in the NFL, where differences in craft, training, and socialization can isolate them from their colleagues. The case of the Bahr brothers, though, shows that the NFL workplace can have its rewards—and that the "real-world" workplace isn't always such a gentle environment either.

In November 1979, Matt earned his black and gold bars for the Steelers. In a key divisional matchup with Cleveland, the Steelers trailed 30–20 in the fourth quarter. Pittsburgh narrowed the gap on a Franco Harris touchdown before Matt kicked a game-tying field goal. In overtime, the rookie boomed a 37-yard game-winner. This time, the entire Steelers team engulfed Matt. I shot Jack Lambert lifting him off the ground in triumph—and I feared that Lambert might accidentally break Matt's ribs.

Pittsburgh won two of their last three games, breezed through the AFC Playoffs, and won their fourth Super Bowl championship in six seasons. Matt earned a Super Bowl ring. Eleven years later, he earned another, this time as a member of the New York Giants. On the road in San Francisco for the NFC Championship, Bahr's 5 field goals accounted for all the Giants' points in a 15–13 upset victory. Before Super Bowl XXV (25), I spoke with Matt during pregame warm-ups. "This could be your last chance in one of these," I said pointedly.

Matt hooked a field-goal attempt wide off Tampa's natural grass surface. "Don't jinx me," he shot back. Later, his 21-yard fourth-quarter field goal gave New York a 20–19 lead. When Bills kicker Scott Norwood missed a late 47-yarder, Matt earned his second Super Bowl ring.

In January 1981, Chris Bahr and the Los Angeles Raiders took on the Philadelphia Eagles in Super Bowl XV (15). Chris accounted for nine Raiders points in a 27–10 victory, earning a championship ring of his own. In Super Bowl XVIII (18), the Raiders wasted Washington, 38–9. Chris scored 8 more points and matched his younger brother's ring total.

Off the field, Thunder Foot was making the most of his down time between football seasons. By the end of his playing career, Chris had earned a law degree from Southwestern University. When I visited Chris with a production crew and introduced myself to him for the first time, our get-together took place at the law firm he'd recently joined in Hawthorne, California. What happened next ranks as the scariest interview in my four-plus-decade NFL Films career.

Chris's general partner and boss informed us that we would have to do the interview in a particular office. No problem. The crew lit the desk area while I prepped Chris on the subjects we would cover. I assured Chris's boss that we would finish everything in one hour, give or take a few minutes. When the boss finally closed the door on his way out, I began my interview.

Shortly thereafter, we all heard a door slam, followed by a loud voice coming from the reception area. I paused the interview. We couldn't quite make out what was being said, but the noise was distracting, and the voice was growing louder and angrier: "I wanna talk to Chris Bahr right now. . . . Where is he? Where the hell is Bahr?" Chris looked confused and concerned. So did my crew. I thought about opening the door to investigate, and I remember thinking, "Pretty tough way to start your career, Chris." Then, things turned ugly.

"Where the f*** is Chris Bahr? I wanna see him *right now*, dammit. Is he in there???" You mean where we were hiding? Yes, he was. And that's when we heard a *gunshot*!

Quickly, Chris ushered us into a large storage closet behind the desk and closed the door. There was no lock. Chris; Hank, my veteran cameraman; and I were huddled in the closet, being as quiet as we could be. Our freelance California soundman was hiding somewhere out in the office.

That's when we smelled gunpowder wafting through the law firm. My cameraman and I both started searching the closet for weapons—an umbrella, a fire extinguisher, anything. I looked at Chris. He was ashen white. I don't remember what Hank and I ended up with, but we grabbed whatever blunt instruments we could find, then positioned ourselves on either side of the closet door. I realized that the angry man was hunting for Chris, not us, but we were in his path. I could hear *all* our hearts pounding.

This terror went on forever. None of us made a peep. We muffled coughs and tried to ignore the gunpowder smells. We all were scared sh*tless! Finally, we heard muffled voices outside. We listened more carefully. We couldn't make out words, but we didn't dare open the door. Then . . . we heard laughter. I looked at Chris. He seemed genuinely confused. So, we opened the door and looked around.

Outside stood an off-duty Hawthorne policeman, Chris's boss, and our soundman. They were laughing their asses off. We'd been "punked," big time! No wonder people don't trust attorneys. I looked at Thunder Foot. The color was slowly returning to his face, and we all breathed again. Suddenly, I realized why Chris's boss had been so concerned about time and had insisted that we sequester ourselves in *this* office. I thought about filing a suit against everybody involved, but eventually, we all laughed it off. Not surprisingly, we all drank alcoholic beverages at lunch.

Connor Barwin *(born 1986)*

Defensive End and Outside Linebacker

- Houston Texans (2009-12) · Philadelphia Eagles (2013-16)
- Los Angeles Rams (2017) · New York Giants (2018)

One of the greatest sound bites I ever got—one that will *never* be seen or heard—involved a former defender-turned–front office executive named Connor Barwin.

Ironically, Barwin was born deaf. Surgery repaired his right ear, but Barwin still struggles to hear much of anything out of his left one. Born in Michigan, he attended the University of Cincinnati on a football scholarship. During an injury epidemic, Cincinnati's basketball team recruited him to join its depleted roster, and he wound up scoring six points in a game against Pittsburgh. The Houston Texans drafted him with their 2009 second-round pick, the forty-sixth overall selection.

As a pro, Barwin's most productive month proved to be November. In 2011, as a Texans outside linebacker, he recorded four sacks in a single November game against the Jacksonville Jaguars, a Texans team record. The AFC named him Defensive Player of the Month. As an Eagle, in November 2014, Barwin collected 6.5 sacks, made 24 tackles, batted down 2 passes, and forced a fumble. This time, the NFC named Barwin its Defensive Player of the Month.

His "Soundbite of the Century" for NFL Films took place late in his tenure with the Texans—probably in November.

One of my favorite tricks was to shoot players sitting near the end of a team's bench area from a position in front of and off to the side of the bench area. Players would spot me and just carry on with their conversations, unaware that my soundman's microphone hung on a boom pole just above their heads. Not so with Barwin, a person who came into this world unable to hear.

In this instance, Barwin saw me kneeling in his purview off to one side, shooting back toward his position. Almost instantly, he glanced up and spotted my soundman's fuzz-covered microphone (fuzz is a windscreen) hanging just above his head. I prepared for something extraordinary. What transpired next still makes me smile.

With all the dignity and aplomb he could muster, he turned toward his nearest Texans teammate and said, "I've noticed I play a lot better on Sunday when I don't jerk off the night before."

I looked up at my soundman just as he looked over at me. We both turned our attention back to Barwin, who could not control himself. He was smiling ear to ear. His teammates were in shock, but Barwin was enjoying our collective discomfiture immensely. See you in Hell, Barwin! Later, standing next to defensive lineman Antonio Smith, he spotted our boom pole again and launched into the same routine and punchline. Why not? He knew we'd never be able to use it.

As of 2022, Barwin is working in the Eagles front office, making his way up the ladder as an NFL executive. I doubt that his classic NFL Films sound bite is included in his résumé. It still ranks as one of my favorite experiences as a sound cameraman. Thanks for the candor, Connor!

Brian Billick *(born 1954)* 🏆

Assistant Coach and Offensive Coordinator

- Minnesota Vikings (1992-98)

Head Coach

- Baltimore Ravens (1999-2007)

Early in 2001, Steve Sabol informed me I would be coproducing and directing a new show for distribution by HBO called *Hard Knocks*. The Baltimore Ravens had agreed to participate without restrictions. I relished the opportunity to work with their head coach, Brian Billick.

The 1998 Minnesota Vikings won fifteen regular-season games (15–1) with Billick as their offensive coordinator. I shot nearly half of them, including the only one they lost, a week-nine road game in Tampa. Billick's offense had scored 556 points, an NFL single-season record at the time. They scored 41 more against the Arizona Cardinals in the first round of the playoffs. But in the NFC Championship, Vikings kicker Gary Anderson hooked a 39-yard game-winning field-goal attempt—

his first miss in two years. Atlanta, not Minnesota, advanced to Super Bowl XXXIII (34), where the Falcons lost to Denver, 34–19. Meanwhile, my good friend Brian Billick became the Baltimore Ravens' new head coach.

Billick inherited a stout defense anchored by future Hall of Fame middle linebacker Ray Lewis. Brian's job was to fix the offense. After an 8–8 finish in 1999 and a 5–4 start in 2000, Billick took action. He benched quarterback Tony Banks and elevated Trent Dilfer to the starting lineup. The Ravens reeled off seven straight wins and made the playoffs as a wild card. In four consecutive road playoff games—a string that included Super Bowl XXXV (35)—the Ravens' stellar defense allowed just one touchdown. Not one per game: *one* total TD over *four* games. Dilfer and NFL Rookie of the Year running back Jamal Lewis controlled the football. And Billick's team beat the New York Giants, 34–7. Billick was a Super Bowl champion.

My lone encounter with Brian that season occurred during his first Super Bowl press conference. Billick had warned the media in advance that he was there to talk about this year's game and *not* Ravens linebacker Ray Lewis's legal issues, a murder charge that was plea-bargained down to obstruction of justice, resulting in a $250,000 NFL fine. When reporters opened the session with questions about Lewis, Billick refused to participate. He stood his ground and reminded them, "I have the podium." The media got the message, and the Ravens prepared for the game minus distractions. Lewis was named Super Bowl MVP. Billick had drawn a clear boundary line around his football team, just as he had promised.

Just a few months later, a Cincinnati-born, Hollywood-based producer named Marty Callner sold the *Hard Knocks* concept to NFL Films and HBO Sports. Somebody wrote Callner a check and promised him a credit before sending him packing. I began researching and developing the debut of "the first sports-based reality series" in American television history: *Hard Knocks: Training Camp with the Baltimore Ravens.* No pressure there!

Fortunately, Billick was very much on board. He was a pragmatist who saw the additional coverage as a marker of success that could work for him rather than against him. During his first team meeting, Billick introduced our NFL Films crew to players and staff while we actively covered the room. He told everybody present to get used to us because we would be around his football team through Labor Day. Then, he addressed his Super Bowl championship team: "We know how to handle adversity. . . . The key now is can we handle success?"

At his first press conference, Billick pointed out our robotic cameras mounted all around the room, then strode about as our remote camera ops dutifully followed him. He told the assembled media that if his players and coaches couldn't deal with cameras in their faces, they couldn't remain focused enough to return to a Super Bowl. At the Ravens' first practice, he summoned me from a distance and complained about the boom microphones hanging over unit drills. When I told him that the solution was wireless microphones, he said, "Then do it." We transitioned that afternoon. He made decisions instantly and decisively. He wanted this TV experiment to work for everybody, but *especially* for his football team. For his part, Steve Sabol seemed far more concerned about possible league office complaints than did Billick or anybody else in the Ravens organization. In particular, Steve worried about the rampant profanity. But this was HBO, and Billick knew that he was no Tony Soprano, even if Sabol did not.

Our deal with the Ravens included an early Wednesday morning screening of each week's new "Rough Cut" before its Wednesday night HBO premiere. In addition to Billick, screenings included one or both Modells, Art and David (Ravens ownership); general manager Ozzie Newsome; and Kevin Byrne from Ravens media relations. As we sat through the second show, I was not surprised when the entire group stood up and issued a collective "Good job, Bob," just as they had after screening the first show. On his way out, Brian turned to me and said candidly, "The show could use a few more gratuitous 'f***s' going forward, just to spice things up." That marked the final time Steve Sabol mentioned profanity.

One of the show's unique qualities was the absence of narration. The Ravens seemed more than adept at telling their own stories. In our interview trailer, I deliberately asked Billick questions, hoping that his words would provide editors with critical storyline transitions. One afternoon when Billick was in a hurry and kept missing my cues, he said flatly, "Bob, just tell me what you need me to say, and I'll say it in my own words for you." That's what I call collaboration! By the show's third episode (out of six), HBO had a hit on its hands. As one Los Angeles TV critic described it, "*Hard Knocks* . . . is a seminal moment in sports television history."

Billick's Ravens did not repeat as Super Bowl champions. A training-camp, season-ending injury to Jamal Lewis seriously limited the Ravens' ball-control capabilities. The release of Dilfer and the signing of veteran quarterback Elvis Grbac—who threw just 15 touchdown passes against 18 interceptions before retiring—hurt the Ravens' offense, and their mighty defense could not make up the slack. Billick won two more AFC North division titles in 2003 and 2006 before a 5–11 finish in 2007 led to his dismissal.

So, Billick transitioned into television, first as a draft analyst for NFL Network and then as a game analyst for Fox Sports (2008–09). He's still active today. In 2016, the year before I retired from NFL Films, I visited Brian's Eastern Shore Maryland home to interview him for a pair of *A Football Life* episodes. When I mentioned *Hard Knocks*, he broke into a smile. The rapport we cemented in time that memorable summer will last both our lifetimes.

Gil Brandt *(born 1932)*

Front Office Executive

- Los Angeles Rams (1955-57) · San Francisco 49ers (1958-59)

Vice President of Player Personnel

- Dallas Cowboys (1960-88)

Ever hear the term *biorhythms*?

The theory dates back to a late-nineteenth-century German physician named Wilhelm Fliess. According to Fliess, each of us lives with three active biological cycles that begin at birth and affect our daily lives. Each has its own duration. Our physical cycle (strength, coordination, well-being) recurs every twenty-three days, our emotional cycle (sensitivity, awareness, mood) every twenty-eight days, and our intellectual cycle (memory, communication, logic) every thirty-three days. Each of these cycles moves between peak periods and low points, and our aptitudes and abilities in various domains are adjusted accordingly. In short, we're biologically predisposed to good days and bad days.

Most modern-day researchers consider biorhythms to be nothing more than pseudoscience, so imagine my surprise in the late 1970s when I learned that Dallas Cowboys executive Gil Brandt was investigating biorhythms as a potential game-planning tool. NBC Sports producers told NFL Films that if Brandt was willing to go public about it, they'd air the segment on their Sunday pregame show.

So, off I went to Dallas. I'd never met Brandt before, but I loved the energy he expended just chewing his gum. NBC's Donna de Varona interviewed Brandt for more than an hour. No, Cowboys coach Tom Landry was not building game plans around biorhythmic data, but Brandt was investigating possibilities. I still vividly remember one thing I learned that day:

In 1972, Pittsburgh's rookie fullback Franco Harris rushed for 100 yards in six straight games. On the day his streak ended, December 10, Harris's biorhythmic readings were "critical," according to biorhythmic theory. On December 23—the day Harris plucked a deflected pass out of the air and then rambled 60 yards for a game-winning touchdown against Oakland in the 1972 AFC Playoffs—Harris's biorhythms all hit peak levels. That event has a name: "the Immaculate Reception," possibly the single-most-memorable play in NFL history. Was it fated to happen?

"So, you can see why it's worth looking into, right?" Brandt asked me pointedly.

Looking back, I can see how biorhythms in particular might have appealed to Brandt. He'd benefitted from having an open mind and looking outside the box. Moreover, he'd seen stars suddenly align several times in his life, brought together by luck or fate, for better and for worse, so I can understand his looking for a science to it all.

Brandt began his NFL career in the mid-1950s as a regional scout for Tex Schramm, an executive with the Los Angeles Rams. When Clint Murchison founded the Dallas Cowboys in 1960, he hired Schramm to organize and run his front office. Schramm made Brandt (then twenty-five years old) and Landry his first two hires. The three of them together controlled the Cowboys' football fate for nearly three decades.

Brandt ran Dallas's player personnel operation. The scouting and evaluation systems that Brandt created and then computerized raised the bar in professional sports. During his tenure, the Cowboys posted twenty consecutive winning seasons (1966–85), still the NFL record. Nine of Brandt's draft picks made the Hall of Fame. Landry's Cowboys played in five Super Bowls, winning two of them (VI [6] and XII [12]), while losing the other three (V [5], X [10], and XIII [13]) by a combined 11 points. Many of Brandt's player selections—Bob Lilly, Tony Dorsett, Troy Aikman—seemed destined for the Hall of Fame from the beginning. Others involved calculated risk; Roger Staubach owed the Navy five years after his graduation from Annapolis, so his future Hall of Fame rights only cost Brandt and Dallas a tenth-round draft pick in 1963.

Of more consequence for the future of NFL team management were the numerous small college players, Historically Black College and University (HBCU) players, and college basketball players Brandt brought to Dallas, with winning results. In 1975, Dallas added *twelve* first-year players to its roster and nearly beat Pittsburgh in Super Bowl X (10). Two years later, Brandt's "Dallas Dirty Dozen" celebrated a victory in Super Bowl XII (12). Randy White, Brandt's first pick in 1975, shared MVP honors with Harvey Martin, a third-round "steal" in 1973.

But it all ended suddenly on February 25, 1989, the day that Jerry Jones bought the Dallas Cowboys. Brandt took his player evaluation expertise to television, most notably with NFL Network, which is where I encountered him again.

In February 2004, NFL Network produced six separate shows, giving American TV audiences their first inside look at the College Player Scouting Combine in Indianapolis. Brandt provided analysis for the broadcast, and I directed it. Nearly a decade later, I worked with Brandt again, this time on a very special project. NFL Network produced a show called *JFK: The Untold (NFL) History of That Day in Dallas.* As biorhythmic fate would have it, Brandt's wife was one of the very last people to shake President John Kennedy's hand before his motorcade made that fateful right turn toward the Texas School Book Depository. I was assigned to produce the segment, so I reconnected with Brandt, now eighty years old.

Together, we visited the very site where Brandt's wife, Sara, shook Kennedy's hand. Then, we transitioned to the sidewalk area between the Book Depository and the Grassy Knoll. Finally, we walked to the highway overpass overlooking the entire plaza. We shot Brandt retelling Sara's story at each stop. Before and after these city locations, we did a lengthy interior interview at a local business and then walk-and-talks in and around the Cotton Bowl. My octogenarian subject never flinched.

In the end, my segment detailing Sara's *Untold Story* followed by Dallas's tense team experiences that weekend in Cleveland made for some pretty good television. In fact, it won a Sports Emmy Award for Outstanding New Approaches Sports Programming Short Format. It was my first solo Emmy as a producer and the last Emmy I won.

I'm proud to know Gil Brandt. I met him in my twenties and worked with him for the last time just months short of my sixty-first birthday. When he was enshrined in the Pro Football Hall of Fame as a contributor in 2019, I couldn't have been happier. Biorhythmically speaking, it was a very good day all around.

Jim Brown *(born 1936)*

Fullback

- Cleveland Browns (1957–65)

> Jim Brown was not a beautiful runner—he was a power runner. But in the end, his power was beautiful to watch.
> —Steve Sabol

Fans of NFL Films know this line well. Steve practically insisted that it be heard in every show or segment our company produced about Cleveland Hall of Fame fullback Jim Brown. In my case, I used it in our syndicated show *The NFL's Best Ever Runners*. And you know what? It's as true today as it was then and ever shall be, amen!

The Cleveland Browns selected the Syracuse All-American (1957) with the sixth overall draft pick. Yes, that's right: Five other players (Paul Hornung, Jon Arnett, John Brodie, Ron Kramer, and Len Dawson) were chosen before quite arguably the greatest pure football player of all time. In 1965, Brown rushed for 1,544 yards and 17 touchdowns before walking away from the game. Indeed, Brown's power was beautiful to watch.

My first professional encounter with him took place at the Stardust Hotel on the old Las Vegas Strip. I'm guessing the year was 1983 or 1984. I spent much of both those off-seasons traveling with CBS Sports analyst Irv Cross, producing his "Legends of the Game" series for *The NFL Today*. As a former Philadelphia Eagle, Cross had played against Brown from 1961 through 1965. I guarantee you that Cross's presence was the only reason Brown had agreed to give me and NFL Films an audience.

At the time, Brown was part of a radio talk show being produced and performed live on a set on the Stardust's ground floor. After observing the arrangement, I concocted a fake call-in from Cross to Brown that we staged and shot prior to the actual broadcast. Brown reluctantly went along with it. When we finished, Brown invited Cross to come upstairs to his private dressing room. Irv motioned for me to follow him. But, sensing this was private time for ex-players and their immediate "peeps," I declined, one of the few times I ever turned down such an intriguing offer.

Later, on our interview set, Brown fixed his intense stare on me and asked, "So, Bob, what are your ambitions?" Nobody had ever asked me that question that way before. I almost said, "Are you kidding, I'm living my dream here." After a moment of reconsideration, I stammered something about wanting to break into feature films someday. Brown, the actor, smiled: "Pretty tough business, hope you have thick skin." Lessons on toughness from a guy with more than 2,600 career touches! Years later, I thought, "You were talking to Jim Brown, stupid!" Veteran screen actor, Jefferson from *The Dirty Dozen*, a Hollywood leading man, probably the first African American actor featured in an interracial love scene (with Raquel Welch in *100 Rifles*). "Quiet, Robert!" The lesson extended well beyond toughness, Hollywood, and whatever else. . . .

Flash forward three decades. This time, around 2016, I was working on an NFL Films *A Football Life* episode. Our subject was Brown's former Cleveland coach Paul Brown, for my money the most innovative head coach in football history. I was sitting in the Browns facility in Berea, Ohio, waiting for my crew to finish lighting the set. We'd been on location for more than two hours, long in advance of our call time for Brown's interview, so I left the set area and wandered toward the lobby.

There, as big as life, sat Mr. Brown. At first, he didn't notice me, so I surveyed the scene. Most of the millennials occupying the lobby wouldn't even look at him—that's how intimidating his presence remained, even in his late seventies. But now, I was sixty-something, so I walked to his chair, stuck out my hand, and said, "Jim, Bob Angelo from NFL Films. We worked together a long time ago at the Stardust in Las Vegas with Irv Cross."

Brown shook my hand as a smile appeared on his face: "I remember." Glad that he didn't ask me how my feature film career panned out. I told him that we were all set up and asked him whether he'd like to do his interview early. The Cleveland Browns media relations director was nowhere in sight, and Brown seemed eager to get on with things, so off we went.

I actually wasn't sure how this interview would play out. Paul Brown was ahead of his time in most regards. He signed fullback Marion Motley and lineman Bill Willis to Cleveland contracts in 1946, the first African Americans to play professional football in the modern era. (Motley's 5.7-yard career rushing average actually exceeds Jim Brown's 5.2.) Some say that Paul Brown was colorblind, especially when it came to good football players. The fact that Jim Brown led the NFL in rushing eight of his nine seasons (Green Bay's Jim Taylor led in 1962) certainly made the future Hall of Famer invaluable to Paul Brown's ball-control, offensive system.

But as the 1950s became the 1960s, and Paul Brown's inability to coach Cleveland to an NFL title despite employing the league's best runner continued, Jim's politics and activism for racial justice probably loomed as a major distraction to Paul's immediate project. (In tribute to both men, I hope I phrased all that properly.) Notwithstanding, Jim couldn't have been more insightful in describing his years with Paul: honest, as always; occasionally critical of certain situations; but in the end, very respectful of Paul Brown's enormous contributions to the game.

At one point, an ESPN producer who had been hovering in the shadows approached the set and said that he was scheduled to interview Brown first. By then, Brown and I had bonded. Without breaking stride, the greatest fullback of all time fixed his still-menacing stare on the ESPN fellow and said quietly but firmly, "We're right in the middle of something here."

On my way out of Cleveland's facility that day, I made certain to avoid the poor young producer and his crew. It would be tough to be in his shoes when he walked back into that room. Perhaps Brown still had some lessons to teach.

Cris Carter *(born 1965)*

Wide Receiver

- Philadelphia Eagles (1987–89) · Minnesota Vikings (1990–2001)
- Miami Dolphins (2002)

Who had the greatest hands of all time? Old-school purists say Raymond Berry, John Unitas's go-to guy for a generation. Seahawk fans counter with Steve Largent, also no slouch as a pass catcher. For my money, the single best pair of ball-receiving hands ever on display in the NFL belonged to Cris Carter—end of statement.

I've worked with Carter numerous times. I've visited his Boca Raton home. I've done several interviews with him, including the three-hour-plus sit-down that runs through his *A Football Life* episode. I've experienced his anger and emotion, his heavy-handedness and light-heartedness firsthand. And I admire the man. His pride and energy are contagious. I always know exactly where I stand.

If you've seen Carter as a sports commentator post-NFL, you know that he brings passion to everything he does. Raised by a single mother in Middletown, Ohio, Carter excelled at two sports and could have played either at Ohio State. He chose football over basketball, then went on to set Buckeye and Rose Bowl receiving records. But when he prematurely signed with an agent, leading to charges of mail fraud and obstruction of justice, he forfeited his final year of eligibility, a long-standing NCAA rule. The Philadelphia Eagles selected Carter in the fourth round of a special 1987 supplemental NFL draft.

His very first professional catch went for a touchdown, and so did 19 others during his first three years in Philadelphia. Then came an existential crisis. In Carter's own words: "I flunked another drug test, not for alcohol or marijuana. . . . It was for cocaine." Just before the 1990 NFL season, Eagles head coach Buddy Ryan cut Carter. When asked about it, Ryan blithely replied, "All he does is catch touchdowns." The Vikings claimed him for the standard $100 NFL waiver fee.

"It was unsettling. We were newly married, I was pregnant with my son. . . . I couldn't believe it, I couldn't believe I had married a drug addict." These were the words his wife, Melanie, spoke to me during that three-hour *A Football Life* interview. Cris was standing nearby in the kitchen while we talked.

Given a second chance, Carter made the absolute most of it. His first Minnesota start came against Philadelphia, on October 15, 1990. During pregame, Carter went out of his way to seek out and shake Ryan's hand. Later that night, he scored 2 long touchdowns, totaling 110 yards against his former team. Afterward, when asked about Ryan, Carter said, "[Ryan] gave me three years, more than most people would have [given me]. I have no bad feelings toward him." In later years, Carter said flatly, "Buddy Ryan saved my life." In my experience, very few NFL players have owned up to shortcomings with more humility or class.

During a dozen Vikings seasons, Carter caught more passes for more touchdowns than anybody in the NFL except Jerry Rice. Many were spectacular. More than a few were off the charts. The skill, courage, and concentration on display in Carter's career highlights reel should be required viewing for anybody who wants to play the position. Even Jerry Rice conceded in his own NFL Films *A Football Life* episode, "Cris Carter had the best hands in the NFL." Rice continued, "Nobody who ever played pro football had better hands than Cris." As Carter told me, "I don't believe in dropping it. . . . I always thought that almost every ball was catchable."

But Carter brought more than receiving skills to the Vikings. For years, he was Minnesota's on-field and locker-room leader. His wirings yielded a treasure trove of sound bites involving teammates and opponents alike. A sampling of Carter's comments to opponents:

"You haven't stopped us yet!"

"Get your teeth fixed!"

"When you go to sleep at night, pray. . . . Pray that you can play as long as me."

He called out teammates when they weren't performing up to his high standards, including Randy Moss—often! He challenged Minnesota's coaches when he believed that they weren't making the best decisions, calling the right plays, or demanding better results.

And he led by example. Nobody worked harder to be successful. NFL Films productions reveal Carter postpractice catching ball after ball from Jugs machines positioned at *very* close range. He made many of these catches one-handed. Aspiring NFL stars often joined Carter in Florida for his lengthy and grueling off-season workouts. As a teenage Vikings ball boy, a big strapping young man named Larry Fitzgerald later admitted, "I watched Cris every day. I try to emulate him."

In 1998, the Vikings finished 15–1 and seemed poised to play in the Super Bowl. Then, they lost the NFC Championship Game at home to the Atlanta Falcons. In Minnesota's postgame locker room, many players were wiping away tears. One superstar was inconsolable—take a guess which one!

The Pro Football Hall of Fame surely welcomed Carter at the end of his career, right? Think again. I know that Pete Rose gambled on baseball, but I've been told that he never gambled against his own team. But only two human beings ever hit safely four-thousand-plus times: Ty Cobb and Pete Rose. To me, Cooperstown without Rose is just not worth visiting. I felt the same about Canton without Carter.

The experts who elect Hall of Fame inductees take more than numbers into consideration. Yes, Carter's decisions at Ohio State damaged the program and probably cost the head coach his job. Yes, Carter dabbled in drugs before Ryan called him out on it. Yes, sometimes he waxed a bit portentous, and his super-strong opinions betrayed the ordained minister that Carter has become since achieving sobriety.

But Carter has been tested by misfortune and risen above every obstacle life has thrown his way. He's blossomed into a full-bodied human being, a man of *true* character and conviction. Like him or not, he's a Pro Football Hall of Famer. Eventually, in 2013, he took his rightful place.

I will always hold Carter in the highest regard for one particular moment in time. When the Vikings emerged from their offensive huddle prior to Carter's 1,000th career catch, Cris spotted my soundman and me in the end zone and then advised us via his wireless microphone,

"Stay right there, it's coming at you." It did! And Carter's million-dollar hands hauled it in. Afterward, we followed Carter and his family around the Metrodome as thunderous applause rained down upon them.

Thank you, CC!

Matt Cavanaugh *(born 1956)*

Quarterback

- New England Patriots (1978-82) · San Francisco 49ers (1983-85)
- Philadelphia Eagles (1986-89) · New York Giants (1990-91)

Assistant Coach

- Arizona Cardinals (1994-95) · San Francisco 49ers (1996)
- New York Jets (2009-12, 2021) · Chicago Bears (2013-14)
- Washington Commanders (2015-16, 2019)

Offensive Coordinator

- Chicago Bears (1997-98) · Baltimore Ravens (1999-2004)
- Pittsburgh Steelers (2005-08) · Washington Commanders (2017-18)

In the NFL, even the ordinary can take your breath away. Folks such as Matt Cavanaugh, who've been around awhile, learn to savor off-field moments, shooting the breeze as it were—oftentimes in locker rooms full of guys, where jocularity is commonplace, and other times in a production trailer with a working film crew, where a certain degree of professionalism might be expected.

As a junior, Cavanaugh quarterbacked the 1976 Pitt Panthers to an undefeated 11–0 season and a consensus National Championship, beating Georgia in the Gator Bowl 27–3 while earning game MVP honors. The New England Patriots selected him in the second round of the 1978 NFL Draft. Over 14 seasons, he earned two Super Bowl rings as a backup. I got to know him during his third season (of six) as the offensive coordinator for Brian Billick's Baltimore Ravens. It was the summer of 2001—and the HBO debut of *Hard Knocks.* I produced and directed the series.

Following the Ravens' 34–7 win over the New York Giants in Super Bowl XXXV (35)—where Cavanaugh earned a third Super Bowl ring—Billick surprisingly replaced incumbent quarterback Trent Dilfer with seven-year veteran Elvis Grbac. Cavanaugh's role in this QB transition seemed critical, so he made frequent visits to our air-conditioned *Hard Knocks* interview trailer.

That trailer served as a refuge from the heat of summer camp and the pressures of *Hard Knocks*. The entire staff knew that I napped there in and around scheduled afternoon interviews. My camera operator and soundman sometimes joined me. We lounged on sound baffling, fashioned pillows out of towels, and lay there digesting our dormitory lunches. And we farted. Frequently. All of us. Every day, while we waited for subjects to arrive. One afternoon, it appeared Cavanaugh was *not* going to make his scheduled interview, so we really let it rip. Toxic gas permeated every inch of our sanctuary. The whole place smelled like ass. And three *grown men* couldn't stop laughing.

That's when Cavanaugh opened the door! "Sorry, I got held up, guys," he said. It was far too late for excuses. The trailer smelled like an abandoned Porta Potty. Cavanaugh tried to be polite, but our laughter became hysterical. As the director, I realized that I needed to "clear the air."

"Sorry, Matt, but my soundman's been farting."

Sanity disappeared. Cavanaugh covered his mouth and nose with his T-shirt. Tears ran down our cheeks. This craziness went on for a while. I quickly opened the door, hoping for a puff of fresh air. No such luck. Eventually, we fanned the fumes out the door so Cavanaugh could do his interview. And the circle of NFL life continued.

Bill Cowher *(born 1957)*

Linebacker

- Philadelphia Eagles (1979, 1983-84) · Cleveland Browns (1980-82)

Assistant Coach

- Cleveland Browns (1985-88) · Kansas City Chiefs (1989-91)

Head Coach

- Pittsburgh Steelers (1992-2006)

I first crossed paths with Bill Cowher—although quite accidentally—in high school. One of our team's toughest games each and every season was against Crafton High School, part of the Ohio Valley Conference, an eight-school, Class B collection of steel towns down river from Pittsburgh, Pennsylvania.

"Sounds like you played against my brother," Cowher commented one day while we were setting up to do an interview. I was working on a Steve Sabol–directed NFL Films crew in Pittsburgh, and my boss was actively concerned that I was distracting Cowher with my high school football talk. "It's OK, Steve, I haven't heard some of these names in years," he said, diffusing the situation.

I've never met a western Pennsylvania high school football player who did *not* want to relive those glory days. Cowher was not one of those personalities for whom life in the NFL diminished the importance of life outside the NFL. And young Cowher had done it all: Western Pennsylvania Interscholastic Athletic League (WPIAL) All-Star linebacker. The 1978 MVP at North Carolina State. But when no NFL team drafted him, Cowher entered the league as a free agent. In his own words, Cowher was a "bubble player," a special teamer whose NFL starts were few and far between—a total of 4 starts in 45 career games. So, he made his impact covering kicks. In late October 1983, in Philadelphia's Veterans Stadium, Cowher made the initial hit on Bears punt returner Jeff Fisher. When two other Eagles piled on, Fisher suffered a broken leg, his first indication that he might make a better coach than a player. Cowher's playing career ended following his own knee injury just one year later, in 1984.

In 1985, Cleveland Browns head coach Marty Schottenheimer hired twenty-eight-year-old Cowher to coordinate the Browns' special teams. Later that year, I shot some isolations of Cowher at a Browns game during kickoffs and punts. Wow! *Intense* doesn't begin to capture what my shots revealed. Cleveland players actually moved out of Cowher's way to avoid being steamrolled. And each time, Cowher welcomed his charges back to the sideline with smacks to their helmets and shoulder pads, frothing, "Let's go!" with unadulterated enthusiasm.

The Browns made the playoffs all four seasons Cowher coached alongside Schottenheimer but failed to advance to a Super Bowl, losing back-to-back AFC Championship Games to the Denver Broncos. When Schottenheimer left Cleveland to coach the Kansas City Chiefs, Cowher became his defensive coordinator. Together, they again won a lot of games yet consistently came up short in postseason competition. But the Pittsburgh Steelers liked Cowher's coaching résumé and his Crafton roots. On January 21, 1992, Cowher replaced Chuck Noll as the Steelers head coach.

Early on, Steve Sabol asked Cowher whether NFL Films could wire him for a regular-season home game. Steve promised that we would air nothing that Cowher didn't preapprove. Cowher responded, "Steve, you can use anything you want." His go-to expression continued to be "Let's go!" He used it when he was happy or pissed off, to encourage or to congratulate—at least six or seven dozen times every game. His menacing, square-jawed, big-chinned stare could intimidate Al Capone. His single-minded focus and his simple directives became NFL Films staples: his "Rush the quarterback!" mantra to linebacker Greg Lloyd, or his sympathy for a rookie special teamer (a fellow "bubble player") making his way back toward the sideline after a very hard collision ("You OK? You alright?" Finally, a smile. "Welcome to the NFL.").

Cowher enjoyed instant success as a head coach, reaching an AFC Championship game in just his third season. In his fourth, Cowher became the youngest head coach ever to take a team to a Super Bowl: Super Bowl XXX (30) a 27–17 Dallas win. Cowher wore a wire. At game's end, our cameras followed him to a rendezvous with his family at the top of the Steelers tunnel. There he kissed his wife Kaye and their daughter in silence. Finally, Kaye said, "I'm sorry. . . . We'll see you in the locker room." At our weekly screening, there was not a dry eye in the house.

Over the next decade, Cowher piled up wins, but Pittsburgh folded in the playoffs. Then along came Ben Roethlisberger—and a realization. Cowher went to training camp in 2004 determined to field a tougher team. He was weary of watching his offensive linemen jab-step, then backpedal into pass protection. That summer, Steeler linemen on both sides of scrimmage fired off the ball in anger—with determination and purpose. And the Steelers got their mojo back.

After a 15–1 finish in Roethlisberger's rookie season (2004), Cowher's 2005 Pittsburgh team made the postseason as a wild card. In three straight road games (at Cincinnati, Indianapolis, and Denver), the Steelers controlled both scrimmage lines while Big Ben threw seven touchdowns. In Super Bowl XL (40), Roethlisberger became the youngest quarterback to win a Super Bowl as Pittsburgh defeated Seattle, 21–10. Soon, our NFL Films wireless microphone picked up "Daddy?" This time, the daughter who had commiserated with her father following a Super Bowl loss ten years earlier hugged and kissed him in triumph. His family surrounded him while Cowher drew up the following play: "On the count of three, let's give a big high five." Afterward, Cowher engulfed them in his arms.

After one final season, Cowher took his intimidating presence and quintessential Pittsburgh accent to CBS Sports in New York and *The NFL Today* show. In July 2010, Cowher's beloved wife Kaye died of complications from skin cancer. She was fifty-four years old. Despite years of rumors, Cowher's only head coaching job after the Steelers came in the movie *The Dark Knight Rises*, with many scenes filmed at Pittsburgh's Heinz Field. In 2014, Cowher remarried. In 2019, the Pro Football Hall of Fame's David Baker announced Cowher's election to the Hall of Fame live on *The NFL Today*.

The curly-haired kid from Crafton now lives and works in New York City. His memoir, titled *Heart and Steel*, came out in 2021. Not bad for a self-proclaimed free-agent "bubble player," an exceptional great big kid from the now-defunct Ohio Valley Conference.

Irv Cross *(1939–2021)*

Cornerback

· Philadelphia Eagles (1961-65, 1969) · Los Angeles Rams (1966-68)

The NFL Today premiered on CBS in the fall of 1975. The original cast included Brent Musberger, Phyllis George, and Irv Cross. Jimmy "The Greek" Snyder joined the team one year later. Each played a particular role.

Cross worked as the Xs and Os guy. His specialty was hard-core football analysis. He, too, traveled and worked with NFL Films crews. And as a former Pro Bowl cornerback (1964–65) and assistant coach (Eagles 1969–70), this steel worker's son from Hammond, Indiana, the eighth of fourteen children, commanded respect from players and coaches wherever he went. In the early 1980s, NFL Films made *me* Cross's primary producer. I was a little shocked.

Although I understood technical football well, I had spent most of my first five years at NFL Films doing segment work, feature shorts for NBC and CBS, show openings for CBS and NFL Films, and longer-form shows, such as *The Super Seventies*, an hour-long documentary on a decade of NFL football that aired on NBC in September 1980. My goal was to grow Cross's segments from the technical analysis he was used to doing, to expose his humanity and personality to CBS Sports audiences. So, when I described the scripted tease and accompanying montage that I was planning for our first segment together, I could sense his concern: "That really doesn't sound like what I do, Bob!" I asked him to trust me and promised that the final segment would contain lots of "real" football. I absolutely do not remember the subject of that montage and tease or anything about the segment, but when it aired that Sunday, not only did the *NFL Today* producer like it, but so did Irv. From that day on, we became a team.

When Jack Whitaker left CBS before the 1982 season, Cross inherited the "Legends of the Game" series, in-depth feature shorts that would air almost weekly on *The NFL Today*. It became our pet project. Our Hall of Fame subjects included Jim Brown, Ray Nitschke, and Larry Wilson, to name just a few. Players who hesitated to commit when first asked would immediately agree when our associate producer mentioned Cross's name. Real football people loved him!

And the more we worked together, the more he trusted me. A shoot with Houston Oilers head coach Bum Phillips in Texas proved to be a foundational moment in our working relationship. After Cross finished interviewing him, Phillips announced that he was taking us all to his favorite seafood restaurant. Cross winced. "This place is simple, but it's got great food. . . . No candlelight and bullsh*t . . . just good old Southern cookin'!" Phillips said in his Texas drawl. Sure enough, the restaurant was built inside an old fishing boat landlocked on a plot of ground near the Oilers facility. When I saw seafood gumbo on the menu, I ordered it. Cross seemed squeamish but curious.

"Wanna try it?" I asked. He nodded, so I passed my entire bowl his way, but Cross didn't have a soup spoon. "Just use mine," I said. He did. Football teammates share blood and sweat. We shared a soup spoon. And he liked the gumbo. Now, we were brothers.

Over time, Irv's natural likable qualities and his healthy sense of mischief broke through his all-business comfort zone as he grew more trusting—and proved to be quite entertaining. One day, deep in the heart of Oklahoma, Cross donned a ten-gallon hat and sat on a quarter horse to do a stand-up about a former Kansas City Chief turned rancher named E. J. Holub. CBS loved it. Irv's innate humility and courage allowed him to evolve from the viewers' teacher to their friend.

On a California football field for another CBS piece, Cross donned a #27 jersey (his number from his playing days), then went head-to-head with former 49ers pass catcher R. C. Owens, also a #27. Together, we staged a number of pass-and-catch shots of Cross defending Owens in a practice field reenactment of the infamous "Alley Oop" play (commonly called a "Fade Route" today) that Owens and quarterback Y. A. Tittle had executed in late-game, must-score situations. By design, of course, my final segment showed Owens making a game-winning grab as Irv looked on helplessly. Beneath it all, TV audiences heard the Hollywood Argyles' 1960s classic "Alley Oop." Again, CBS loved it.

By the fall of 1986, my NFL Films in-house duties prohibited me from all but weekend travel. But when *The NFL Today* producer George Veras insisted that I free myself up to direct Cross in Michigan in early November for a Thanksgiving Day special about George Plimpton's classic book *Paper Lion*, Steve Sabol set me free. Plimpton's 1966 nonfiction work details his very real attempt to learn to play quarterback during the 1963 Detroit Lions training camp.

First, I needed permission to shoot Irv's stand-up at the Cranbrook Educational Community, an exclusive prep school in Bloomfield Hills, Michigan, home of Detroit's 1963 summer camp. I needed to book Irv's interview with Plimpton. I needed access to a quality print of the 1968 movie *Paper Lion*, featuring Alan Alda as Plimpton. And, most importantly, I needed to confirm the author's suspicion that Lions veteran linebacker Carl Brettschneider was, in fact, "The Creeper," a lone, mysterious nocturnal prowler who hid in closets or under beds, then leaped out in the darkness to scare the fecal matter out of unsuspecting teammates. It all came together.

Cranbrook welcomed the publicity, Plimpton agreed to a sit-down, NFL Films procured the movie, and Brettschneider confirmed his sordid past. On camera with Cross, he said, "I admit it, Irv. . . . I was the Creeper." When I scored Hollywood's depiction of Brettschneider with the Tokens' 1960s classic "The Lion Sleeps Tonight," Veras dubbed it "the finest segment we'll air all season." Sadly, it was the last time I worked with my dear friend and comrade Irv Cross.

In 1990, Cross left CBS. In subsequent years, he worked as the athletic director for Idaho State University (1996–98), then Macalester College in St. Paul, Minnesota (through 2005). In 2009, the Pro Football Hall of Fame named Cross the winner of its Pete Rozelle Radio-Television Award, given annually for long-time and exceptional contributions to pro football coverage. In 2017, Cross cowrote *Bearing the Cross: My Inspiring Journey from Poverty to the NFL and Sports Television*. In the book's foreword, Dallas Cowboys Hall of Fame front office executive Gil Brandt says that Cross could have been the first Black general manager in the NFL.

I thank Irv Cross—the first full-time African American sports analyst on a national television network—for trusting part of his future to a young producer trying to make a name for himself.

The Crowders

Randy Crowder *(father, born 1952)*

Defensive Lineman

- Miami Dolphins (1974-76) · Tampa Bay Buccaneers (1978-80)

Channing Crowder *(son, born 1983)*

Linebacker

- Miami Dolphins (2005-10)

Over the years, the NFL has hosted some iconic families with sons following their fathers into the league: This book discusses the Mannings, the Longs, the Harbaughs, the Sharpes, and the Bahrs, and perhaps my new favorite family—the Crowders.

In the early 1970s, Penn State University required all incoming freshmen to take a swimming test. It involved two minutes of treading water followed by navigating one length of a swimming pool by any means possible. That's where I first encountered Randy Crowder.

Randy played college football at Penn State under Joe Paterno, who would later write, "Randy was one of the finest players I have ever coached." As a senior, Crowder made numerous All-American teams. The two-time reigning Super Bowl champion Miami Dolphins selected Randy in the sixth round of the 1974 NFL draft. He played three seasons for Don Shula, and beginning in 1978, he played three more seasons for the Tampa Bay Buccaneers. In between, Randy sold a pound of cocaine to an undercover narcotics agent. He and his Miami Dolphins teammate Don Reese spent a year in jail as a result.

Three decades later, during a pregame warm-up on a Sunday morning in Miami, I again saw the name CROWDER emblazoned on a Dolphins jersey. "Has to be," I thought. So, I strolled over with my camera to get a closer look. Eventually, Channing Crowder took notice.

Channing: "Something I can do for you?" He seemed perturbed by my presence. Maybe I'd caught him at a bad moment. But I pushed on.

Me: "Is your dad named Randy?"

Channing: "Who's asking?"

With all the Nittany Lion pride I could muster, I told him simply, "Your dad and I failed our swimming tests at Penn State." Channing smiled and said, "My old man still can't f***ing swim."

Following his career, Channing sat down for an interview with another NFL Films producer. When asked about any "hidden talents" he might have brought to the game, Channing admitted to urinating down his leg in pregame in every contest he appeared in for six NFL seasons. Glad I never took a swim test alongside the younger Crowder.

Ben Davidson *(1940–2012)*

Defensive End

- Green Bay Packers (1961) · Washington Commanders (1962-63)
- Oakland Raiders (1964-71)

Len Dawson *(1935–2022)*

Quarterback

- Pittsburgh Steelers (1957-59) · Cleveland Browns (1960-61)
- Kansas City Chiefs (1962-75)

Near the end of my NFL career, I shot at least one game per year in Kansas City, Missouri. Each time I went, I made the trek from the field through the labyrinth of tunnels inside Arrowhead Stadium to the elevator, then up to the Chiefs media lounge. I had two reasons for this: first, Kansas City served a terrific pregame breakfast, and second, I wanted to visit Len Dawson.

A 1957 first-round draft selection of the Pittsburgh Steelers, Dawson was traded to Cleveland in 1960. The Purdue All-American quarterback made little impact in either city. In Kansas City, as part of an American Football League franchise newly renamed the Chiefs, Dawson flourished.

In Super Bowl I (1), Dawson kept the Chiefs competitive against Vince Lombardi's Packers until a second-half interception triggered a runaway 35–10 Green Bay win. In Super Bowl IV (4), against the heavily favored Minnesota Vikings, Dawson engineered a 23–7 upset, the final game in which the American Football League (1960–69) was officially separate from the National Football League. He retired from football in 1975 and was inducted into the Pro Football Hall of Fame in 1987.

Generation Xers may know Dawson from his quarter-century stint cohosting HBO's *Inside the NFL* (1977–2001). Chiefs fans know him from five-decades-plus on KMBC-TV in Kansas City. I teamed up with Dawson in the late seventies, when he was working for NBC Sports as a game analyst. In a week in which the Chiefs would face the Raiders, NBC dispatched Dawson to San Francisco to work with me on a feature about the fabled 1960s Chiefs–Raiders rivalry.

But first, Dawson and I rode the San Francisco cable cars. It was a picture-perfect postcard day in the Bay Area. As we climbed and then descended the city's hills, I noticed people looking in our direction. The more we talked pro football, the more folks gathered around or leaned in to listen. Finally, an elegant older woman approached us: "That's a beautiful ring you have on. What's it for?"

"It's a Super Bowl championship ring," Dawson replied.

"I've heard of that," she said. After a pause: "What sport is that again?"

"Professional football, ma'am," replied the Most Valuable Player of Super Bowl IV (4).

Next up was our location shoot. Our destination was a private home across the Bay Bridge, outside Oakland. Our subject was former Raiders defensive end Ben Davidson. Dawson was concerned: "You know, Bob . . . Ben and I aren't necessarily on the best of speaking terms."

In his playing days, "Big" Ben Davidson stood six feet eight inches tall and weighed in at 275 pounds. He wore a distinctive handlebar mustache that he stroked meticulously on the sidelines before face-slamming quarterbacks. His sparkling eyes radiated menace and mayhem all at once. He was a dominant and destructive defensive force, an intimidating pass-rusher who epitomized the "Raiders Mystique." And he was *not* a fan of Dawson or his Kansas City Chiefs.

On November 1, 1970, the Chiefs led the Raiders 17–14 late in the fourth quarter. On third down and long, Dawson scrambled and ran, picking up the first down before being tackled on a play that should have sealed a Chiefs victory. Then, Davidson arrived. As Dawson lay on the ground, Davidson "speared" him with his helmet. Kansas City wide receiver Otis Taylor attacked Davidson and started pounding him. A veritable on-field riot ensued: "Holy Toledo, it's a free for all," screamed Raiders radio voice Bill King. Ironically, AFL rules negated the play *and* its aftermath. Dawson's first-down run was nullified, the Chiefs were forced to punt, and the Raiders tied the game before the clock ran out. This result eventually elevated Oakland to the division championship. It cost Dawson and his Chiefs—the defending Super Bowl champions, mind you—a 1970 playoff berth.

Davidson's tough-guy persona didn't end there. In *Conan the Barbarian*, he plays the bad guy opposite Arnold Schwarzenegger. In the adult film *Behind the Green Door*, featuring former Ivory Snow pitchwoman Marilyn Chambers, Davidson portrays a tuxedoed, ill-tempered bouncer named Porter. Davidson's finest screen moments are in the twenty-plus commercials he did for Miller Lite beer. The famous ensemble spot titled "First Lite Beer Bowling Tournament" is my favorite. With the score tied and Rodney Dangerfield about to roll his ball, Davidson advises him in his raspy, intimidating voice, "All we need is one pin, Rodney!" Dangerfield nets none—his ball bounces off them. Once again, no respect for Dangerfield!

On this late-1970s afternoon in California, Davidson answered his door, and Dawson shook his hand, possibly for the first and last time ever. As my crew lit a semi-outdoors patio set, I observed from a distance, hoping that Dawson and Davidson's playdate would turn out well. I wasn't really certain that this meeting was a good idea, but Dawson had agreed to it, so what the hell?

My concerns were unwarranted. Dawson and Davidson addressed each other with mutual respect. Soon they were reminiscing about the AFL's good old days. When they discussed the "unpleasant business" detailed earlier, Davidson offered no remorse, and Dawson expected none. For the duration of our visit, Davidson wore his tough-guy persona on his sleeve, Dawson his quarterback cool. Neither could be anything else. By the time of the interview, I was pretty sure that Davidson would *not* toss us into the pool.

Eventually, Lenny laid my list of questions aside, and the two began ad-libbing about all things AFL. Like Muhammad Ali and Joe Frazier after their three epic fights, the two very different gridiron warriors made a peace that was truly beautiful to behold. I watched it happen in real time, knowing that my final segment was going to light up the NBC Sports switchboard when it aired on Sunday afternoon.

That's why I always made time to seek out Leonard Dawson on Sunday mornings at Arrowhead. He would smile warmly each time I mentioned our magical day by the San Francisco Bay. And when I glanced at Dawson's Super Bowl ring—something Davidson never owned—how could I not remember his female admirer on the cable car? Sorry, Big Ben. Sometimes nice guys do finish first—and get to wear a big ring to prove it. Good for you, Len Dawson.

Fred Dean *(1952–2020)*

Defensive End

· San Diego Chargers (1975-81) · San Francisco 49ers (1981-85)

catalyst (n., *kat*-uh-list): a person or thing that precipitates an event

In October 1981, defensive end and pass-rush specialist Fred Dean arrived in San Francisco. At the time, the 49ers' record stood at 3–2. In Dean's first game with the team (October 11), head coach Bill Walsh had planned to use Dean sparingly. Instead, Dean played most of the game, logging two sacks and numerous pressures and keying San Francisco's 45–14 victory over the Dallas Cowboys. The 49ers won twelve of their next thirteen games, culminating with a 26–21 victory over the Cincinnati Bengals in Super Bowl XVI (16). A pro football dynasty was taking shape. Fred Dean was its *catalyst*.

Dean started his career in San Diego, one of three defensive linemen selected by the Chargers early in the 1975 NFL Draft (Southern Methodist University's Louie Kelcher and Grambling State's Gary "Big Hands" Johnson were the others). All three earned All-Pro honors during their NFL careers, but Dean was special: a lean, mean, pass-rushing machine who rebuffed the Chargers' efforts to convert him to outside linebacker. As a rookie (1975), Dean recorded 7.5 sacks. In 1978, he hit 15.5. That season, Don Coryell took over as the team's head coach. Quarterback Dan Fouts began to flourish as part of "Air Coryell," a potent vertical passing game that led the NFL in passing yards and total offense for six consecutive seasons (1978–83). With Dean spearheading the pass rush, San Diego seemed poised to be an annual Super Bowl contender.

But in 1981, Dean felt very betrayed by the Chargers.

During a 2015 interview with me in Ruston, Louisiana, Dean said, "My brother-in-law, he drives eighteen-wheelers. And he makes more money than me." He added, "I had been promised something, and it just didn't pan out. My thing was—either pay me or else. And they [the Chargers] took the 'or else.'"—one of the worst player personnel decisions by any NFL team ever!

The San Francisco 49ers gave Dean the money he wanted, Fred gave the 49ers the outside pass rush they needed, and the 49ers dynasty dominated the decade. They won Lombardi Trophies in two of Dean's five years with the team (1981 and 1984) and fell one win shy of a Super Bowl in a third (1983), losing the NFC Championship Game to Washington. During that 1983 season, Dean recorded 6 sacks against the New Orleans Saints, a single-game NFL record at the time. His 17.5 sacks led the NFC.

In 1984, Johnson and Kelcher joined Dean in San Francisco in time for Super Bowl XIX (19). On January 20, 1985, the 49ers pass rush sacked Dan Marino four times in a 38–16 rout, prompting this moment of amused anguish from Dan Fouts, Dean's former San Diego teammate: "That '75 Chargers draft gave us a defensive line that ended up being Pro Bowlers before they became Super Bowlers . . . in *San Francisco*!" Fouts and the Chargers never did play in a Super Bowl, but both Fouts and Dean made the Hall of Fame.

As Dean told me that day in Ruston, "I just wanted to prove to the Chargers that I was that caliber of player that could make a difference." That's what "catalysts" get paid to do.

Jack Del Rio Jr. *(born 1963)* 🏆

Linebacker

- New Orleans Saints (1985-86) · Kansas City Chiefs (1987-88)
- Dallas Cowboys (1989-91) · Minnesota Vikings (1992-95) · Miami Dolphins (1996)

Assistant Coach

- New Orleans Saints (1997-98) · Baltimore Ravens (1999-2001)

Defensive Coordinator

- Carolina Panthers (2002) · Denver Broncos (2012-14)
- Washington Commanders (2020-Present)

Head Coach

- Jacksonville Jaguars (2003-11) · Oakland Raiders (2015-17)

I knew a lot about Jack Del Rio before we met. Most college scholarship athletes commit to their best single sport and concentrate on it year-round, riding it as far as they can. By his own choice, Del Rio played football and baseball at the University of Southern California, excelling at both. On the diamond, Del Rio was a catcher on the same Trojans team as Randy Johnson. He caught the Big Unit while hitting .340 as a two-year starter. On the gridiron, Del Rio played linebacker. As a senior, he was a consensus All-American, co-MVP in a Rose Bowl, and the runner-up for the Lombardi Award, presented annually to the nation's best lineman or linebacker.

My first professional experience with Del Rio came in 1995, his next-to-last season as a player for the Vikings. TNT Sports had contracted NFL Films to produce a variation on our *Six Days to Sunday* show called *Six Days to Sunday Night*. Essentially, it was a behind-the-scenes look at the Vikings' and Cowboys' week-long preparations for their Week 3 Sunday night game on September 17, 1995.

I produced the Vikings' side of the event. Vikings head coach Dennis Green opened up his entire football operation, granting us total access. I arrived with three crews on September 9, shot the Lions–Vikings game on September 10, and then set up shop in the giant equipment shed at the Vikings' Eden Prairie, Minnesota, training facility. We brought dozens of rolls of Kodak film; every manner of camera, lens, light, and microphone; and enough beer to satisfy not only my crew but also curious Vikings players for the entire week—after hours, of course.

For most of our time there, Del Rio was conspicuous by his anonymity—until Friday's team lunch. By Coach Green's decree, Vikings rookies were responsible for providing catered meals every Friday for all football personnel. This feast was to be set up in the locker room and ready to go immediately following morning team activities. Special meal orders were an accepted part of the process. Del Rio ordered red beans and rice. Rookie safety Orlando Thomas—who went on to lead the league in interceptions and make several All-Pro teams—seemed to be in charge of this particular week's meal. For whatever reason, he forgot to order Del Rio's favorite dish.

So, Del Rio took action. After lunch, he and a group of Vikings veterans surrounded the rookie, then methodically taped him to his own locker. I'm talking yards and yards of ultra-adhesive athletic tape, designed to survive sweat and sticky enough to remove all body hair upon removal. Del Rio applied it liberally until Thomas could move only his mouth.

"You know why this is happening, don't you?" Del Rio asked Thomas, who hung his head in shame. "Next time, don't forget the red beans and rice!"

After retiring as a player, Del Rio went into coaching. By the summer of 2001, he was in his third season as the linebackers coach for the Baltimore Ravens, a group that included Ray Lewis. The Ravens went to camp as defending Super Bowl champions. Brimming with confidence and open to new challenges, they allowed NFL Films total access to their summer camp for the inaugural season of HBO's *Hard Knocks*, which I produced and directed for NFL Films.

When I asked the Ravens for input on potential story subjects, they suggested a rookie free-agent linebacker named Kenny Jackson, an elementary school teacher from California. His chances of making the final roster appeared slim, but his good looks and radiant personality made him an instant favorite with television audiences. That meant that Del Rio would be heavily featured as well, as the coach Jackson was trying to please.

For six weeks, Coach Del Rio tried to turn this great big, fast, likable athlete into a functional pro football linebacker. I wired Del Rio and Jackson at least twice a week and was privy to Del Rio's ongoing frustration: Jackson just couldn't master simple fundamentals. But Del Rio persisted, day in, day out. One afternoon toward the end of camp, while interviewing Del Rio in our isolated air-conditioned trailer, I turned off the camera and asked him bluntly, "Kenny's got no chance at all, does he?"

Del Rio responded diplomatically, "Hopefully he'll be a special teamer." He would not admit defeat.

Then, I ventured into uncharted territory: "You've got head-coaching ambitions, don't you?"

Without hesitation, Del Rio replied, "That's the plan, Bob." Despite Del Rio's best efforts, Jackson failed to crack the Ravens' talent-laden roster, but two years later, Del Rio replaced Tom Coughlin as head coach of the Jacksonville Jaguars. I couldn't have been happier for him.

If my NFL Films career taught me one thing, it was this: *Everybody* on NFL sidelines takes their cues from the head coach. Jacksonville's on-field security people could be difficult, but after Del Rio walked me through his bench area, reminiscing about *Hard Knocks*, I suddenly sensed fewer rent-a-cops disturbing me while I worked. The same went for the respect we received from players. On a rainy December day in 2010, I was shooting the Jaguars defensive line coach reaming his group over a long Raiders touchdown run. As a Jaguar lineman stared menacingly at my soundman's microphone, Del Rio approached.

"They're doing their job," Del Rio said sternly. "So how about you guys start doing yours?" Just like that, I was invisible. After that game, a thrilling 38–31 Jaguars win decided in the closing seconds, Del Rio noticed my crew in pursuit. He deliberately slowed down to give us a sound bite.

"That's a big one for us, Bob," (paraphrasing) he announced. He delivered his postgame locker room speech with verve and passion. His players cleared a lane so "Bob" could capture the moment with an unobstructed view. Then, Jack thanked my crew for being there.

As of 2022, Del Rio is coordinating the Washington Commanders' defense. I fully expect him to get another chance at head coaching. In the interim, one of these days, I just may surprise him with an online order of red beans and rice. It's the least I can do after his years of on-field cooperation.

Dan Dierdorf *(born 1949)*

Offensive Tackle

- St. Louis Cardinals (1971-83)

For many years, I only knew Dan Dierdorf from a distance, but I'd heard things about him. An NFL general manager once told me, "He wasn't even the best offensive lineman on his own team." Yet the National Football League Players Association (NFLPA) named him the game's "Best Blocker" three years in a row (1976–78). Player recognition is no accident, nor is the fact that during that period, the Cardinals allowed the fewest sacks in football *five* years in a row.

After football, Dierdorf transitioned into broadcasting, first as a radio analyst for football and hockey in St. Louis (1984), then as an NFL game analyst for CBS Sports (1985–86). In 1987, he became the third man in the booth with Al Michaels and Frank Gifford on ABC's *Monday Night Football*, the Rolls-Royce of NFL telecasts at the time. Dierdorf's concise language and candid insights appealed to the football fan in me, but his idle chatter about crew hotels and gourmet meals seemed a bit pretentious. Again, all of this occurred at a distance.

Near the end of the 1987 season, NFL Films assigned me to direct a series of live-to-tape stand-ups with Dierdorf on location in San Diego for its annual *Road to the Super Bowl* show. These stand-ups involved big-time interior and exterior lighting, tracking shots, teleprompters, makeup, and all the other trappings to which network talent is accustomed. Dierdorf's official credit would read "Hosted by Dan Dierdorf." Everything else was up to me.

I remember shaking Dierdorf's hand for the first time—I'd never seen bigger fingers. Preproduction went smoothly enough, but when we set up for our first shot—a hilltop exterior looking down on Jack Murphy Stadium—the trouble began. Dierdorf's copy mentioned "a farewell to Walter Payton, a guy who showed us what style and grace really are." But I wasn't sure how much actual Payton footage was in the segment—if any. Unfortunately, I said this out loud.

Dierdorf drew a hard line in the sand. "You've got to pay tribute to the guy," he insisted. When we struck the set to move into the stadium, I found a pay phone and called Steve Sabol. "He's the *host*," Sabol reminded me. "*We'll* produce the show." Needless to say, none of this went over well with Dierdorf: "You gotta tell your boss Payton's retirement has to be a part of the segment we just did, Bob. Or we've got a problem!" His dogged determination was genuine.

This back-and-forth went on most of the day. With each new setup, Dierdorf wanted a progress report. And each time, I had to find a pay phone, call Steve, give him an update, and then report back to Dierdorf. Oh, yes—and walk the camera operator, the soundman, the track rigger, the lighting crew, the prompter guy, and so forth through the next setup and shot. My meticulous shooting schedule turned to crap in a hurry. Every phone call and discussion cost us another ten to twenty minutes. By the time we reached my fully sunlit late-afternoon-San-Diego-skyline-in-the-background payoff dolly shot, it was early evening. We rushed through the setup, accepted a less-than-perfect final take, then headed off to the airport to catch a red-eye home. I was thoroughly disillusioned.

In retrospect, Dierdorf and ABC did NFL Films a favor. Eventually, Steve Sabol authorized changes to the segment to include Payton's retirement, and all seemed right with the world. When I ran into Dierdorf on the field during the pregame of Super Bowl XXII (22), his huge mitt again enveloped my hand. "Nice job, Bob. It all worked out well," he said.

In retrospect, Dierdorf's candor in standing his ground was admirable. The 1987 season included a month-long players strike. NFL owners countered by hiring replacement players. As I watched our editors sprinkle Dierdorf's segments into our NFL Films production, I finally heard the *meaning* rather than the *words* in ABC's well-crafted scripts. Even better was Dierdorf's sincerity in delivering observations: "A disastrous strike for the players who had no chance of winning . . . and they didn't. . . . NFL owners embarked on a policy of replacement games that would count in the standings and in doing so—I think—seriously damaged the credibility of the game."

NFL Films couldn't say these things without repercussions. Dierdorf could and did. Dierdorf lasted eleven seasons on *Monday Night Football* (1987–97). In 1996, he was voted into the Pro Football Hall of Fame. I remembered the NFL executive who questioned Dierdorf's talent level. I heard a new complaint, paraphrased here: "Of course he made the hall . . . he campaigned for years on Monday nights." Again, someone was faulting Dierdorf's dogged determination. And again, standing his ground and expressing himself honestly paid off.

As irony would have it, Dierdorf grew up in Canton, Ohio, just blocks from the Hall of Fame. As a youth, he witnessed Pete Rozelle's 1962 ground-breaking ceremony. What I remember most about his acceptance speech involved the hall's alleged seven-minute time limit on speeches. In Dierdorf's words, "We're told we have seven minutes when we come up here. . . . They have a red light and a white light. . . . The white one goes on when you have a minute left . . . and the red one when you're supposed to finish. I just want you to know . . . I unscrewed them [both]!"

In the late 1990s, when the *new* Cleveland Browns were building their new waterfront stadium, Dierdorf signed on to help the Browns sell seat licenses. I produced a film for the marketing group promoting those licenses and selling those seats. Once again, Dierdorf and I would work together. This time, I wrote all of Dan's scripts. The marketing firm even hired a helicopter to shoot cityscapes and aerials of the construction site. I decided to make a dramatic descent into old Municipal Stadium timed with Dierdorf's emergence from one of the dugouts. It almost worked.

The chopper's engine made the audio useless, but Dierdorf braved the breeze from the whirling blades and walked out to his spot in the infield amid the din and dust just as I designed. I knew that we couldn't possibly coordinate Dierdorf's walkout with the helicopter's lengthy landing procedure. I'm not even sure why I insisted that Dierdorf do it—payback, probably! But in final postproduction, we made the whole jagged, disjointed thing work—this time, it was NFL Films showing dogged determination.

I haven't seen Thick Fingers since. In retrospect, Dierdorf's induction into the Hall of Fame was inevitable. Not only was he a "Best Blocker"; he was a man of true integrity, whose words carried real weight. He represents all the things that are "right" about America's love affair with pro football. And, like Payton, Dierdorf's dogged determination has always allowed for "style and grace."

John Elway *(born 1960)*

Quarterback

- Denver Broncos (1983–98)

I resented John Elway before he took his first NFL snap. How dare this great big talented kid from Stanford threaten to play major league baseball and force a trade rather than report to the lowly Baltimore Colts, the team that selected him with the first overall pick in the 1983 NFL Draft?

Sometimes, in our zeal to tell a story, we storytellers fail to recognize that, given the right opportunity, great players will tell their own. Elway didn't like being "sentenced" to a bad team. But once he gave his commitment, he honored it for a lifetime.

I shot his NFL regular-season debut against the Pittsburgh Steelers, on September 4, 1983. As Pittsburgh fans taunted him, Elway stuck his hands behind a Broncos guard rather than his center. No football forthcoming there! From an end-zone angle, I watched Pittsburgh linebacker Jack Lambert faking blitzes on nearly every snap. Eventually, Lambert came and leveled Mr. Too-Good-for-Baltimore for a major loss. I cheered the moment. Before being replaced, Elway completed one pass for 14 yards with an interception. Welcome to the NFL.

His rookie season numbers were not impressive: 7 touchdown passes against 14 interceptions, with a 54.9 passer rating. I shed no tears over his year-long struggles, and I wasn't satisfied yet. When he started winning games with fourth-quarter comebacks, I pointed out, "That's because he plays horribly for three quarters." In his first NFL decade, he threw more interceptions than touchdowns and only once posted a passer rating above the league average of 80. In three Super Bowls (XXI [21], XXII [22], and XXIV [24]), he led Denver's offense to just 40 total points in those defeats.

After a 55–10 drubbing by the 49ers in Super Bowl XXIV (24), I did not see Elway in person again until January 9, 1994. That day, I shot a Broncos–Raiders playoff game in the LA Coliseum. Raiders fans were shoveling more verbal sh*t Elway's way than even he deserved. After documenting the profane abuse, I scurried over and knelt down in front of Elway for a reaction.

"Looks like you've got a fan club?" I said out loud. Elway studied me, smiled broadly at all the hoopla going on behind him, then uttered a response that immediately changed my feelings: "LA mutants!" He glanced down again to gauge my reaction. I smiled. Quick wit!

The Raiders beat the Broncos that day, 42–24. But Elway eclipsed 4,000 passing yards in a season for the first time in his career. Slowly, my attitude toward Elway began to morph into respect. I realized that he was stuck in an old-school system with little support from skill players. In 1995, all that changed when Mike Shanahan became Denver's head coach and general manager. First, he drafted Georgia running back Terrell Davis. Then, he installed his "Stretch Play" running-game system, turning Davis into an instant star and giving Elway the offensive help he'd always needed.

In 1996, the Associated Press named Davis the NFL Offensive Player of the Year. Denver won thirteen games before an upset loss to Jacksonville in the playoffs. In 1997 and 1998, Elway and the Denver Broncos became the sixth team ever to win back-to-back Super Bowls. Prior to Super Bowl XXXII (32), I spent a week in Denver directing "Super Bowl Diaries," a pregame segment series for NFL Network. My crew spent one lovely evening as guests of John and Janet Elway at their suburban Denver home—or at least, that's how things got started. As Elway served us beers, I decided not to share my feelings regarding his early years. Instead, I listened with curiosity (and sympathy) as Elway described his son Jack's football aspirations: "Guess what? He wants to be a quarterback!" he lamented. Not many Hall of Fame passers want their sons to follow in their footsteps.

Later that evening, Elway gathered his family and whisked them all off to a Denver-based Dave and Buster's. I remember just two things about that night. First, everybody in the establishment recognized Elway instantly, but not one person sidled up to him or asked for an autograph. When I asked store managers whether they'd made an announcement or advised patrons to keep their distance, they all replied, "Nope . . . we didn't even know he was coming."

Even better was watching father John compete with his son Jack at various ball-throwing events. John allowed Jack to keep scores close, but ultimately, father always made one more basket or rolled up five more points than son. To make up for it later, Elway became Jack's quarterback coach during his senior year at Cherry Creek High School. Jack made Colorado All-State and then accepted a full ride to quarterback at Arizona State University. But living up to Dad's standards proved to be difficult. Today, Jack owns a company called Mint Tradition that sells designer hats.

As for Elway, in Super Bowl XXXII (32), his now-famous "whirlybird" first-down leap late in the fourth quarter became the calling-card moment of Denver's 31–24 win over Mike Holmgren's Green Bay Packers. After the game, Broncos owner Pat Bowlen elevated the Lombardi Trophy and then announced, "This one's for John!" The following year, in Super Bowl XXXIII (33), Elway's 80-yard touchdown pass to wide receiver Rod Smith propelled Denver to a 34–19 victory over Atlanta. Elway was named the game's MVP. Shortly thereafter, he retired.

NFL players dream about "going out on top." Elway actually did it. Five years after Elway's second Super Bowl triumph, the Pro Football Hall of Fame enshrined him in his first year of eligibility. Then, in 2011, Broncos owner Bowlen hired Elway to become the team's general manager and executive vice president of Football Operations. Elway was back in the game.

When the Indianapolis Colts made Peyton Manning a free agent, Elway welcomed the veteran passer to Denver. Manning led the Broncos to four consecutive AFC Western Division titles (2012–15) and a pair of Super Bowls. After enduring a blowout defeat to Seattle in Super Bowl XLVIII (48), GM Elway signed free-agent defenders DeMarcus Ware, Aqib Talib, and T. J. Ward. One year later, he dismissed head coach John Fox, then replaced him with his own former backup quarterback, Broncos offensive coordinator Gary Kubiak. Veteran defensive coordinator Wade Phillips and pass rusher extraordinaire Von Miller completed Elway's front office masterpiece.

In Super Bowl 50, Denver beat Carolina 24–10 to win the team's third Lombardi Trophy. Von Miller was named MVP, and it was Manning's turn to go out on top—very fitting. I could *not* have been more wrong about Elway's football mission.

Norman "Boomer" Esiason *(born 1961)*

Quarterback

- Cincinnati Bengals (1984-92, 1997) · New York Jets (1993-95)
- Arizona Cardinals (1996)

Nobody ever looked more like the old-fashioned stereotype of an NFL quarterback than Norman "Boomer" Esiason: six feet five inches, 220 pounds, blonde hair, blue eyes, and a perfect left-handed throwing motion! Seriously, if I were writing a movie about a mad geneticist trying to clone the prototypical professional passer, he would use Esiason's DNA.

And what hasn't he done? In 1988, he won the league's MVP award while leading Sam Wyche's Bengals to Super Bowl XXIII (23). Only Joe Montana's last-second heroics prevented Esiason from adding a world championship to his resume. He played for fourteen seasons, made four Pro Bowls, retired with just under 38,000 career passing yards, and earned the prestigious Walter Payton NFL Man of the Year Award in 1995 for his noteworthy charitable endeavors.

After football, he transitioned into broadcasting as a game analyst on *Monday Night Football.* He's been a regular on CBS's *The NFL Today* and Showtime's *Inside the NFL.* In 2007, Esiason began work on WFAN's (New York City) morning sports talk show, the top-rated program in its time period. He's appeared in dozens of television shows and commercials. He cohosted a Miss America pageant and a Macy's Thanksgiving Day parade. He's guest-starred on episodes of *Family Feud* and *Blue Bloods.* He's coauthored books and grown his Boomer Esiason Foundation (benefiting cystic-fibrosis patients) into a major philanthropic force. Nassau County, New York, inducted him into its Hall of Fame. He may walk on water.

But it took three encounters and three decades for Esiason and me to find our groove. Esiason's growth over that period was gratifying to behold.

In the late 1980s, a fellow NFL Films producer and I made *NFL Kids: A Field of Dreams.* We wrote a script about a dream world in which four children would interact with and learn from their NFL heroes. We employed artists and set designers to turn our sound stage into a combination kid's bedroom and football fantasy land. We matched four players (Esiason, Ronnie Lott, Michael Irvin, and Christian Okoye) with four children ages eight to eleven. Finally, without the benefit of rehearsal, we started shooting: two days with the four young people, and one day apiece with each of the NFL players matched with one individual youngster. Good luck to us.

The moment Esiason arrived, he started offering free advice. The problem was that his child actor and partner on set was *not* the most agreeable kid I've ever encountered. We didn't need Esiason making things more difficult: "There's too much in this script for one day" (that's because we couldn't afford two days of your fee). "You guys should be recording your voiceover while I'm in makeup" (it's not finalized yet, sir!). "There's not very much room out there on that stage" (no sh*t, Sherlock! Now help us wrangle your little costar, would you please?!).

In the spring of 2005, at a Fort Lauderdale resort, NFL Films produced *EA Sports NFL Quarterback Challenge*. We asked Esiason to do analysis and commentary alongside Rich Eisen (play by play) and Bonnie Bernstein (color commentary and interviews). I directed the entire event. The original *Quarterback Challenge* concept used NFL passers and a slew of lifeless standing and moving targets. Despite some strong casts, most of those events went on to yield very lackluster TV shows, so the league asked us to revamp the format. A fellow producer and I went to lunch at a Boston Market and came up with the following.

First, we added real-life NFL receivers for two of the four events. Second, I insisted on wiring the quarterbacks so they could hear the broadcast team and respond to them during actual events. Finally, and most importantly, we weighted scoring in the final event to make certain that the winner would be decided in the show's closing minutes. We even revamped the "Legends" component, adding some alumni quarterbacks, including Esiason.

Boomer loved it. He said, "Look at all these guys with arthritis" before finishing second to John Elway in the "Legends Accuracy" competition. When Carson Palmer hollered, "Bad ball!" after overthrowing a wide-open receiver, Esiason advised, "Don't tell *him* [the receiver] that." When Drew Brees's first pass in the "Long Distance" event came up way short, Esiason said, "Hey, Joe Montana couldn't throw 40 yards either." Panthers QB Jake Delhomme won the grand prize in our finale, the "Prilosec No-Huddle Drill," a mouthful even for Eisen. Before it began, Delhomme complained, "You've got to start again, Boomer's bothering me." It made for some interesting TV, only this time, Esiason was getting under everybody else's skin.

In 2015, Esiason and I met again. The NFL was celebrating five decades of Super Bowls and had commissioned Wilson Sporting Goods to create three thousand golden-skin footballs, one for every living player and coach who'd participated in the ultimate game. *CBS This Morning* offered NFL Films major coin to produce ten segments involving Golden Football recipients at various awards ceremonies. Because WFAN is a CBS station, Esiason became one of our subjects.

Norman Esiason had attended East Islip High School on Long Island. At our preproduction meeting the day before Boomer was scheduled to receive his football, the principal and staff of East Islip offered us unconditional cooperation. They scheduled a mid-morning pep rally involving the entire student body; they shuttered the gymnasium and then covered the walls with signs welcoming home their conquering hero; and they swore every teacher, janitor, and cafeteria worker to secrecy. That night, the president of the school board announced to all present that "Boomer is coming."

When the band started playing and Esiason emerged from the gymnasium bowels, East Islip HS went bananas. Tall, blond, and beautiful, Esiason strode through a gauntlet of cheerleaders and well-wishers like the respectful, well-meaning East Islip boy he truly is. As the director, I knew instantly that this segment would be a cinch to edit and a pleasure to watch. And Esiason didn't piss off anybody.

When it aired on *CBS This Morning*, the network's producers opened the program block with Esiason live in WFAN's studio. Next came my segment, followed by an interview with Boomer still on set. The program block ran nearly twelve minutes, an eternity for live morning television. And throughout, Esiason was all smiles. Our third time was truly a charm.

Leslie Frazier *(born 1959)* 🏆

Cornerback

- Chicago Bears (1981-85)

Assistant Coach

- Philadelphia Eagles (1999-2002) · Cincinnati Bengals (2003-04)
- Indianapolis Colts (2005-06) · Baltimore Ravens (2016)

Defensive Coordinator

- Minnesota Vikings (2007-10) · Tampa Bay Buccaneers (2014-15)
- Buffalo Bills (2017-23)

Head Coach

- Minnesota Vikings (2011-13)

NFL trivia: Who led the vaunted 1985 Chicago Bears defense in interceptions? And who is the only member of that defense to become a Super Bowl champion as a player *and* a coach? The answer to both is Leslie Frazier. His six picks paced that record-breaking Bears defense, and his coaching helped the 2006 Indianapolis Colts win Super Bowl XLI (41).

I spent time around Frazier at each of his NFL stops. Not only did I have no idea who he was; I had no actual recollection of his time with Buddy Ryan's incredible 1985 Bears defense. I just knew that Frazier knew his stuff and that his players respected him. When Frazier replaced Brad Childress as the Vikings head coach before the end of the 2010 season, I studied his résumé. This guy was the real deal, both as a player and as a mentor of men. We became first-name colleagues.

In 2013, the Discovery Channel decided to become an active broadcast partner with the NFL. In particular, the network wanted NFL Films to dust off and then redeploy our tried and proven *Six Days to Sunday* format with that season's two Wembley Stadium regular-season NFL contests.

On September 22, 2013, I shot the Vikings' 31–27 home loss to Cleveland. That made Minnesota 0–3 on the season, with a trip to London coming up. Ben Roethlisberger and the 0–3 Pittsburgh Steelers would be their Wembley opponent. My job was to make things work with the Vikings so NFL Films could cash the Discovery Channel's check in good conscience.

The NFL set up the Vikings contingent at the Grove Hotel in Watford, a charming eighteenth-century landmark eighteen miles outside London. The Vikings seemed inspired by the enchanted surroundings . . . until I handed Minnesota's media relations executive Bob Hagan a lengthy laundry list of things I wanted to accomplish: daily interviews, practice wirings, multiple on-field cameras shooting player and coach subjects from up-close vantage points, prearranged off-field activity shoots, league-sponsored events at London landmarks, and more.

Surprisingly, Hagan agreed to pretty much all of it—until we actually started working. Then, the proverbial poop hit the propeller: "Bob, my owner and my general manager are all over me." In my experience, additional coverage often makes players clam up and seek cover. Organizations worry that it will distract or embarrass them. In the end, it usually comes down to trust, and trust comes down to relationships. Like most media relations folks dealing with an aggressive director during an unexpected and dreadful losing streak, Hagan was desperate to reconcile his promises to me with his reality.

"Let me talk to them," I said.

I spoke to Vikings owner and president Mark Wilf and general manager Rick Spielman jointly, my camera still mounted on my shoulder. Together, they asked whether Pittsburgh was allowing similar access across the pond in the Steel City. Although I answered, "Yes," I knew that Pittsburgh head coach Mike Tomlin was making my colleagues beg for table scraps. Wilf and Spielman questioned why I had microphones scattered all over the practice field. I diplomatically responded, "So we can hear what our cameras are seeing." I assured them that nothing we captured would be used without their consent, although I had no idea whether that was enforceable. Then, I took a calculated risk. Luckily, I had an existing relationship with a member of the organization who understood teamwork and people.

"Why don't you ask Coach Frazier how he feels about all this?"

Spielman liked that idea, so off he went toward Frazier, who was standing on the other side of the field complex. I resumed working, keeping one eye on that distant conversation. Sometimes, it pays to roll the dice. I saw Leslie look my way and then turn back to Spielman and speak his mind. A few moments later, Spielman reported to Wilf, who spoke to a very relieved Bob Hagan. Apparently, Frazier told them (in summary), "The players seem very relaxed and haven't practiced this well since training camp." Bacon saved. The rest of our week went swimmingly.

We shot Jared Allen playing golf with quarterback Matt Cassel. Later that night, Allen and his fellow defensive linemen drank with my crew until curfew. Adrian Peterson allowed a producer to tag along with him as he toured Piccadilly. Every interview I scheduled with Vikings players and coaches went off without a hitch. And the Vikings showed up on Sunday mentally relaxed and ready to reverse their fortunes against an equally determined Steelers team.

In the end, in front of eighty-three-thousand-plus at the world-famous Wembley Stadium, Minnesota prevailed, 34–27. Thanks to my recently tested ties with the Vikings, we wired Peterson and Allen for the game. Peterson ran for 140 yards and 2 touchdowns, one from 60 yards out. Allen made good on a pregame promise, recording 2 sacks and several other quarterback hits. He even got his hand on the fumbled football that terminated the Steelers' potential game-tying drive as time ran out.

When the show aired a week later on Discovery, NFL Films folks said, "Well, of course, Angelo gets to do whatever he wants with the Vikings." I'm not sure whether I ever told anybody about my twelve long minutes on the practice field waiting for Frazier to pass judgment on our enterprise. I'm not even sure why I knew that Leslie would let us keep working. I just did. Unfortunately, Frazier barely survived the season.

After three less-than-successful seasons as an assistant in Baltimore and a coordinator in Tampa Bay, in 2017 Frazier joined the staff of the Buffalo Bills. Buffalo made the NFL playoffs five times during Leslie's six years with the team. Four of Frazier's defenses ranked in the league's top five in fewest yards allowed. His 2021 defense ranked as the NFL's overall best.

By his own choice, he won't return to Buffalo in 2023. But he will be back. And with any luck, he'll get another shot in a Super Bowl. Good for you, Leslie Frazier. Keep plying your trade. And thanks for the vote of confidence.

Frank Gifford *(1930–2015)*

Halfback/Wide Receiver

- New York Giants (1952–60, 1962–64)

In my early years at NFL Films, a senior colleague wrote these words about Hall of Famer Frank Gifford: "He was a diamond stickpin in the lapel of pro football."

I barely remember Gifford as a player. I recall seeing him on *Captain Kangaroo* one morning when I was home sick from school. I read that he won the NFL's Most Valuable Player Award in 1956, helping the Giants win their first NFL championship since 1938. I produced a segment on "The Dynasty That Never Happened," chronicling the team's five consecutive championship-game losses in six years (1958, 1959, and 1961–63), four of which Gifford played in. And I learned about Eagles linebacker Chuck Bednarik's knockout tackle that sidelined the game's "diamond stickpin" for eighteen months, paving the way for the Philadelphia Eagles' 1960 NFL championship season.

Yes, I watched and liked Gifford when he was part of CBS's pioneering 1960s Sunday pregame shows. NFL Films produced segments for these original programs. Gifford also did lead-ins for our highlight films and syndicated specials. To me, Gifford's voice "sounded" like NFL football, much the way the voices of Pat Summerall, Ray Scott, or Curt Gowdy did.

In 1971, however, I discovered another side of Gifford. As a college student aspiring to do something NFL-related after graduation, I was disturbed by Gifford's *Monday Night Football* presence. My issue: How could a play-by-play announcer make *so many mistakes*? Don't believe me? Go to YouTube and call up any Monday night telecast involving Gifford doing play by play. I promise you'll hear a minimum of five mistakes per quarter—and he prepared for all these events! After joining NFL Films, I observed him one workday at the NFL's Park Avenue corporate offices, sitting alone in a lobby with a clipboard of information, boning up for the following week's telecast.

Until 1982, my feelings toward Gifford were more annoyance than real disdain. Then, I began working on the 1981 New York Giants highlight film, which Gifford would narrate. As I edited and wrote the film, I made every effort to confirm each fact and temper every judgment in my script. Prior to Gifford's scheduled narration, Steve Sabol prepared me to meet NFL royalty, but a veteran fellow producer warned me to wear my "thickest skin."

Every narrator does things differently. Some like to do complete read-throughs before going back for pickups. Others prefer to read single pages or clearly delineated sections before stopping. A few want to do one line at a time, wait for approval, then move on to the next line, so there's nothing left to do when finished. And a handful consider their first reads to be perfect unless they stop themselves for undisclosed reasons. Guess which kind Gifford was?

"I've been doing these a long time," he reminded me early on. Too bad, pal. I was editing the film, and I knew what I wanted. Near the end of Part 1, I underlined the word *first*. When Gifford finished, I hit my talkback button and asked him to read the line again, emphasizing *first*, as in "The *first* Giants playoff team in nearly two decades." I don't remember his exact response, but paraphrasing from memory: "If you're going to keep stopping me like this, we're never going to get through this." Later, I asked him to reread one line a bit slower. Again, he bristled, became condescending, then reminded me that he was doing television long before I was born. Yeah, *Captain Kangaroo*. By then, I'd grown immune to his caustic temperament. I also couldn't stop wondering why his face was covered with pancake makeup for a voiceover session.

When he left, Steve Sabol summoned me for a debriefing. I described my issues, but Steve insisted that I was being too picky, that every line does not have to be read a certain way, and that, ultimately, Gifford's voice recognition would enhance the film and elevate its impact. I thought, "Bullsh*t," but stifled my resentment and went about my business while Steve and Gifford went to lunch.

A month or so later, the Giants public relations staff invited me and Steve to the 1981 Giants highlight film media premiere at the Meadowlands. When I learned that Gifford would also be there, holding court and shimmering in the spotlight, I declined the invite, but Steve made it quite clear that refusal was not an option. So, one early spring day in 1982, we piled into a well-marked NFL Films van and drove up the Jersey Turnpike to the premiere.

Lunch included an open bar. I ordered a second cocktail while I was swallowing my first. Lots of media folks had gathered around Gifford. At one point, I heard Gifford proclaim, "They [NFL Films] usually do a good job matching pictures to my words." I contemplated ordering a third drink.

First off, visual storytelling drives good filmmaking. Quality images and natural original sound come first. They are primary. Music comes second. It establishes tone and tempo, and it creates mood and services cinematic dynamics. And *my* script—not *your* words—sets up and foreshadows cinematic high points, provides context for and interprets images and montages, and describes, details, and delineates visual storytelling as necessary. If anything, I thought, *your* words make me want to pour my double vodka on your thinning hair, then watch your makeup wash away that pompous, conceited smirk on your face. I quickly ordered another drink for the screening.

When the film ended, the media folks, who earlier had surrounded Gifford, suddenly wanted to hear what *I* had to say. I was flattered—and tipsy. Steve eventually joined me and shared the stage. When the writers were finished, along came Gifford. Without much ado, he looked me in the eyes, extended his hand, and said, "That really turned out pretty well, Bob."

On the way to the van, Steve put his arm around me and told me how much the Giants and all the media folks liked the film. He, too, had downed a few vodkas! I was truly enjoying the moment. But deep inside, I was feeling like a smacked ass. I realized that Gifford's comforting voice had, in fact, made my little highlight film a legitimate football movie. All my resentment and stifled rage seemed like one great big overreaction. I'd been suffering for naught.

In the end, the "diamond stickpin" delivered in the only way he knew how: with his charmed radiance at the center of it all. I tried hard to make this event a learning experience—but in the end, I failed.

Jerry Glanville (*born 1941*)

Head Coach

- Houston Oilers (1985-89) • Atlanta Falcons (1990-93)

Steve Sabol had a name for such coaches as Jerry Glanville: "meal tickets." When other teams wouldn't allow game-day wirings, player interviews, or potentially invasive special projects, we could always count on Glanville. The man enjoyed the spotlight—and, usually, so did his teams.

At a 1988 preseason game in Dallas, Glanville and his Houston Oilers were in winning form. Glanville was wearing a wire and thoroughly enjoying his team's 54–10 annihilation of Tom Landry's Dallas Cowboys. I was shooting handheld action while listening to the wire. Over the years, Glanville's sharp tongue and biting wit yielded dozens of amusing sound bites.

Speaking to a rookie: "All your friends here tonight?" Pause. "Where they both sittin'?"

Excoriating a rookie game official: "This is the N-F-L, which means Not For Long when you make those f***ing calls. . . . [Keep up these calls and] I'll be selling groceries!"

And finally, the ultimate setup: "See that guy over there?" He pointed out an opponent whose jersey nameplate read KOWALKOWSKI. "I coached his dad in Detroit." The unsuspecting assistant coach fell for it. "What was his dad's name?" he asked. "Kowalkowski," Glanville replied.

Glanville's Oilers played aggressively—and that's putting it nicely. Houston's division rivals used such terms as *dirty* and *cheap-shot artists* to describe them. AFC Central games often ended in controversy. On December 17, 1989, Sam Wyche's Bengals deliberately ran up the score in Cincinnati, thrashing Houston, 61–7. In his postgame interview, when asked whether he thought less of Wyche, Glanville replied succinctly, "I don't think any less of Sam now than I ever did."

Pittsburgh Steelers Hall of Fame head coach Chuck Noll took things one step further. Following a late-season 1987 loss to the Oilers, the usually stoic Noll pointed his index finger at Glanville during a postgame handshake while uttering a thinly veiled threat: "Your f***ing guys coming over and jumping people like that are gonna get your ass in trouble. Just know that, I'm serious."

Glanville evoked strong responses. He carefully cultivated a "bad boy" image, wearing nothing but black, driving Harley-Davidsons, and leaving tickets for James Dean and Elvis Presley at stadium will-call windows. Nonetheless, his Oilers became contenders. But in playoff games, Houston never advanced beyond the divisional round. A 26–23 overtime loss to the Steelers on New Year's Eve in 1989 ended Glanville's tenure in Texas.

One week later, Glanville signed a contract to coach the Atlanta Falcons. That summer (1990), Glanville invited Buddy Ryan's Philadelphia Eagles to Georgia for a good old-fashioned training-camp scrimmage. I took an NFL Films crew there to document Glanville's latest adventures. Soon after the scrimmage began, a near riot erupted.

Two groups of very large angry men were going at it while Glanville screamed obscenities at Eagles coaches. No cops or grown-ups were anywhere to be found. I literally feared for the lives of my crew. Fortunately, after the initial surge and lots of helmet punches and such, cooler heads prevailed.

That same trip, we shot a Saturday morning offensive walk-through session with a stedicam, several handheld cameras, and a sound mixer literally mired in the middle of it all, forcing players to maneuver around us. No NFL head coach, friend or foe, ever granted us that kind of all-encompassing and intrusive access. Like I said, "meal ticket."

In four tumultuous years with the Falcons, Glanville posted just one winning season—1991—and even that year carries a huge asterisk. In 1991, Atlanta selected University of Southern Mississippi quarterback Brett Favre in the second round of the NFL Draft (thirty-third overall pick), but Favre took his time showing up in Atlanta. Favre's agent, Bus Cook, shopped him to Canadian teams, hoping to drive up his Falcons contract. Glanville reportedly said, "F*** that kid," often within the confines of the team facility. When Favre finally did show up, on July 17, Glanville said that "it would take a plane crash" for Favre to appear in an NFL game. Glanville was kidding, but just barely.

In 1991, Favre threw just 4 passes for the Falcons, 2 of which were intercepted. Atlanta, meanwhile, won ten games and generated quite a following. MC Hammer's chart-topping hit "2 Legit 2 Quit" became the team's theme song and mantra. Deion Sanders hit a 3-run homer for the Atlanta Braves one day, then reported to the Falcons' facility the next.

Atlanta actually won a playoff game against New Orleans before losing a divisional round game to Washington. The future looked bright for Glanville and his Falcons.

But after back-to-back 6–10 finishes, Atlanta and Glanville parted ways. He would never again coach an NFL team. Favre played nineteen seasons and completed 6,000-plus passes for 70,000-plus yards and 500-plus touchdowns faster than any quarterback before him. Favre also remains the only player to have won the Associated Press MVP Award three years in succession (1995–97). He played in back-to-back Super Bowls, won Super Bowl XXXI (31), and joined the Pro Football Hall of Fame in 2016. Even "meal tickets" don't get a pass on decisions like that one.

After three decades of coaching in the NFL, Glanville took up college coaching, Canadian Football League coaching, XFL coaching, sports broadcasting, and, last but not least—auto racing. In my final decade at NFL Films, I traveled to his Georgia home in the hills several times to interview him for assorted shows. I was there one fateful day in Minnesota when he hopped on a Harley, drove into a bystander, and incurred a lawsuit.

Yes, Glanville relishes the spotlight—sometimes a bit too much for his own good.

Otto Graham *(1921–2003)*

Quarterback

- Cleveland Browns (1946-55)

NFL trivia: Who's the winningest quarterback (by percentage of games won) in NFL history? Your first ten guesses don't count.

In my role as the coordinating producer of the "NFL Storybook" segments for HBO Sports's weekly show *Inside the NFL*, I interviewed Otto Graham three times late in his life, around the turn of the millennium at his home in Sarasota, Florida. Graham's win percentage of .810 ranks at the top of the heap. In short, Graham won four out of every five pro football games in which he played—impressive even in Graham's leather-helmet era. And there's more. In his decade-long pro playing career, Graham took his Cleveland Browns to championship games *ten times*. That's every year he played. He won *seven* of those ten games. That's 70 percent! And that's absolutely incredible!

The Cleveland Browns spent the first four years of their existence in the All-American Football Conference (AAFC), a rival league to the NFL. My interviews with Graham covered three events in Graham's combined AAFC and NFL careers: (1) a 1948 road trip during which the Browns won three games in eight days; (2) the Browns' first-ever NFL game in 1950, an opening-night contest against the 1949 NFL champion Philadelphia Eagles; and (3) Graham's last career appearance, the Browns' 1955 NFL Championship Game victory over the Rams in Los Angeles.

During the four years the AAFC existed (1946–49), Cleveland won four straight championships. Their cumulative regular season record over those years was 47–4–3. Twice (1947–48) Graham earned MVP honors. In 1948, Cleveland finished the season undefeated (14–0) then beat Buffalo, 49–7, for the AAFC Championship. Along the way, they won three road games in eight days. On November 21, they dispatched the New York Yankees in Yankee Stadium, 34–21. Next came a cross-country trip to Los Angeles for a 31–14 Thanksgiving Day (November 25) win over the LA Dons. That Sunday, November 28, the Browns closed out their trifecta with a 31–28 victory over the 11–1 San Francisco 49ers in old Kezar Stadium. Graham played through a knee injury he suffered on Thanksgiving, rallying the Browns from a 21–10 third-quarter deficit.

"We were running on fumes," Graham told me during one of our interviews. "We were all soaking in pools in Los Angeles to try to get our muscles back. And I didn't even know if I could play because of my knee. But, you know, with Paul Brown, there was no such thing as giving up." Afterward, Cleveland coach Paul Brown called it simply "Otto's greatest performance."

Following the 1949 season, the AAFC folded. Cleveland and two other teams (San Francisco and the Baltimore Colts) joined the NFL. For years, NFL players and coaches looked down their collective noses at the AAFC and its teams. To validate their disdain, the 1950 NFL schedule matched the Browns against the NFL champion Eagles on opening day, September 16. On a Saturday night in Philadelphia, more than seventy-one thousand paying customers jammed into Municipal Stadium to watch the Eagles show the upstart Browns how *real* football was played.

But the humbling never happened. When Philly's opening drive stalled, the Eagles punted to Cleveland's Don Phelps, who returned it 64 yards for a touchdown. A clipping penalty nullified the score, but no matter. After spotting Philadelphia a field goal, three Graham touchdown passes accounted for the game's next three scores. In the final quarter, Graham ran for a touchdown and engineered one final long salt-in-the-open-wound scoring drive. Cleveland won, 35–10.

As Graham remembered it, "Paul Brown told us before the game that 'Four years of achievement were at stake.' And we sure didn't want to let him or us down." NFL commissioner Bert Bell named Graham the game's Most Valuable Player and presented him with a trophy that Graham prized deeply. Bell called the Cleveland Browns "the greatest team to ever play the game." "That game really got us off to a good start!" Graham recalled with a smile.

At season's end, Cleveland trailed the Los Angeles Rams 28–27 late in the fourth quarter of the NFL Championship Game. Graham picked that moment to fumble the ball back to LA.

"I was so discouraged. . . . I thought . . . our first year in the NFL . . . and I lost the football," he recounted in our interview. "I avoided Paul Brown." So, Brown found Graham, patted him on the shoulder pads, then said, "Don't worry, Ott [Brown's nickname for his quarterback], we're still gonna get 'em." Sure enough, the Rams punted the ball with one minute forty-nine seconds left in the game. In the clutch, Graham ran once for big yards and hit 4 huge passes, driving to the Rams' 11-yard line. Lou Groza's short field goal won the game, the first of three NFL Championships the Browns would win in their first NFL decade.

The second came in 1954, a 56–10 shellacking of the Detroit Lions. Graham accounted for 6 Browns touchdowns: 3 passes and 3 runs. After the game, Graham announced his retirement. But when Brown offered Graham $25,000 (the largest salary in league history at the time) to play one final season (1955), Graham came back, won his third NFL Most Valuable Player Award (1951, 1953, and 1955), and led the Browns to their *tenth straight* championship-game berth.

This time, nearly eighty-eight thousand football fans turned out to see the gridiron miracle that was Otto Graham. The winningest quarterback of any era yet did not disappoint, throwing for 2 scores and running for 2 more, besting his Hall of Fame counterpart Norm Van Brocklin and the Rams, 38–14. Near game's end, Brown gave Graham the ultimate tribute.

BROWN: We were so far ahead that I took him out with a couple minutes to play just as a courtesy to him. . . . These were rival fans, but they gave him a standing ovation.

GRAHAM: So, I went over to the sideline and just shook his hand and said, "Thanks, Paul."

BROWN: And I said, "Thank you, too, Otto." And that's all that was said.

GRAHAM: And the opposing eighty thousand people cheering for you . . . it impressed me, believe me. . . . I've got tears in my eyes right now even thinking about it.

Me, too, Mr. Graham.

Bud Grant *(1927–2023)*

Offensive End

· Philadelphia Eagles (1951-52) · Winnipeg Blue Bombers (1953-56)

Head Coach

· Winnipeg Blue Bombers (1957-66) · Minnesota Vikings (1967-83, 1985)

On a Thursday night in January 2016, my cell phone rang. "Bob . . . it's Bud Grant. . . . I wanted to know . . . are you shooting our game this Sunday?" He was referring to the January 10 NFC Wild Card Game featuring the Minnesota Vikings and the Seattle Seahawks, slated to take place at TPC Stadium, the University of Minnesota's quaint open-air venue. Meteorologists were already warning fans to expect subzero air temperatures, with gusting winds capable of dropping wind chills to twenty-five below or thereabouts. "Yes, Bud. I'll be there," I said. "Will I be seeing you?"

"You might want to shoot this: I'm going to be walking out for the coin toss in short sleeves."

"Of course you are, Coach!" This was the Minnesota Vikings' identity back when they played in Super Bowls. It began and ended with the eighty-eight-year-old man on the other end of this phone call.

Harry Peter "Bud" Grant is truly one of a kind. Born in 1927 in the working-class lake town of Superior, Wisconsin, "Buddy Boy" (his father's nickname for him) suffered from childhood polio. So, his dad bought him a baseball glove, then sent him outside to work through it. In high school, Grant's polio was gone, and he was a three-sport letterman. During World War II, Grant played football for Paul Brown's Great Lakes Naval Training Center team. After the war, Grant played three varsity sports at the University of Minnesota, excelling in all of them. He rounded out his calendar by pitching each summer for several semipro baseball teams in two different leagues and states. On several occasions, Grant threw two complete games in a single day.

In the 1950 NFL Draft, the Philadelphia Eagles picked Bud Grant in the first round. Instead, he opted for pro basketball and played for the Minneapolis Lakers' 1950 NBA Championship team. In 1951, Grant moved onto pro football in Philadelphia. In 1952, his 997 receiving yards ranked second in the NFL. But when Philly refused to meet Grant's 1953 salary demands, he "played out his option," the first professional athlete in any sport to do so. (To this day, Grant remains the only person to have played professionally in both the NFL and the NBA, despite erroneous reports that Otto Graham did it first. The NBA began officially in 1949.)

Upon leaving the Eagles, Grant signed with the Canadian Football League's Winnipeg Blue Bombers, then spent the next fifteen years in Canada, first as a player, then as the team's four-time Grey Cup champion head coach (1958–59, 1961–62). For his efforts, Grant was inducted into the Canadian Football Hall of Fame. Today, there's a twelve-foot statue of Bud outside Winnipeg's pro football stadium. How many other athletes or coaches experience such reverence and acknowledgment in their own lifetimes?

So, how did I become so intimately involved in Grant's life that he wanted me to know what cut and style of shirt he'd be wearing at one of the NFL's all-time coldest games?

It all dates back to an interview I did at Grant's lake home one summer day sometime after the turn of the century. Mike Grant (his son) coached football at Eden Prairie High School in Bloomington, Minnesota. His teams had won numerous state championships. Mike's son Ryan happened to be visiting Grant's lake home the day I took a crew there to interview his Grandpa Bud. At the time, Ryan was quarterbacking his father's Eden Prairie team. Naturally, when I finished working, I couldn't resist tossing some passes with Ryan. Pretty soon, both of us were pouring sweat. From that day forward, I was part of Grant's football family. Our interactions at Vikings games became more personal. Late in my career, when NFL Films started producing the show *A Football Life*, I asked Bud whether he would be a willing subject. He laughed and then replied pointedly, "You better get started, Bob. I'm eighty-eight years old."

So, when NFL Films gave me preliminary approval, I started producing the project. Quite suddenly, NFL Films announced that Grant's *A Football Life* episode would now become a half-hour special for our weekly Fox Sports syndicated series *This Is the NFL*. I challenged our program planners to reverse their decision. When they refused, I asked Vikings ownership to intervene on Grant's and my behalf. My efforts did nothing but piss people off. "You're taking this much harder than I am," Bud said to me calmly one day in a phone call. He was used to being left out in the cold.

So, I shot Grant at the 2015 CFL Championship Game in Winnipeg. Later, I did a three-hour long, two-camera interview with Grant at his Bloomington, Minnesota, home. Then, I researched nearly nine decades of still photographs, home movies, archival footage, and college and pro action from Grant's collection as well as U.S. and Canadian sources. Finally, I shot Grant duck hunting, once in Minnesota, and a second time in Arkansas. The Fox special came together nicely.

The show's emotional apex features Grant walking to midfield in short sleeves for that coin toss. When the stadium public address system announces Grant's name, the capacity crowd roars. It is heartwarming. The Vikings lost that day, 10–9. With time running out, Vikings kicker Blair Walsh shanked a 27-yard field goal that would have won it. No, these were definitely *not* Grant's Vikings.

That night, I reflected on Grant's NFC Championship Vikings teams. I remembered how they beat the odds to win frigid home playoff games against seemingly superior foes. I remembered Grant's words describing how he fashioned the Vikings' enduring identity and marveled at their simplicity:

"We're the Vikings, so let's be a cold-weather team," Grant said at one of his first team meetings. "We're gonna be cold . . . we're gonna practice in the cold . . . you're gonna get *used* to the cold because we won't have any heaters. . . . Look at what the other team is doing. . . . They've got heaters over there. . . . They're not even watching the game—they're trying to get warm."

If you combine Grant's Winnipeg wins with his Vikings wins, only three men in North American pro football history (Don Shula, George Halas, and Bill Belichick) have more career coaching victories than Bud

Grant. He played in three professional leagues and is one of only two men (along with Warren Moon) to be enshrined in two pro football Halls of Fame. He's a one-of-a-kind champion, a true North American original. It warms my chilled bones to think of him.

Dennis Green *(1949–2016)*

Head Coach

- Minnesota Vikings (1992-2001) - Arizona Cardinals (2004-06)

On the final weekend of the 1992 regular season, rookie head coach Dennis Green's Minnesota Vikings blew out the visiting Green Bay Packers, 27–7. Anticipating a Gatorade shower for the new coach, I bolted onto the field before the final gun and positioned myself in front of him. Sure enough, the Vikings soaked him good. It marked the first time in NFL Films history that a cameraman also got drenched. Green seemed to enjoy the moment as much as I did.

Green ushered in the "Purple Pride" era of Vikings football. Some coaches run football operations like military bunkers, trying not to mess up while denying outsiders access, lest they reveal faulty leadership and suspect commands. Not surprisingly, organizations that emphasize pride tend to be less suspicious of visiting production teams. In turn, they build higher-achieving teams themselves. I suspected that Green was such a builder.

Over the next quarter century, I shot as many Vikings home games as NFL Films would allow. In 1994, when Fox Sports became the NFC's new broadcast partner, it hired NFL Films to shoot a preseason training-camp special in Dallas, Arizona, and Minnesota. Given my choice, I quickly opted for Mankato State, summer home to Green's Vikings. Scott Scharf was my soundman. As usual, Green gave us total access. We wired players and coaches at will. We attended meetings and hung out in the dorms until bed check. One day after practice, Green took us out fishing in his boat. Quite literally, we were welcome anywhere onsite. The Fox producer tagging along, who specialized in covering ice-skating, stayed out of our way as we delivered the goods.

We returned in 1995 to shoot and produce *Six Days to Sunday Night* for TNT Sports. For this show, NFL Films dispatched crews to Dallas and Minnesota as the two teams prepared to play each other in a Sunday-night matchup on September 17. Once again, I chose the Vikings. This time, we literally lived with the Vikings. We traveled to their homes, partied on the road with them in St. Cloud, and wired players and coaches for all meetings and practices. When doors momentarily closed, Green reopened them. We visited the set of Green's weekly television show. We filmed him playing a drum solo on the full kit he kept downstairs near the Vikings weight room. No muss, no fuss, no censorship, and absolutely no typically intrusive and paranoid NFL oversight. Early on, Green explained to his assembled team, "The main reason I'm allowing all this is the cameraman." Then, he pointed directly at me. Talk about instant credibility.

On game day, Dallas defeated the Vikings in overtime, 23–17. The final edited version of *Six Days* aired in a ninety-minute primetime slot later that month. Green called me the morning after to report how much the entire organization had enjoyed the show and exposure. By the time Green put his vision for the Vikings together, my bond with him and his team was strong.

Flash forward to the 1998 NFL season, when a Texas multimillionaire named Red McCombs bought the Vikings. When twenty teams passed on proud and flamboyant Marshall wide receiver Randy Moss in the draft, the Vikings sprinted to the stage to make him the team's first pick. Journeyman Randall Cunningham became the starting quarterback. Suddenly, magical things began to happen in the Twin Cities. The Vikings were winning football games. "Purple Pride" was in full bloom.

Minnesota finished the 1998 regular season with a record of 15–1. In their first playoff game, the Vikes dispatched the Cardinals, 41–21. The stage was set. Minnesota hosted Atlanta for the NFC Championship. Once again, Green agreed to wear a wire. My soundman and I met him privately in a little-used men's room adjacent to the Vikings' locker room. Green glanced at us while Scott mic'd him up. In his distinctive lovable, raspy voice, he said, "We certainly have come a long way together, haven't we guys?" Indeed we had—within reach of a Super Bowl.

In my perfect world, the Vikings would have defeated the Falcons and advanced to Super Bowl XXXIII (33), where they'd have run Denver's mediocre defense off the field. But things didn't play out as I hoped. Late in the game, Minnesota held the ball deep in Denver territory. Placekicker Gary Anderson hadn't missed a field-goal attempt since the previous season (1997). So, when Green sent Anderson out and told his offensive coordinator Brian Billick, "This is to win the game, Coach," I knew that Anderson would blast it through from 39 yards—but he missed it.

The ensuing nightmare haunted Green the rest of his career. Several of his subsequent Vikings teams qualified for the postseason, but in the

Twin Cities, "Purple Pride" remains an unfulfilled dream. The Vikings eventually parted ways with Green, who then did a three-year stint as head coach of the Arizona Cardinals. When I greeted him at the NFL Combine in Indianapolis, I said, "You just don't look the same in all that red." But our bond remained strong to the end.

In 2016, Green died suddenly from complications due to cardiac arrest. At the time, I was too stunned to believe it and too busy with the season to be emotionally affected by it.

Later that year, as I sat surrounded by my camera equipment in Minnesota's new domed stadium, the public address announcer began introducing Green's immediate surviving family. When his wife and children walked onto the field, I thought about that day in the Metrodome when we had wired Green in the abandoned bathroom. I also thought about my late soundman Scott Scharf, another colleague who had departed this world suddenly, unexpectedly, and far too early.

I covered my face with a towel and sobbed for cherished old times and dear old friends.

Jon Gruden *(born 1963)* 🏆

Head Coach

- Oakland Raiders (1998-2001, 2018-21) - Tampa Bay Buccaneers (2002-08)

During the first and only interview I ever did with Jon Gruden, he told me bluntly, "You keep saying things like that, and we're going to be rolling around on the floor." He was, famously, intense. But before you jump to conclusions . . .

Remember that snowy night in New England when America first heard the term *Tuck Rule*? It was January 19, 2002. In a New England blizzard, Oakland Raiders Hall of Fame cornerback Charles Woodson forced a Tom Brady fumble that the Raiders recovered, seemingly clinching a victory that would have sent Gruden's Raiders to the AFC Championship Game. But after further review, the officials gave the ball back to the Patriots, who drove it into field-goal range, tied the game in regulation, then eventually went on to win Super Bowl XXXVI (36). The Patriots dynasty was born—and Gruden's Oakland Raiders got screwed by enforcement of a bad rule that's still causing problems!

Even worse, Al Davis orchestrated a trade sending Gruden to the Tampa Bay Buccaneers for a slew of first- and second-round draft picks and $8 million in cash. Critics questioned Davis's motives and the Bucs' sanity. Yes, Gruden turned Raiders quarterback Rich Gannon into a Pro Bowler and the Silver and Black again seemed poised to challenge for a Super Bowl. Meanwhile, Gruden inherited a Tony Dungy Bucs team that had made it to the NFL playoffs four times in the previous five seasons (1997, 1999, 2000, and 2001). Talk about intrigue!

In 2002, Gruden worked his magic with veteran Bucs quarterback Brad Johnson. Tampa Bay's defense dominated, and the Bucs advanced to Super Bowl XXXVII (37). There, they would face Gruden's former team with Gannon, 2002's unanimous choice as the NFL's MVP. Storylines pulsated with irony. But Tampa Bay possessed a secret weapon: *Chucky*!

While in Oakland, Gruden's contorted facial expressions and intensity had earned him the nickname "Chucky," a reference to the diabolical doll from the horror film *Child's Play*. The name stuck. Also still fresh in Gruden's mind was the wisdom he'd passed along to the Raiders' all-star quarterback. At a Bucs practice during Super Bowl week, Chucky (an ex-college quarterback out of Dayton) ran the Raiders' Scout Team's offense to show his Bucs' defense how Gannon would likely use pump fakes and look-offs to draw Tampa's defensive backs out of position. Like Gruden's nickname, Chucky's lessons stuck(ied).

On game day, NFL Films wired Gruden and future Hall of Fame safety John Lynch. On the Bucs' sideline early in the game, Lynch said, "Every play they've run, we ran in practice [with Gruden playing the role of Gannon]. It's unreal." Later, Lynch did his pre-snap read and then told Bucs safety Dexter Jackson to watch out for a specific route called a "Sluggo" ("Slant and Go"). Gruden's closed-practice fingerprints were all over that insight too. On the play, Gannon did all the tricks that Gruden had emphasized while in Oakland—the same tricks that had earned Gannon MVP honors. But his look-off attempt and pump fake did not influence Jackson. Gannon's "Sluggo" pass sailed directly into Jackson's waiting hands, as if he knew it was coming. Later, Jackson picked off a second pass en route to MVP honors.

In all, Tampa Bay picked five Gannon passes because Gruden had shown them what to expect. Tampa Bay beat Oakland, 48–21, the Bucs' first Super Bowl title. At age thirty-nine, Gruden became the youngest head coach to win a Lombardi Trophy. But an aging defense and salary-cap issues soon diluted Gruden's roster. Over the next six seasons, Chucky managed just two more divisional titles with zero postseason victories. Following a third-place finish in 2008, Tampa fired him. A tenure that began brilliantly ended in mediocrity and disarray.

Shortly thereafter came the birth of Gruden's "Fired Football Coaches Association" (FFCA) think tank. In the 2010s, I took an NFL Films crew to Tampa to interview him for an NFL Network *Top 10* episode on Brett Favre, but our GPS could not find his offices. We passed in and through a suburban Tampa strip mall numerous times. "This place looks like it should have a check-cashing agency and a pawn shop!" I hollered over the phone at our talent coordinator. So, we knocked on doors. Finally, Gruden appeared: "Where the hell you guys been?"

While my cameraman lit an interview set, Gruden screened game tape of college football players aspiring to the NFL. He paid no attention to us except to offer us as many FFCA T-shirts as we could carry out. I gravitated toward his editing area to check out his operation. Basically, Gruden, a "Fired Football Coach," was studying college game tape focused on individual players. When he witnessed something noteworthy, he would "clip" the play to a compilation reel he was building on a second recorder nearby. In TV jargon, Gruden was making "machine-to-machine" edits, the most tedious, time-consuming, torturous way of building a reel. His focus was laser sharp.

"You need some help here, Coach," I suggested.

"No way!" he replied. "I learn what I need to know about all these guys by watching them myself." I knew that he ran a quarterback camp for prospective pros. I also knew that his *Monday Night Football* analyst position made him the highest-paid personality at the network. Yet here he was, watching play after play by himself, building clip reels in a run-down strip mall, passing out T-shirts nobody wanted.

When Gruden sat down to be interviewed, I explained that I was producing a show on Brett Favre. He reminded me that he and Favre had arrived in Green Bay the same year, 1992. Favre had come in as a quarterback, and Gruden as an offensive assistant/quality-control coach. I described the *Top 10* show as "fast-paced and loaded with controversy." My explanation didn't register. After my third or fourth question concerning Favre's shortcomings, Chucky fixed his maniacal gaze on me and announced in front of the entire crew, "You keep saying things like that, and we're going to be rolling around on the floor." The man was intense—although not serious. (I think!)

Over many years, I screened hours of Gruden's wirings and never once detected a hint of prejudice or hate. Intensity, yes. Malice or genuine evil? No way. His summary dismissal by the Raiders (2021) for alleged abusive emails surprised many in the pro football world, myself included.

In time, I hope that he can recover a measure of respect. Few human beings have worked longer hours to master a demanding craft. His intense work ethic allowed him to survive a "Tuck Rule" fiasco, a cash-and-carry trade, and a not-so-complimentary nickname. It would not surprise me to see Chucky coaching again some day at some level. It's hard to imagine him without some form of football in his life. I wouldn't root against him.

George Halas *(1895–1983)* 

End

- Decatur Staleys/Chicago Staleys/Chicago Bears (1920-29)

Head Coach

- Decatur Staleys/Chicago Staleys/Chicago Bears (1920-29, 1933-42, 1946-55, 1958-67)

Owner

- Decatur Staleys/Chicago Staleys/Chicago Bears (1920-83)

During the 1981 NFL season, I produced a segment on the National Football League's founding father, the longtime owner and head coach of the Chicago Bears, George Halas. *The NFL Today*'s Jack Whitaker was my talent. Our subject was approaching his eighty-eighth birthday and rarely did interviews, but when the Bears learned that Whitaker was involved, they agreed to give us an hour of Papa Bear's time at their downtown Chicago office. I couldn't wait.

Halas was the son of immigrants from Austria-Hungary. He grew up in Chicago and played football, baseball, and basketball at the University of Illinois. During World War I, he joined the Great Lakes Naval Training Center football team (1918) that won that year's Rose Bowl. Halas returned an interception 77 yards *without* scoring, the longest nonscoring play in Rose Bowl history. Halas was named MVP, and his entire team received military discharges.

In 1919, at age twenty-four, Halas signed with the New York Yankees. A serious leg injury short-circuited the speedy right fielder's career. In the twelve games he played, he slapped two Walter Johnson fastballs over the wall (both went foul!) and picked a fight with Ty Cobb. Although he rehabbed in the minors, he never played for New York again. At season's end, the Yankees acquired a new right fielder named George from the Boston Red Sox: George Herman Ruth—"The Babe."

In search of a future in sports, on August 20, 1920, Halas and a dozen or so football aficionados gathered at a Hupmobile auto dealership in Canton, Ohio, drank beer while sitting on the running boards of $3,000 vehicles, and formed a professional football league. Canton Bulldogs star Jim Thorpe was elected president. Two years later, the operation officially became the National Football League. Halas played for and coached the Decatur Staleys—who would eventually become "Da Bears."

Our interview covered Halas's Rose Bowl triumph, his Yankees career, that day in Canton . . . Red Grange, Bronko Nagurski, Sid Luckman . . . Chicago's 73–0 victory over Washington in the 1940 NFL Championship, four more NFL titles over the next seven seasons, Papa Bear's final championship team in 1963 . . . Doug Atkins, Dick Butkus, Gale Sayers, and his latest Canton-bound phenomenon, Walter Payton. I sent him our questions in advance, so Coach Halas was prepared. His responses lacked the fire and acrimony he had unleashed routinely on NFL opponents and officials, but they also reflected his deep-rooted love for America's new national pastime. It aired nationally on Thanksgiving Day 1981.

My last question asked about his fondest memory: "Oh, that's easy, just to have been a part of the growth of the National Football League." When we finished, he said to me, "You don't look Italian." I told him that my mother's family hailed from the same sector of southeastern Europe as his own. He asked me her maiden name. I replied, "Chastko." He smiled and said, "Sounds like somebody shaved a few letters off that one." Then, he taught me the proper pronunciation of his own name: GER-ta STAN-i-slawsh ha-LAWSH. George Stanley Halas. The founding father of pro football was an immigrant's son. What could be more American than that?

John Hannah *(born 1951)*

Guard

- New England Patriots (1973-85)

When I was growing up, Kodak Corporation sponsored an annual syndicated television special called *The Kodak College Football All-American Team.* I looked forward to it every season. During my junior year at Penn State, I watched the 1972 team. Near the end, the narrator gave a short tribute to University of Alabama guard John Hannah, the gist of which was: "This guy could be very special in the NFL." An offensive guard, really? So, I tucked that information away and awaited further developments.

The New England Patriots selected Hannah in the first round (fourth overall pick) of the 1973 NFL Draft. That got my attention. I watched him play twice, in 1974 and 1976, against the Pittsburgh Steelers. He more than held his own against Pittsburgh's vaunted front four. In the 1976 game, he dominated Pittsburgh defensive tackle Ernie Holmes in a 30–27 Patriots win in Pittsburgh.

I started shooting games in 1977. By then, Hannah (at left guard) and Leon Gray (at left tackle) were Pro Bowlers. Some considered the two of them together to be the best left side in pro football. Part of my job in pregame was to capture close-ups of All Pros, so one Sunday afternoon, I strolled toward the Pats offensive linemen while they warmed up in the end zone.

"GET THAT CAMERA OUTTA HERE!" Hannah demanded in a tone that literally shocked me. He stared at me until I vacated the area. What was his deal? He had this reaction every time I got close to him for the rest of his career. I'd never met the guy before. I'd never said anything bad about him or his loved ones. In fact, I was a huge fan of those Chuck Fairbanks–coached 1970s Patriots teams. Despite Hannah's expressed rancor, I rooted for the Pats to win most every week. But I hadn't gotten the shot I needed, and the season was nearing its end. What to do?

Then, it came to me. One day in Foxboro, I waited for the national anthem to begin, then I slid into position directly in front of Hannah and shot from my knees about ten feet from his bulking presence. He stood there helpless with his hand on his heart, seething with thinly veiled anger. He wanted to abandon his position and crush the life out of me. I could feel his animus. But I kept doing slow zooms into full-face close-ups because I knew that he wouldn't budge during the song.

When the singer belted out "O'er the land of the free," I bolted toward the opposite sideline and didn't turn around until I felt safe. Looking back, it was worth the risk.

Later in my career, an NFL Films producer invited Hannah and his brother Charley to our facility, so I walked into the interview room and introduced myself. When I asked Hannah whether he remembered my national anthem shot or my abandoned warm-up attempts, he shook his head and said, "Not really . . . I would just get so pumped up and nervous before games that I didn't want anybody around." I shook his hand and thanked him for not running me down. In 1991, Hannah became the first New England Patriot enshrined in the Hall of Fame. Guess which Kodak moment opened the Hannah segment that NFL Films produced for the occasion?

The Harbaugh Brothers

John Harbaugh *(born 1962)* 🏆

Special Teams Coordinator

- Philadelphia Eagles (1998-2006)

Defensive Backs Coach

- Philadelphia Eagles (2007)

Head Coach

- Baltimore Ravens (2008-Present)

Jim Harbaugh *(born 1963)*

Quarterback

- Chicago Bears (1987-93) · Indianapolis Colts (1994-97)
- Baltimore Ravens (1998) · San Diego Chargers (1999-2000)
- Detroit Lions and Carolina Panthers (2001)

Head Coach

- San Francisco 49ers (2011-14)

It's the sad fate of brothers working in the same profession to be compared to one another. It's not fair, but it happens. Of the Harbaugh brothers, Jim has the reputation for being more intense. John hides his intensity better, which makes it all the more disturbing when it suddenly appears.

My one on-field experience with quarterback Jim Harbaugh occurred during an NFL playoff game in Pittsburgh (AFC Championship: Colts vs. Steelers, January 14, 1996). Bud Light's popular national advertising campaign featured the closing tag line "I love you, man!" Colts security didn't share the sentiment. They patrolled their bench area with single-minded purpose, chasing anybody who even slowed down to look or listen. That day, I saw Jim approaching his teammate tight end Ken Dilger after a lengthy Colts scoring drive. While walking, I lifted my camera in time to capture Harbaugh saying, "I love you, man!" Colts security arrived too late.

John Harbaugh came into my life in 1999. I was producing, directing, and shooting a week-long documentary with Andy Reid's Philadelphia Eagles. John was serving as Andy's special teams coordinator, a position he held for a decade (1998–2007). I particularly enjoyed John's kickers' meeting, a three-person affair involving placekicker David Akers, punter Sean Landeta, and John—quite quaint in the modern NFL. John seemed very focused and comfortable in his skin.

Post–beer commercial reference, Jim didn't show up in my life again until 2011. I was working the Combine in Indianapolis, doing interviews for the NFL Films *Top 100* series. Jim was the newly appointed head coach of the San Francisco 49ers. He visited our interview suite to talk about veteran running back Frank Gore, a player he probably hadn't met yet. The interview did not go well. At one point, Jim, who showed up wearing a less-than-flattering skull cap, asked "You got enough, yet?," reflecting his growing impatience with my entire operation. A 49ers PR person ushered him out of there ASAP. I tucked that experience away for future reference.

That same year, older brother John began his fourth season as the Baltimore Ravens head coach. Never in league history had two brothers coached different NFL teams simultaneously. In 2012, John's Ravens defeated Jim's 49ers 16–6 on Thanksgiving Day in Baltimore. NFL Films wired both coaches and numerous players from each team for an NFL Network *Sounds of the Game* special that would air the following week. I worked the Ravens' sideline that day. Terrell Suggs and the Ravens recorded nine sacks on an exciting second-year quarterback named Colin Kaepernick. Baltimore's Joe Flacco accounted for the game's only touchdown, with an 8-yard pass. And when things got tough, from across the field I saw Jim tear off his microphone. Patience was not his strong suit.

Little did I suspect that these same two teams would meet again in Super Bowl XLVII (47)! On that day, I worked the 49ers' sideline. Once again, when things started going against his team, Jim tore off his wireless microphone. Understandably, my young soundman was reluctant to crowd Jim with his boom microphone. Despite my encouragement, his hesitation went on for most of the game. Finally, with the 49ers trailing 34–29 but perched on the Ravens' 7-yard line with two minutes remaining in the contest, I said something about it. Paraphrasing:

"Please, get your mic in there for this. . . . He's so focused on the game that you could hit him in the head with your boom pole and he wouldn't even look up."

In fact, if Jim had suffered a heart attack and his ticker had blown out through his chest cavity and landed on the 20-yard line, he would have kept coaching for another ten minutes before he even noticed. Some questionable calls and some very tight pass coverage cost Jim's 49ers any chance at victory. John's Ravens prevailed over Jim's 49ers again, this time 34–31.

As for John, the Ravens head coach approved a 2011 in-season *A Football Life* episode in advance. He knew that our crews would visit his facility regularly. He was totally upfront about boundaries—very tough, but also transparent. And, like his brother, his patience and good humor eroded quickly when he was upset or bothered.

The very last Ravens game of my career took place sometime between 2014 and 2016. As per NFL policy, I requested permission to follow John into their winning locker room. Unbeknownst to me, the previous week a CBS Sports camera had captured a locker-room speech during which John had said some unflattering things about an upcoming opponent. Without consulting the Ravens, CBS had aired John's words during its postgame show, and he was rightfully pissed.

Nonetheless, Ravens PR ushered me into his locker room. Network cameras were blocked at the door. When John appeared, I raised my camera and started shooting. John launched into his speech, then paused and stared directly at me and my camera. "Turn that camera off," he said bluntly. I was surprised. Not wanting to exacerbate things, I placed the camera on the floor, pointed away from Coach Harbaugh.

"He said turn it *off*." The words came from Steve Smith Sr., a player I had once trusted. It ranks as the single-most-humiliating locker-room experience in my career. In my haste to comply with John's wishes, I truly had forgotten to hit the on/off switch, so now I was seen as a "sneaky sh*t" cameraman.

When John finished, he realized that we had history. Perhaps he recalled our three-person special teams get-togethers in Philly or my regular Ray Lewis *A Football Life* visits to Baltimore. He pasted a phony smile on his face and put his arm around me. I brushed it off with malice and walked away, my last professional encounter with the Harbaugh brothers.

Franco Harris *(1950–2022)*

Fullback

· Pittsburgh Steelers (1972–83) · Seattle Seahawks (1984)

"The Immaculate Reception."

A marker event for western Pennsylvania sports fans. Folks from my generation remember it the way we remember John Kennedy's assassination, the way our parents remember Pearl Harbor. I was home for Christmas break from Penn State, but NFL rules blacked out my area from the upcoming AFC Championship Game (Raiders vs. Steelers) during which it would occur. So, I drove my father's car to my college apartment, where my hometown friend and I watched the game on my black-and-white portable, capturing a distant signal from Johnstown's WJAC-TV.

Near game's end, my friend and I sat in silence and despair. Trailing 7–6, the Steelers faced a fourth down on their own 40-yard line with just twenty-two seconds left on the clock. We watched as quarterback Terry Bradshaw evaded the pass rush and then launched a desperation pass. Suddenly, Franco Harris appeared from out of nowhere, plucked the ball out of mid-air, then ran it into the end zone for the unlikeliest of game-winning plays: the Immaculate Reception. My friend and fellow Penn Stater jumped up and down on one of my roommate's beds, breaking the frame. We opened the windows and screamed like wild animals to anybody listening. We chugged our Iron City beers and basked in victory's glow. I remember it all as if it just happened yesterday.

In Pittsburgh, Steelers rookie fullback Harris was already well on his way to sports icon status. The Immaculate Reception solidified that status—forever! The 1972 Rookie of the Year's game-winning play against Oakland still strikes a chord with Pittsburgh folks as well as students of the game. Several NFL Films productions have identified it as the single-most-memorable moment in league history. As late Steelers owner Dan

Rooney told me during one of his many oversight visits to NFL Films, "Bob, that play changed everything for the Pittsburgh Steelers."

I had met Harris as a fellow student at Penn State—in a phys-ed course, of all things. A large, likable guy with a manicured beard and sculpted face, he was hard to mistake for anybody else. When I arrived in 1970, he was a junior. He and Lydell Mitchell lined up in the same backfield three years in a row, but while Lydell clearly should have won the 1971 Heisman Trophy, with 1,567 rushing yards and 29 touchdowns, Harris's college stats fell well short of his counterpart's.

So, when Pittsburgh used the thirteenth overall pick on Harris, I questioned their judgment. I presumed the Steelers had drafted him because of his size and speed, envisioning the possibilities. I never imagined just how right they would be. During his rookie season, Harris reeled off six consecutive 100-yard rushing performances. Pittsburgh steamrolled unsuspecting opponents en route to the franchise's first postseason appearance in its six decades of existence! Two years later, the once-lowly Steelers played in their very first Super Bowl.

In Super Bowl IX (9), the Minnesota Vikings could not and would not sustain drives against Pittsburgh's original "Steel Curtain" defense. At intermission, the Steelers led, 2–0. After halftime, the Steelers' ground game wore out the Vikings' undersized defense, and Harris took charge. Franco scored on a 9-yard run, the Steel Curtain shut out the Vikings' offense, and Pittsburgh prevailed in Super Bowl IX, 16–6. My former Penn State classmate was named the game's Most Valuable Player.

In the fall of 1975, I began my career at NFL Films. Harris continued his slow-and-steady assault on Jim Brown's career rushing record. And by decade's end, the Steelers had won three more Super Bowls, an unparalleled—and still unequaled—four Lombardi Trophies in six seasons. I finally encountered Harris in person near the end of the 1976 season, lying on a trainer's table, hoping to work through cracked ribs suffered in a 40–14 playoff victory over the Baltimore Colts. He could not recover in time to suit up for the AFC Championship Game against the Raiders, and with him went Pittsburgh's chances of an unprecedented Super Bowl "three-peat."

The following season, I started shooting NFL games. In 1978, I began writing and editing Pittsburgh Steelers highlight films. In one, I included a slow zoom into a Harris close-up I'd shot that season during the national anthem. NFL Films's legendary narrator John Facenda intoned, "Faces that will make handsome busts in the Pro Football Hall of Fame," and later, "Before Franco Harris, the Pittsburgh Steelers never once made the playoffs. With him, they've never missed."

By 1984, Harris's eight 1,000-yard rushing seasons stood as the new NFL record. His 11,950 rushing yards ranked second all-time to Brown's 12,312. This was Hank Aaron closing in on Babe Ruth—until Harris held out to negotiate a pay raise. Things were said. Tempers flared. I ran into Dan Rooney at a preseason game in Dallas, where he told me bluntly, "Franco's finished with us, Bob." Talk about the ultimate anticlimax to a Hall of Fame career.

When my own NFL career ended, I taught sports segment production for three semesters at the University of Delaware and one COVID-abbreviated term at Penn State. In an effort to help students find story subjects, I reached out to Harris and discovered his involvement with a business venture called Super Bakery that dates back to 1990. Turns out that Franco, Mitchell, and a third former Penn Stater named Ron Rossi had been making nutritious foods for school children for three decades—long before such items were fashionable! Harris agreed to help one of my students with a feature.

Then, along came COVID-19. Classes were canceled, instructors resorted to Zoom technology, promising segments never materialized, and America went into extended hibernation.

But Franco Harris's memory lives on. If you ever fly into Greater Pittsburgh Airport, your journey just may take you into the grand concourse toward the escalators. There, you will find a life-size replica of Harris reaching down to make the Immaculate Reception.

Pittsburgh will never forget.

Bob Hayes *(1942–2002)*

Wide Receiver

- Dallas Cowboys (1965-74) · San Francisco 49ers (1975)

"Bullet" Bob Hayes was a bona fide American sports hero of enormous proportions. On a hot 1984 summer night in Texas Stadium, I recognized Hayes standing on the Dallas Cowboys' sideline. Like everybody else, Hayes was applauding Mary Lou Retton and her fellow medal winners from the triumphant U.S. Summer Olympics gymnastics team. The Cowboys marched them onto the field prior to kickoff in a star-spangled celebration complete with dancing cheerleaders and patriotic music. Few noticed Hayes, another great Olympian onsite.

Bullet Bob attended Florida A&M University, where he lettered in track and football. As a college sprinter, he never lost a 100 yard or 100-meter race. When his college football coach, Jake Gaither, balked at allowing Hayes time to train for the 1964 Summer Olympics, President Lyndon Johnson telephoned Gaither to help him reorder his priorities. At those games, Hayes set world records in the 100-meter dash and the 4×100 relay, anchoring the gold medal–winning U.S. team with an unofficial time of between 8.5 and 8.9 seconds, the fastest time ever recorded—still!

Always willing to gamble on exceptional athleticism, the Cowboys used a seventh-round pick to add the "Fastest Man on Earth" to their roster. Their investment yielded immediate dividends: In his first two NFL seasons (1965–66), Hayes scored 25 touchdowns. One day in Yankee Stadium, he caught a quick slant against New York Giants cornerback Clarence Childs, also a world-class sprinter. Hayes outran him with relative ease. No event did more to advance "Bump-and-Run" and "Zone Coverage" schemes among NFL defensive coaches. Hard to play man-to-man against someone who can outrun everybody else!

Hayes played eleven pro seasons, recording 371 career catches and 74 touchdowns. He played in three Pro Bowls and is permanently enshrined in the Dallas Cowboys Ring of Honor. He remains the only athlete to earn Olympic gold *and* a Super Bowl ring (for Super Bowl VI [6]).

But his critics reduced Hayes's talents to one dimension: speed. They pointed to a missed block on a final meaningful play of the 1966 NFL Championship Game that doomed the Cowboys' chances in a 34–27 loss to Vince Lombardi's Green Bay Packers. One year later, in the famous "Ice Bowl," NFL Films's isolations showed Hayes with both hands stuffed in his hand-warmer on Dallas running plays. Green Bay won both games as well as the first two Super Bowls. Other critics complained that Hayes wasn't clever enough. Once, when asked how he and teammate Dan Reeves complemented each other, Hayes answered, "When Dan does something good, I compliment him, and when I do something good, he compliments me." He may not have caught the questioner's meaning, but it wasn't a bad policy.

Then came Hayes's legal problems. After retirement, he sold cocaine to an undercover narcotics agent. A Texas judge sentenced him to five years in prison. Once an American hero, Hayes became "that guy" who couldn't keep himself "clean" after a football career: an All-American tragedy.

But I remembered Hayes as an Olympic hero. I respected his contributions to and his impact on the NFL. I knew about his hard times after prison. I sensed that sports fans would respond to a fallen idol TV movie on Hayes if it were properly framed. So, after that 1984 preseason game in Dallas, I contacted Hayes and explained my interest. Turns out another filmmaker had similar ideas, a native Texan turned Hollywood professional named Hal Trussell.

Trussell had just served as the director of photography on *Bachelor Party*, starring Tom Hanks. When I tracked him down and described the teleplay I was writing, he volunteered to meet me the next time I traveled to California. That night happened in 1985. Trussell was impressed with my emerging storyline, but he was talking about a low-budget feature film. I believed that a ninety-six-minute TV movie was the way to go. We could not resolve our different approaches.

Eventually, I found a sympathetic ear in Brig Owens, a former Hayes teammate in Dallas (1965) who had played twelve seasons at safety for Washington. Owens knew about Hayes's legal issues and purported alcoholism. He listened carefully to my pitch. He even brought in a money man familiar with TV projects. Therein lay the issue. Although Owens's commercial real estate development company had earned him considerable wealth, in that era, few telepics were funded by outside sources. He was willing to give me an audience, but despite his familiarity with Hayes and sympathy for his plight, he was not willing to finance the project.

Despite obstacles and setbacks, I plowed forward. I communicated with Hayes monthly to develop the script. I made arrangements to meet with a Las Colinas, Texas, studio to "cost out" a Lone Star State location shoot. And I continued to shop the idea with TV network movie execs.

As Thanksgiving 1985 approached, I volunteered to shoot the Cowboys' traditional holiday game so I could meet with Hayes the night before at the DFW Marriott. I waited patiently in the lobby. I called his home number over and over again. Nothing. On Thanksgiving morning, I realized that he wasn't coming. When I returned home, I'd made up my mind. I gathered months of hard work on the movie, loaded it all into a large cardboard box, then put it out in the trash.

In 2002, after battling prostate cancer and liver ailments, Hayes died of kidney failure. In 2004, when the Hall of Fame Selection Committee refused to elect Hayes to Canton, long-time, well-respected *Sports Illustrated* writer Paul Zimmerman temporarily resigned his position in protest. In 2009, the members righted their wrong and voted the original

"Fastest Man on Earth" into the hall. I smiled as I thought of what might have been.

Time has not tempered my enthusiasm for Hayes's tragic story. I still think that somebody should tell his story as a reminder. Fame is fleeting—and sometimes fatal. In retrospect, seeing him standing there on a sideline, applauding politely for new Olympic heroes, I can only imagine how lonely and abandoned he must have felt. He died three months shy of his sixtieth birthday.

Football and athletic heroism serve some men and women well. For others, adjusting to life after the limelight is not a given. "Bullet" Bob Hayes may well have been the "Fastest Man on Earth." But in the end, the world-class sprinter could not outrun his demons—and no one outruns time.

Paul Hornung *(1935–2020)*

Halfback and Placekicker

- Green Bay Packers (1957-66)

During the 1980s, I worked with Paul Hornung three times in eight years. Our first encounter took place in Louisville circa 1982. At the time, I envisioned it as I would a screenplay:

INT. OFFICE—DAY

We see PAUL HORNUNG dressed in business attire, seated behind a desk. We hear David Rose & His Orchestra's "The Stripper" in the background, a bawdy burlesque tune. A good-looking, well-dressed *Woman* in heels struts toward the desk and invites Paul to lunch. They exit stage left, revealing CBS analyst IRV CROSS, who steps out and addresses the camera: "The Golden Boy and his reputation for living the good life. . . ." CUT!

Hornung let Irv Cross finish his line and then asked me what had just happened. I assured him that I was planning a "tasteful tease that would be playfully provocative." The room went silent. Finally, Hornung spoke: "This is my wife, OK. Make sure you don't make me look like an ass!" If life had taught him anything, it was how to protect himself. That night, at one of Louisville's finest restaurants, Hornung stuck Irv Cross with the tab for dinner and lots of drinks. A little payback—just in case!

In 1956, as Notre Dame's senior starting quarterback, Hornung won a Heisman Trophy on a team that won two games. But Green Bay's visionary head coach Vince Lombardi valued Hornung's size, athleticism, and versatility. Lombardi selected Hornung with the first overall pick in that year's NFL Draft. Then, he fashioned a football dynasty around an offensive design he called the "Power Sweep," which suited Hornung's skill set perfectly. By 1960, it all came together.

Hornung and fullback Jim Taylor combined for nearly 1,800 yards rushing and two dozen rushing touchdowns. Hornung caught 2 touchdown passes and threw for 2 others. He added 86 more points as Green Bay's placekicker. In all, Hornung accounted for *176 points* in twelve regular-season games. Not until 2006 was Hornung's total eclipsed, and it took LaDainian Tomlinson *sixteen* games to score *his* 186 points. Green Bay played in the NFL Championship for the first time since 1944, losing to Philadelphia 17–13, Lombardi's only postseason loss ever.

The following season, in 1961, Green Bay won it all, thrashing the New York Giants in the title game 37–0. Despite spending his weekdays serving in the U.S. Army, Hornung led the league in scoring again en route to winning the NFL's Most Valuable Player award. In 1962, Green Bay lost only once en route to a second-straight NFL crown, beating New York 16–7.

But there would be no Packers "three-peat." In April 1963, NFL commissioner Pete Rozelle suspended Hornung and Detroit Lions defensive tackle Alex Karras for gambling on NFL games. Neither bet against his own team, and both were reinstated one year later. But while Karras carried a grudge to his grave, Hornung gave up gambling, avoided Las Vegas, and refrained from attending the Kentucky Derby for the remainder of his NFL career. The "Golden Boy" had learned his lesson.

Which brings me to my second Hornung encounter, this time in Canton, Ohio, around 1985. For reasons I don't recall, I directed several Hornung stand-ups outside the Pro Football Hall of Fame. I *do* remember Hornung's aggravation level rising. After one not-so-good take, Hornung lowered his stick microphone and complained out loud, "We gotta get through this, Bob. . . . I mean, I don't know why I'm here. . . . I'm not even *in* this damn place."

When we finished, he said something along the lines of "I guess some sins are never forgiven." I assumed that he was referring to his gambling suspension and its possible effects on Hall of Fame voters and their ballots, but I couldn't feel much sympathy. His legendary high-life stories reached me in my tiny island hometown downriver from Pittsburgh. I also knew what really mattered to Hall of Fame electors, and Hornung had played a vital role in Lombardi's winning formula.

After a pair of non-playoff seasons (1963–64), in 1965 the Packers returned to the top. Hornung's presence proved to be more than symbolic. In a December road win against the Baltimore Colts, the twenty-nine-year-old scored 5 touchdowns in a crucial 42–27 divisional victory. Less than a month later—on Green Bay's first second-half possession in the NFL Championship Game—Hornung took the handoff on a perfectly executed power sweep, followed Jerry Kramer's crushing block, then strode into the end zone for a 20–12 Packers lead. Green Bay beat Cleveland, 23–12, the team's third NFL title in five seasons. Steve Sabol commissioned a composition to celebrate the occasion. That stirring piece of music bears the title "A Golden Boy Again."

Which brings me to my third and final Hornung encounter. In 1988, Steve asked now Hall-of-Famer Hornung to cohost *The NFL Film-Star Awards*, a live-to-tape, studio-audience event that I produced. The show paid tribute to former and active NFL players in such categories as Best Original Score (Jim Marshall's Wrong Way Run). I'd like to think that today's sports TV galas stole our original idea—but probably not. We never did a sequel.

What I recall most about the three days of creating *The NFL Film-Star Awards*—the orientation meeting and meal, the golf tournament, and the actual show—is how younger players looked at my famous cohost, as if to say, "That's Paul Hornung. . . . He played for Vince Lombardi." Among those players present, only Marshall came from Hornung's generation. Even Larry Csonka, the MVP of Miami's Super Bowl VIII (8) win over Marshall's Vikings, treated Hornung with an extra measure of respect. Hornung didn't play in Super Bowl I, but he stood there on the sidelines and made sure that Max McGee made Bart Starr look good—despite what might have taken place the night before, involving flight attendants, alcoholic beverages, and so forth.

In more than four decades of working games at Green Bay's Lambeau Field, I shot crowd reactions to Hornung's presence many times. I watched women flirt with him from the bleachers. I watched their men cheer for him. One thing I know for certain: off-field allegations aside, Hornung ranks as one of the most versatile and complete football players ever to play the professional game. Lombardi loved the guy. The Paul Hornung Award is given annually to recognize America's most versatile, high-level college football player. Just envision Hornung in a modern-day "Punt, Pass, and Kick" competition. The man was a veritable scoring machine in every possible way.

Sam Huff (*1934–2021*)

Middle Linebacker

- New York Giants (1956-63) • Washington Commanders (1964-67, 1969)

True or false: The late Sam Huff was the NFL's first "real" middle linebacker. Depends on what *real* means, right? Some background: In 1956, the New York Giants' coaching staff included two future Hall of Fame head coaches still learning their trade. Vince Lombardi ran the Giants' offense, and Tom Landry coordinated New York's defense. (If you can name the head coach, Jim Lee Howell, I'd sure like to know why.)

Anyway, that's the year the Giants used their third-round pick to acquire Huff, an All-American tackle from West Virginia University. Initially, Coach Howell could not decide where Huff might fit in the Giants' defensive scheme. Frustrated, Huff left the team's Vermont training camp. Fortunately, Lombardi caught up with him and convinced him to return.

In the 1950s, NFL teams used five-man defensive fronts with a "middle guard" lined up over the offensive center. Landry was tinkering with a novel alignment called the 4–3 defense: just *four* down lineman (in three-point stances) surrounded by *three* linebackers. In Landry's scheme, the "middle guard" backed away from the offensive center and stood upright prior to the snap, thus becoming a "middle linebacker." In the third game of his rookie season, Huff took over the position and never relinquished it. New York's defense keyed five straight wins, the Giants finished 8–3–1, then beat the Chicago Bears for the NFL Championship, 47–7.

Huff's status skyrocketed. The New York media made much of Landry's innovative new scheme and the stand-up rookie star who made it work. Pro football pundits predicted a Giants dynasty with Huff literally in the middle of it. But over the next seven seasons, New York played in five more NFL title games and lost them all. Even the arrival of future Hall of Fame quarterback Y. A. Tittle couldn't tip championship-game results in the Giants' favor.

In the early 1980s, Irv Cross and I journeyed to Huff's farm to interview him for a CBS Sports "Legends of the Game" feature for *The NFL Today*. We covered all the above and then some. Huff even drove his tractor in the background of Irv's stand-up. Then, he sat down to be interviewed. The West Virginia country boy had grown accustomed to these profiles. "I grew up in a mining camp," Huff replied to question #1. America already knew that; *TIME Magazine* had done a cover story on Huff in 1959, the first NFL player ever to be so honored.

Not to be outdone, CBS News featured Huff in a 1960 hour-long episode of its award-winning series *The Twentieth Century*, hosted by Walter Cronkite. Cronkite and his CBS team tagged along to cover "The Violent World of Sam Huff," the story of his fifth New York Giants summer camp. The televised special offered American audiences a never-before-seen glimpse of this environment, the *Hard Knocks* of its era. Cronkite intoned, "Today, you will play professional football riding on Sam Huff's broad back. We've wired him for sound with a tiny transistorized radio transmitter." The very first NFL game wiring ever!

"I felt honored they asked me," Huff told us. "It was about time people got to see what we go through out there." I borrowed liberally from "Violent World" for Irv's segment, such as Huff's not-so-subtle assessment of Sunday afternoons: "Any time you play football, there's no place for nice guys. . . . When we're out on that field, it's either kill or be killed." A bit of an overstatement for such a truly nice guy—yet spoken with a straight face and pure conviction.

The most telling wired moment in "Violent World" involved Huff and Chicago Bears tight end Willard Dewveall (who left the Bears to join the Houston Oilers in 1961, the first NFL player to jump leagues). At the end of a running play, Dewveall shoved Huff backward with both hands, making contact with his chin, mouth, and nose. Suddenly, the transmission static disappeared! Huff's response: "What are you doin' that for, 88? You do that one more time, and I'm gonna sock you one. Now don't do that. . . . You do that again, you'll get a broken nose. . . . I'm not gonna warn you no more now." Even when angered, Huff didn't use profanity.

By design, Landry's "middle linebacker" received protection from down linemen, allowing Huff to move laterally and be the first to arrive at the offense's point of attack. That brought Huff into contact with some of the era's strongest backs, most notably Cleveland's Jim Brown and Green Bay's Jim Taylor. In the late 1950s, New York held Brown to under 50 yards rushing in five straight games. Huff was involved in most of those stops. On one memorable occasion, Huff made the tackle and then politely told Brown, "You stink!" On the next play, Brown ripped off a 65-yard touchdown, allegedly countering with "How do I smell now, Sam?"

In the 1962 NFL Championship Game, Huff's job was to shadow Packers fullback Taylor. In subfreezing conditions at sold-out Yankee Stadium, Huff pounded Taylor play after play. Taylor later remarked, "I don't ever remember being hit so hard. . . . I bled all game." The one time Huff overran the play, Taylor scored a 7-yard TD—then invited Huff to insert the ball "where the sun doesn't shine!" (Taylor told me this story on camera.)

The following year, Huff and the Giants again played for an NFL title. In the third quarter, New York led Chicago, 10–7, but quarterback Y. A. Tittle was limping badly from an earlier hit on his knee. Huff offered Tittle this advice: "They can't score on us, so don't give the ball away." Shortly thereafter, Tittle threw an errant screen pass that Bears defensive end Ed O'Bradovich returned deep into Giants territory. Chicago scored on a QB sneak and held on to win, 14–10. The following season, Giants head coach Allie Sherman traded Huff to Washington, where he finished his playing career in 1969. A decade later, he joined former quarterback Sonny Jurgenson in the team's radio broadcast booth—a job he enjoyed for thirty-four seasons. He died in 2021.

So, was Huff the first "real" middle linebacker? In 1954, Chicago nose guard Bill George stood up and backpedaled into pass coverage against Philadelphia, allegedly the first time such a maneuver had been tried. Landry stood Huff up by design, and the 4–3 defensive scheme Huff anchored in its infancy is still very prevalent in pro football today. All three men are in the Hall of Fame and deserved the recognition. So, you decide what constitutes *real* and how and why a guy who lined up in the middle of it all remained such a "nice guy."

Michael Irvin *(born 1966)*

Wide Receiver

- Dallas Cowboys (1988-99)

Innocence is a word rarely associated with Michael Irvin, yet there was a time when he marveled at new experiences with childlike joy. Following his rookie season in 1989, he participated in the NFL Films *NFL Kids: A Field of Dreams* production that also included Boomer Esiason, Christian Okoye, and Ronnie Lott. During his single day at our facility, Irvin seemed fascinated by control room operations and enthralled by the elaborate child's bedroom set we'd created for the shoot. The "innocent young man" in Irvin remarked, "Man, this is *large*!"

The child actor with whom he worked loved him. So did everybody else in the building. He took direction well and insisted on seeing replays of his takes to make sure that he was satisfied. In short, he bought into the project and took ownership. As the fifteenth of seventeen siblings in a Fort Lauderdale household, Irvin grew up learning about sharing, teamwork, and humility.

So, as Dallas built an all-star supporting cast around him, I enjoyed watching the University of Miami All-American blossom into a Super Bowl champion. Few receivers *ever* used their body and reach better. Irvin perfected offensive pass interference. He rarely dropped a pass. As the "playmaker" in the Troy Aikman–Emmitt Smith–Michael Irvin troika, he was integral to Dallas's three Super Bowl titles in four seasons (1992–93, 1995). He truly earned his Hall of Fame enshrinement.

I'm not sure where the dark side of Irvin's legacy came from. A 1996 sexual assault allegation. The 1998 "Scissorgate" incident in which he allegedly stabbed a teammate over a haircut. Various drug possession and paraphernalia charges. A 2007 sexual assault charge that was settled out of court. A 2017 Fort Lauderdale sexual assault allegation in which charges were dropped.

Irvin's better angels always seem to help him win. Like him or not, his candor as an NFL analyst keeps getting him network jobs. His foxtrot with Anna Demidova earned the duo the single-highest score in the 2009 season of *Dancing with the Stars*. And his tearful Hall of Fame acceptance speech, in which he brutally castigated himself for his numerous brushes with the law, remains one of the most emotional, cathartic orations Canton has ever heard.

In 2016, I met Mike at his alma mater: Saint Thomas Aquinas High School in Fort Lauderdale, Florida. I went there to produce a Golden Football Super Bowl anniversary segment for *CBS This Morning*. We shot campus scenics, B-roll, and an interview with his old football coach before painstakingly lighting an enormous athletic awards hall for Irvin's interview. The place was *large*! It took hours. When we finished, we sent a production assistant to find our subject.

Irvin was gone, nowhere to be found. When he finally answered his cell phone, he promised to be back by 3:00 P.M. Unfortunately, the school needed the awards hall for another event. By the time we lit a much smaller set in a crowded classroom, the prodigal son finally returned. After conciliatory handshakes and hugs all around, Irvin sat down and gave us one of the best interviews in the series. Despite his foibles, Irvin is hard to dislike! It's all that *innocence*.

Brad Johnson *(born 1968)* 🏆

Quarterback

- Minnesota Vikings (1992-98, 2005-06) • Washington Commanders (1999-2000)
- Tampa Bay Buccaneers (2001-04) • Dallas Cowboys (2007-08)

Following Tampa Bay's victory over Oakland in Super Bowl XXXVII (37), Bucs quarterback Brad Johnson was doing his postgame interview. He noticed me waving from a distance. Class act that he is, he smiled warmly and waved back. Extremely gratifying.

In 1994, the Minnesota Vikings acquired veteran quarterback Warren Moon to take charge of the team's offense and help them advance to the postseason.

For insurance, the Vikes imported a pair of Heisman Trophy–winning quarterbacks to serve as Moon's backups: Andre Ware (University of Houston, 1989) and Gino Torretta (University of Miami, 1992). Also on their roster was a six-foot-five-inch 1992 Florida State graduate by the name of Brad Johnson. Can't say for certain, but I don't think the Vikings expected him to make the cut.

That's where I met him in July 1994, at Minnesota's Mankato State University, the one-time summer home of the Vikings. I traveled there to shoot part of a preseason special for Fox Sports, the latest network to secure rights to broadcast NFL games. My primary assignment was to document Moon's arrival and impact on the Vikings' offense.

Things progressed nicely. Dennis Green, as always, granted me almost unlimited access. Every time Moon took a snap, I was there to cover it. When Moon talked football with Green and his staff, his wireless microphone sent the signal directly to my soundman, who hardwired it into my camera (and headset). When Moon watched his fellow quarterbacks do their thing, I listened to his observations and compared them to what I was seeing.

Guess what? Johnson looked much better to me than either of the Heisman Trophy winners. One day, as I climbed the steps to the dining hall, Johnson was walking down toward me. I stopped him and introduced myself. Then, I blurted out the following (paraphrasing): "I hope you're not intimidated by those two Heisman Trophy guys ahead of you on the depth chart, because from what I'm seeing, you're better than both of them."

I praised his superior ball handling, his quick reads and decision making, and his arm strength and accuracy. Johnson seemed stunned. He thanked me, promised me he was doing his best, then shook my hand again before bouncing down the steps. From that day on, we were on a first-name basis.

In Tampa, Johnson benefited from his exposure to Buccaneers head coach Jon Gruden, one of the NFL's most detail-oriented offensive minds and play designers. In Super Bowl XXXVII, Johnson bested Raiders quarterback and NFL Player of the Year Rich Gannon 48–21. This time, America got to see what I'd witnessed at Mankato State nearly a decade earlier.

As I passed by his Super Bowl champion postgame press conference and stopped to wave, I truly hoped that our stairway conversation popped into his head.

Chad Johnson *(born 1978)*

Wide Receiver

- Cincinnati Bengals (2001-10) · New England Patriots (2011)
- Miami Dolphins (2012)

The greatest receiving hands of all time? To me, that's a no-brainer: Cris Carter. In my opinion, the second-best pass-catching hands I ever saw belonged to former Cincinnati Bengals receiver Chad Johnson.

Johnson polarized NFL fans. He loved attention on the field and made trouble off it. Sadly, his reputation was undermined. The respect his football achievements deserved often never came his way. This guy was dedicated to his craft. He rarely dropped a pass that counted. If the ball was catchable, he caught it. When he needed to contort his body to adjust to an errant throw, he did it. He exposed his rib cage over the middle to make leaping grabs. He mastered the two-toe-tap on sideline routes. And, as he once famously demonstrated during an NFL Films wiring, "I can tell people my routes . . . and they still can't stop me." He did this once while mic'd up.

His pregame sound bites were gold. The moment I saw him emerge from the tunnel, I sought him out and positioned myself in front of him while he stretched. Whatever thoughts he hatched during his practice week would pour out, such as "Three things in life that's certain . . . death, taxes . . . and number 85 gonna always be open." Or "I'm like 7–11 . . . I'm always open." And my all-time favorite: When a Bengals trainer asked Johnson whether he had taken anything before the game, his response was immediate and definitive: "Viagra."

In seven of his ten Bengals seasons, he eclipsed 1,000 receiving yards. He led the AFC in this category four consecutive years en route to six Pro Bowls, and his touchdown celebrations became required viewing. In addition to his "River Dance," Johnson resuscitated dead footballs, putted balls with the nearest available pylon, proposed to a Bengals cheerleader on bended knee, donned a yellow "Future Hall of Famer" jacket he had planted on the Bengals' sideline, and so forth. One day, he issued this pregame statement to an NFL Films colleague: "If I get in the end zone today, make sure you keep the camera on me." Later that day when Johnson scored, he took control of a network hard camera and then gleefully turned it on Bengals fans. Brilliant maneuver.

"This is how I feel the game of football is supposed to be played. . . . It's about entertainment," Johnson once told an interviewer. "People who pay for a $75 ticket . . . you mean to tell me I'm not gonna give them a show? . . . I'm gonna give you your money's worth!"

Had the Bengals won anything during Johnson's tenure in Cincinnati, perhaps NFL fans would have accepted his idiosyncratic behavior more readily. Hard-core purists dismissed him as a selfish individualist in a team-sport setting. But this I can promise you: Had the Bengals put Johnson out to pasture, thirty-one NFL general managers would have made offers. Bill Belichick underscores my assertion. He once told NFL Films, "His [Chad's] quickness was a major problem. I didn't want to be in man coverage. . . . I didn't care who we had on him."

In the mid-2000s, I directed several editions of the NFL's *Quarterback Challenge* series, a made-for-TV competition for NFL passers. To make it better, we redesigned events to include active NFL wide receivers. In the summer of 2005, Johnson was one of four NFL pass catchers we invited to join us for the show's two-day shoot in southern California.

Over the four or five years I was involved with *QC*, a handful of receivers distinguished themselves. Torry Holt and Keenan McCardell were very focused. Most at least tried to pull in wild-high or off-the-mark throws. One NFL pass catcher showed up on Day 2 of the event so hungover that quarterbacks moaned when they were matched up with him. And then there was Chad.

As usual, he caught every ball he could reach. If a quarterback overthrew him, he leaped flat out in his attempts to catch the passes. Even his pass-catching colleagues seemed surprised. The passers all applauded his effort. I personally thanked him for giving his all. Even in an off-season "trash-sport" situation, Johnson was completely committed to his craft. He simply wouldn't allow himself to be less. To all the purists out there, I'm pretty sure that works in *every* team context.

In 2007, Johnson amassed 1,440 receiving yards, his best single-season total as a pro. But according to the NFL rumor mill, his relationship with the Bengals was strained beyond repair. One report alleged that Johnson blew up at head coach Marvin Lewis and trashed his team's locker room during the halftime of a game. Johnson's days in Cincinnati appeared to be numbered. Shortly after the Bengals concluded their 7–9 season on January 13, 2008, Johnson appeared on ESPN's popular *Mike & Mike* call-in talk-radio show and poured his heart out:

"I was labeled selfish and a cancer, and it hurt. Fingers were pointed at me this year. 'If the team and the organization want to further themselves . . . you need to get rid of the problem.' It hurt me. To do me that way and not have my back . . . and nobody came to my defense."

So began Johnson's metamorphosis. Privately, he threatened to sit out the 2008 season. Several teams reportedly made trade offers. Johnson hinted that a "change of scenery" might benefit everybody. But his head coach wasn't having it. So, on August 29, 2008, Johnson legally changed his last name to "Ochocinco." In the end, Bengals quarterback Carson Palmer suffered a season-ending injury, the Bengals lost their first eight games, and Ochocinco went down with the ship.

He rebounded in 2009, fell off in 2010, played for Belichick in 2011, then changed his last name back to "Johnson" before joining the Miami

Dolphins in time for the team's *Hard Knocks* debut on HBO in August 2012. But after a much-publicized arrest on domestic-battery charges, the Dolphins released him. Although he never returned to the NFL, he did play football for the Montreal Alouettes (2014–15) in the Canadian Football League, the Monterrey Fundidores (2017) of the Liga de Fútbol Americano Profesional in Mexico, and semiprofessional soccer for the Boca Raton Field Club (2018–19). Yes, Johnson's legendary quickness served him well in multiple sports.

Vocal, visible, vital professional athletes such as Johnson provoke strong reactions. No, domestic battery isn't acceptable *ever*. Egotistical behavior breeds contempt. Even showboating can go too far. But *nobody* can deny Johnson's pass-catching brilliance or his total commitment to his craft.

Jimmy Johnson *(born 1943)*

Head Coach

- Dallas Cowboys (1989-93) · Miami Dolphins (1996-99)

Jerry Jones *(born 1942)*

Owner, President, and General Manager

- Dallas Cowboys (1989-Present)

One of the NFL's most storied owner-coach relationships went far deeper than many realized. Jerry Jones and Jimmy Johnson played college football together at the University of Arkansas. Johnson was an All-Conference defensive lineman. Jones was an offensive lineman and team co-captain. Under head coach Frank Broyles, the 1964 Razorbacks finished undefeated at 11–0, then beat Nebraska in the Cotton Bowl 10–7 to clinch college football's mythical National Championship. Johnson committed to football and worked his way up through the collegiate coaching ranks. Jones created an oil and gas exploration business in Arkansas and became a billionaire. Three decades later, their paths would cross again.

Johnson's top-ranked Miami Hurricanes arrived for the 1987 Fiesta Bowl wearing combat fatigues, quite confident they would defeat Penn State. But on New Year's Day, the Lions rushed three linemen and dropped eight defenders into coverage. Miami quarterback Vinny Testaverde never quite figured things out. With eighteen seconds left in the game, Penn State picked off Testaverde for the fifth time to preserve a 14–10 victory and win a National Championship.

That fall, Johnson's Hurricanes went undefeated and then beat Barry Switzer's Oklahoma Sooners in the Orange Bowl on January 1, 1988, for their own National Championship. Jones took notice. In 1989, when the billionaire oilman bought the Dallas Cowboys, he fired Hall of Fame head coach Tom Landry, then named his former Arkansas teammate to replace him, only the second head coach in team history. They drafted wisely and imported free agents with purpose. By 1991, Jones and Johnson's team was ready to compete again.

On November 24, Dallas (7–5) arrived in Washington's (11–0) RFK Stadium. It was my first season shooting sound. When I drew the assignment, I predicted that Dallas would win the game. When they did (24–21), I asked the Cowboys' public relations executive Rich Dalrymple to allow me to shoot in his winning locker room. It marked the very first time NFL Films recorded Johnson's trademark rhetorical rant "How about them Cowboys?"

In 1992, the Johnson–Jones juggernaut finished the regular season 14–2, beat San Francisco 30–20 in the NFC Championship Game, then thrashed Buffalo 52–17 in Super Bowl XXVII (27). Near game's end, I cozied up next to Johnson on the sideline with my wide-angle lens. In that instant, Emmitt Smith decided to mess up Johnson's always perfectly coiffed hair. Networks show that shot every time they revisit the Cowboys' glory days. It still amuses me.

In Super Bowl XXVIII (28), Dallas again manhandled Buffalo, this time 30–13. Then, quite abruptly, the Arkansas Alliance dissolved. At the time, I could not comprehend why two grown men could not sublimate their egos with so much NFL history at stake. After Johnson left, Jones replaced him with Switzer, whose 1995 Cowboys beat Pittsburgh for their third Lombardi Trophy in four seasons, the first NFL team to accomplish this. They haven't won since.

As of 2022, seven different coaches have guided the Cowboys since Johnson. Jones remains the face of the franchise. Throughout the 1990s, I knew Jones from afar as the very visible owner who showed up on the sidelines just in time to celebrate or commiserate with his team. That changed one 2002 late spring day in Dallas. In a downtown hotel overlooking Dealey Plaza (the site of John F. Kennedy's assassination), HBO and NFL

Films sponsored a luncheon to announce Dallas's participation in the second season of *Hard Knocks.*

The impression Jones and his son Stephen made on me that afternoon remains with me to this day. Each is a stand-up guy—comfortable in his own skin, approachable, and likable. Both promised my crews full cooperation. At first I was skeptical, but as the Cowboys' San Antonio summer camp unfolded, NFL Films was afforded the same access to which we'd become accustomed in Maryland with the Ravens during *Hard Knocks*'s inaugural season in 2001. To paraphrase the Cowboys' media relations executive Rich Dalrymple: "Hey, it's free national publicity."

Few understand better than Jones what an asset publicity can be. Before the team broke camp, Jones invited my crew and all the other local and national media to join him at a San Antonio restaurant for "happy hour." By then, my wife had joined me for a brief "working vacation," so I took her to the event. When I left early to take care of business, Barbara remained behind with the crew and friends.

After several Cosmos, Barb made a bathroom run. On her way back to her table, she encountered Jerry one on one, introduced herself, then asked if she could take a picture with him. A friend snapped the photo. Afterwards, Jerry resumed his laps around the room and Barb acquired an image that hangs amidst a collage in our guest bathroom for all our friends and family to behold. To this day, she laments the inexpensive Walmart summer dress she was wearing for the occasion.

Jones inspires criticism. Some say that he only hires head coaches he can control. Others say that he and his son Stephen meddle in matters they don't fully understand. During the second season of *Hard Knocks*, I was surprised the Cowboys allowed us to do multiple camera shoots of their scouting operation. Stephen ran these meetings. Jerry, of course, oversaw everything.

Then, it hit me. Jones *wanted* America to see all this, to demonstrate that "America's Team" was doing everything possible to win. And he was at the center of it. Why *not* let NFL Films shovel a promotion at viewing audiences rather than Cowboys PR? No wonder the ratings tanked. When programming crosses the line into promotion, viewers shy away, and dynasties disappear.

Johnson is in the Pro Football Hall of Fame but not the Cowboys' Ring of Honor. Jones's team has not played in a Super Bowl in a quarter century. Egos can wreck empires.

The Kalil Brothers

Ryan Kalil *(born 1985)*

Center

- Carolina Panthers (2007-18) · New York Jets (2019)

Matt Kalil *(born 1989)*

Offensive Tackle

- Minnesota Vikings (2012-16) · Carolina Panthers (2017-18)
- Houston Texans (2019)

In 2007, the Carolina Panthers used their second-round draft choice (the forty-seventh pick overall) to select USC Trojans center Ryan Kalil. By his fifth NFL season, Ryan had signed the largest contract for a center in history at the time. So, when NFL Films asked me to do a segment on the Kalil family in the summer of 2014, I went online to learn more about Ryan, his siblings, and his parents.

Overachievers didn't quite capture it. Ryan's father, Frank, had played professionally in the World Football League (1982–85), also as a center. Ryan's mother, Cheryl (maiden name Van Cleave), had served as Miss California in 1981 and competed in that year's Miss America pageant. Ryan's sister, Danielle, had performed in the West Coast finals of

American Idol. Ryan's younger brother Matthew had been the Minnesota Vikings' first-round draft selection (the fourth pick overall) in 2012. And Ryan turned out to be a man of many talents, a truly versatile human being. A week before my crew and I traveled to California to produce my Kalil family segment, Ryan emailed me a detailed schedule for our two-day shoot. Yes, a pro player I'd never met did my preproduction work for me—which made July 18, 2014, one of the longest and hardest days in my career.

It started at a vacation home in Newport Beach that Ryan and Matthew had rented specifically for a family vacation. It ended fourteen hours and many miles of bumper-to-bumper driving later at the Kalil family residence somewhere due east of LA in the California foothills. In between, we captured (1) Ryan's two toddler daughters shaving their father's beard with real double-edged razors; (2) the brothers lifting weights, pushing sleds, and flipping airplane tires at a nearby gym; (3) Danielle recording her composition "The Water" at a sound studio, with her two brothers in attendance; (4) Frank and Cheryl hosting a family picnic featuring enough barbecue to feed a Roman legion; and (5) four lengthy interviews, all of which required lots of lighting. "You're right on schedule, Bob," Ryan kept reminding me. He would know—he drew it up.

Along the way, Ryan encouraged Danielle before her recording session: "I thought I'd give you a pep talk. . . . Don't suck!" To which his sister responded, "I'll try not to disappoint the family." We learned from Frank, "When he [Ryan] was playing football early, it didn't look promising." According to Ryan, "Part of it was because . . . I wasn't any good." And no family segment is complete without some pointed candor. Said Ryan, "Athletically, he's a lot more gifted than me. Looks-wise, I'm much more handsome." They could turn a phrase, too, as Matt pointed out in discussing his parents: "My dad got lucky with her. She was Miss California. . . . He definitely outkicked his coverage."

The segment's payoff showed Ryan's Panthers on the road against Matt's Vikings, on October 13, 2013. Between them, in a Fox Sports three-way split-screen, appeared Danielle singing the national anthem. Looking on from the end zone were Frank and Cheryl: a complete football family affair. Reflecting on her children's paths leading them each to this moment together on top of the world, Cheryl exclaimed to the camera, "I've never been prouder!" To which Frank added, "Or more nervous . . . I ain't rooting for nobody!"

As the piece showed Frank in an upstairs end zone booth following the action intently, Matt's voiceover added context: "There's never a moment he's not grading us. . . . He's that guy with the binoculars." To which Ryan added, "It's a win-win for me when we both play well and we [Ryan's Panthers] can still win." Diplomatically stated, another of Ryan's virtues. After my segment aired nationally on Fox Sports's *This Is the NFL*, my on-field encounters with Matt and Ryan pretty much all followed the same script:

"Good morning, Ryan [or Matt]. Your folks here today?" To which each would reply, "Pop's up there watching us somewhere!" Perhaps Frank never watched with as much nervousness or trepidation as on February 7, 2016, the day of Super Bowl 50: Carolina versus Denver. I ran into Ryan prior to pregame outside the Panthers' locker room.

"Why not?" I said as we man-hugged. "Exactly, why not?" Ryan replied. To my dismay (I shot the Panthers' sideline), Denver prevailed, 24–10. Ryan wore his disappointment on his face. My camera could feel it. I can only imagine how the rest of the family suffered in the bleachers.

I'm not certain how Danielle's career is progressing. As for Ryan and Matt, both have retired from the NFL. But in 2017–18, Matt played alongside Ryan on the Carolina Panthers' offensive line. Both benefited from their father's expertise and training. I smile when I envision Frank trying to follow both sons simultaneously through binoculars. How does one grade pass protection and footwork for two? I'm pretty certain that's not even possible.

In the coming years, I would not be surprised if Ryan receives some Hall of Fame consideration. It's also possible he may gravitate toward TV production. He certainly knows how to max out a production crew's workday. Regardless, Ryan, Matt, Danielle, Frank, and Cheryl rank as one of the most accomplished families I've ever had the privilege to profile. Even better is how they conduct themselves with each other—even with tired, sweaty, and overworked production-crew guests in their home.

As Frank underscored in the final image of my segment, an on-field family photo shot at the end of the Panthers–Vikings game in 2013, "I'd love people to know that these two guys and my daughter are such good kids outside of what they do. . . . It's just been a great ride so far for the Kalil family."

These more-than-worthy subjects were a joy to coproduce! Thank you, Kalil family! And a special nod to Ryan, the best coproducer I've ever inherited—like it or not!

Paul Krause *(born 1942)*

Safety

- Washington Commanders (1964-67) · Minnesota Vikings (1968-79)

This is a story about love and loyalty.

Paul Krause grew up on the poor side of Flint, Michigan, but no matter—he had strong faith, good friends, and incredible athletic ability. He loved sports and excelled in every one he played. At Bendle High School, in Burton, Michigan, Krause earned All-State honors in baseball, football, basketball, and track, but he listed baseball and football as his two favorites.

He also fancied a neighborhood girl named Pamela Henry. Paul grew up playing sports in Pam's backyard. They've known each other since they were four years old. They married in 1963, Krause's final year at the University of Iowa, where he earned All-American recognition in both of his favorite sports. But a bad shoulder injury suffered during his junior year of football canceled the center fielder's baseball prospects, so Krause focused on playing safety.

As a rookie with Washington in 1964, Krause intercepted 12 passes, including at least one in seven consecutive games. He finished second in Rookie of the Year balloting to teammate Charley Taylor. Despite his 28 interceptions in his first four NFL seasons, in 1968 Washington traded Krause to the Minnesota Vikings. He played his final twelve seasons for Bud Grant, a man who appreciated Krause's superb ball-hawking, "centerfielder" instincts.

In the final month of the 1979 season, Krause became the NFL's all-time interception leader with 81 career picks. Emlen Tunnell (Giants and Packers, 1948–61) recorded 79. The next closest number is Rod Woodson's 71. There's no such a thing as an unbreakable NFL record, but Krause's 81 career picks are as close to untouchable as any individual record in the book. Tack on his durability—only two games missed due to injury in sixteen seasons—and you've got one incredible football player, right?

So, what took the Pro Football Hall of Fame voters so long to recognize Krause's achievements? As a semi-regular at Vikings home games, I witnessed quite a few of the team's annual alumni gatherings. Among the Hall of Famers and future enshrinees present were Fran Tarkenton, Mick Tingelhoff, Carl Eller, Alan Page, Chris Doleman, John Randle, Cris Carter, and head coach Bud Grant. Dozens of former NFC champions, Pro Bowlers, and just plain old teammates also took a bow, far too many to name individually. As did, of course, Krause, the league's all-time interception leader.

So, I struck up several conversations with Krause, and then I asked colleagues why he wasn't in the hall. I suspected that Minnesota's four Super Bowl defeats and Krause's alleged dislike for tackling were the primary reasons. But, as Krause explained to me, "I gave the ball to my offensive team 81 times. And I stopped 81 offensive drives." And as Grant reminded Krause on Day 1 and many times after, "Just don't get beat deep." The 1969 Vikings allowed an NFL record (at the time) 133 points in 14 games. That's fewer than ten points in a contest. Think about that for a moment: Maybe football's best "center fielder" had some real impact.

Eventually, the Hall of Fame selection committee realized that Krause, this veritable "Willie Mays of NFL defensive backs," belonged in the hall with his peers. So after a long, two-decade wait, in 1998, Krause was enshrined. That's when I met Pamela Krause. During Krause's acceptance speech, he broke into tears describing the near-death experience that his wife, Pam, had endured. I knew nothing about this. Several days later, I learned the details from the Vikings' media relations staff, then asked whether I could tell the Krause family's story. Paul Krause agreed.

In 1996, a truck slammed into Pam Krause's car as she was driving the family dog to a kennel. First responders found her barely alive and totally unresponsive. She remained in a coma for nearly *six months*! Very few people recover from such trauma.

This is where love and loyalty merged. When Pam did regain consciousness, medical and long-term health care professionals recommended that the family commit her to a facility. Instead, Paul and his daughter Zendi brought Pam home. The two of them fed her, clothed her, cared for her, and taught her how to walk with a cane. As Zendi told me, "We were always a very close family. Things like this can make a family closer, or they can drive you apart."

When I interviewed Paul and Pamela, I insisted that they sit together. Pam said very little until Paul prompted her. When she spoke, she formed her words carefully and spoke as well as her near-fatal, brain-stem trauma would allow. Paul's loving smile never faded, and his resolve to assist her never wavered. Later, Zendi took her outside for some therapeutic walking. Then, Paul showed me his high school yearbook. That's when I realized I was producing something special.

As Krause explained in his Hall of Fame enshrinement speech, "This past year, Pam made the statement that this was going to be my year [to be elected to the Hall of Fame] because God wanted her to be present." When television cameras cut to a close-up of Pam sitting in the audience, she signaled "OK" with her thumb and index finger. Sustained applause filled the air in Canton.

Every semester I taught at the University of Delaware and Penn State, I screened my Paul and Pamela Krause segment in my video production class. Each time, I fought back tears. And it all goes back to the two precious things I mentioned up top—love and loyalty—as well as two remarkable quotations attributed to Paul and Pam next to their individual yearbook pictures.

Paul Krause, the four-sport letterman and future NFL Hall of Famer, wrote prophetically, "Great athletes are rare and always will be."

With even more uncanny farsightedness, Pamela Henry wrote, "A true friend is forever a friend."

The segment opens with their yearbook pictures, followed by Krause's rags-to-riches story. The segment ends with the two statements highlighted above. And as a sentimental piece of music reaches its emotional climax—as Paul and Pamela's faded pictures are layered over their old, timeworn yearbook cover, the narrator says, "Sometimes, these people are one and the same."

I've won some awards in my career, and yet somehow, this segment didn't measure up. But for me, the love and loyalty I experienced in the Krauses' presence will live with me long after any trophy.

Jack Lambert *(born 1952)*

Middle Linebacker

- Pittsburgh Steelers (1974–84)

Jack Lambert was as simple as he was complex, a tough, no-nonsense middle linebacker with malice in his competitive heart yet mischief in his eyes. Despite his toothless, madman persona, Lambert was an intelligent, multidimensional player *and* human being who both cultivated and disdained the spotlight that so often found him. Without Lambert, there's no way the 1970s Pittsburgh Steelers would have won four Super Bowls in six years. They may not have won any. My opinion echoes that of Bud Carson, coordinator of Pittsburgh's "Steel Curtain" defenses of that decade, to which Carson added, "If Joe Greene was the cornerstone of our defense, Lambert was the catalyst." He also ranks as my second-favorite NFL player friend of all time.

I got to know Lambert slowly, as most people outside the Steelers' locker room did. A second-round pick in Pittsburgh's historic 1974 NFL draft (Lynn Swann, John Stallworth, and Mike Webster were among the team's other selections, all Hall of Famers), Lambert played himself into a starting role during the preseason. By season's end, he was the NFL's Defensive Rookie of the Year, the Steelers were Super Bowl champions, and this eastern Ohio country boy was famous.

One of my earliest exposures to Lambert came during a pregame warm-up at Three Rivers Stadium. While shooting with my camera, I noticed Lambert standing in my foreground, backed by a banner draped over the stadium wall behind him that read "Lambert's Lunatics." I zoomed in on the sign and focused on the boisterous, zealous fans trying to get Jack's attention. When I pulled back to reveal Lambert, he turned and acknowledged them with a wave of his taped-up hand. That banner hung in Three Rivers for a decade.

During Lambert's heyday, his front teeth were conspicuously absent in several national magazine photos, so, while producing a Steelers highlight film, I paired one of our best tight-lens close-ups of Lambert's missing bicuspids with a descriptive line from the great John Facenda: "Count Dracula in Cleats." Steelers fans turned that into a stadium banner as well.

By 1984, the Steelers were no longer annual Super Bowl contenders, but Lambert was still plying his trade at an All-Pro level. At a preseason game in Dallas, we made arrangements to wire Lambert's shoulder pads for a mic'd-up feature. In Pittsburgh's locker room, our best soundman placed the microphone, ran the wire to the transmitter attached to the back of Lambert's pads, then sealed the unit in place with a durable protective metal plate and an entire roll of gaffer tape.

Lambert walked in, smoking a cigarette. When he sat down beside his locker, he pulled out his pads, fit them over his head, then stood up and rolled his arms. He looked at me menacingly, puffing smoke out of the corner of his mouth. In his gravelly baritone, he let me know, "Pretty f***ing heavy, Bob." I explained this was all standard operating procedure. I lied and said that quarterbacks wore this identical package. I did all I could do to defuse the situation. Lambert dragged on his cigarette, exhaled, then stared coldly in my direction. "Pretty f***ing heavy, Bob," he repeated.

I went into sales mode. I reminded him that he'd promised to do this, which was why we had flown an entire crew to Dallas in the preseason, set up an elaborate transmission receiving station behind the Steelers' bench, and spent nearly an hour fitting and refitting the microphone, transmitter, and wires on his shoulder pads. He snuffed out his cigarette. "I didn't say I wouldn't wear it, but it's still pretty f***ing heavy, Bob!" He walked away, quite pleased with himself.

Two of Lambert's better interview sound bites came on *Monday Night Football* telecasts. In ABC's "Talking Heads" intro format, he announced, without snickering, that he was "Jack Lambert from Buzzard's Breath, Wyoming." Another time, he suggested, "Quarterbacks should have to wear dresses," although he couldn't keep a straight face after that one.

When he retired, I interviewed him at his rural home in Worthington, Pennsylvania. I learned how much he liked beer, hunting, and the absence of media types like myself. So, when a fellow producer went there years later, I told him to take Lambert a case of Michelob, admire his mounted antlers collection, and don't waste his time. The interview went swimmingly.

In the summer of 1986, near the end of a two-week production trip, I scheduled my crew's final stop at Lambert's football camp somewhere in eastern Ohio. Back then, ATMs didn't honor local bank cards, so my soundman and I showed up at Lambert's watering hole flat broke. Within minutes, Lambert was on the phone with one of his camp assistants: "I'm sitting here with two assholes from NFL Films, and they don't have a plug nickel between them."

The Michelob flowed that night. Lambert told me about a Pro Bowl in which he glanced around a defensive huddle and counted seven other black Steelers helmets in addition to his own: "One of the proudest moments of my career." Several beers later, he confessed that by the end of most seasons, he barely weighed two hundred pounds and that Mel Blount, Pittsburgh's Hall of Fame cornerback, actually outweighed him. He was *not* the prototypical NFL middle linebacker.

The next morning at Lambert's camp, he showed up with a softball bat and demonstrated his left-handed swing. He then asked me, "Think I could play the part of Jimbo?" What? When the cobwebs cleared, I realized that the night before, I'd described a softball screenplay I'd written and had offered Lambert one of the supporting roles—that of Jimbo. And he really wanted it!

My final Lambert encounter took place the day the Steelers played their final game in Three Rivers Stadium. Lambert was among the last players introduced. As Pittsburgh's all-time greats took one final victory lap and Lambert approached, I placed my camera on the ground. Lambert hugged me, then said, "In case I never see you again, Angelo, it's been good knowing you." Colleagues standing nearby seemed stunned. "Is he sick?" they asked me. Nope! But he was through playing games. He was headed back to his country home to hunt, drink beer, and savor his solitude. That's Jack Lambert.

Ray Lewis *(born 1975)*

Middle Linebacker

- Baltimore Ravens (1996-2012)

In 2011, NFL Films decided to do its second in-season version of *A Football Life*, and I was picked to produce and direct. My subject was Baltimore Ravens middle linebacker Ray Lewis. Ravens head coach John Harbaugh signed off on the project—with certain stipulations: I could work with Lewis outside the Ravens' complex as I saw fit, but at the team's facility, I needed Harbaugh's permission in advance. All parties agreed, and production immediately commenced.

Over the next five months, NFL Films mic'd up Lewis for every 2011 Ravens game, including those that he missed after fracturing his big toe while playing the Seahawks on November 13. Off the field, I shot every other aspect of Lewis's existence—or so I thought. I did what I could at Baltimore's training facility. Along the way, I learned that Lewis excelled in many roles.

As a father, Lewis maintained great relations with his six children. At a Florida high school football game in October, he prowled the sideline like a caged tiger, watching his first-born son Ray III run for 3 touchdowns. At a Florida public park in November, he arranged a gala affair that included water sports and live entertainment for his son Ralin's eleventh birthday. At Christmas, he joined his daughter, Diaymon Desiree, at one of her fitness sessions, groaning in agony as he tried to match her sit-up for sit-up.

As a preacher, Lewis learned about a White, blue-collar Ravens fan suffering from late-stage cancer whose dying wish was to meet him. So, Ray began visiting John Doe at his suburban Baltimore home. There, he led Doe's family in prayer while beseeching the Lord to use his healing powers. My entire crew was mesmerized by the heartfelt evangelical experience.

As a leader, Lewis provided complete Thanksgiving Day meals to needy Baltimore families, many *hundreds* of them. One day at the team's facility, an Operation Desert Storm war hero inspired by Lewis showed up to present Ray the Purple Heart he had won in the line of duty. At a Saturday night team meeting in Pittsburgh, just hours before a crucial divisional game, Lewis stood up in front of his teammates and delivered an emotional sermon that had me and my crew ready to suit up and join the fray.

If you're reading this, you most likely know about Lewis's legal issues. If not, I'll summarize: Lewis attended Super Bowl XXXIV (34) in Atlanta as a spectator. In the wee hours of the morning on January 31, 2000, a group of men partying with Lewis became involved in an altercation that resulted in two deaths and several murder charges. In court, Lewis eventually pled guilty to obstruction of justice. The NFL fined him a quarter of a million dollars.

At no point during 2011 did I mention these events in Lewis's presence—I'd been waiting for our final interview together to broach the subject. I knew that if our final show failed to address these issues, sports television critics would lambaste NFL Films, saying that we had covered up or whitewashed Lewis's association with the tragedy. Ray sensed that. One day in January 2014, very late in the show's production process, Lewis sent me an email announcing a speaking engagement he'd agreed to do for Black Harvard law school students in mid-February. He advised me to join him on campus with a crew. In his words: "You really need to be there for this, Bob."

Sure enough, Lewis recounted his Atlanta nightmare in detail for NFL Films and Harvard's Black legal eagles. As he spoke, I felt a great weight being lifted, from the production and from Lewis himself. I would not need a narrator to rehash events from a script. Even better, any and all Ravens objections had been preempted—after all, Lewis had invited NFL Films to meet him at Harvard, away from team facilities. He wanted us to hear his version and record his account of those fateful events. He spoke openly and honestly for an entire morning for the aspiring attorneys in attendance and the American TV audiences who would eventually hear his words. He'd met head on the event that I'd wisely chosen not to mention in his presence for five months.

Now, my editing partner and I could start fashioning forty-four minutes of rough cut out of the mountain of original material we had generated. By the time we finished in the late winter of 2012, I was fairly certain that our show would be well received, so imagine my surprise when the four-person NFL Films team who supervised production on all *A Football Life* episodes interrupted us about one-third of the way through our first pass: "I was OK with everything up 'til now, but this is too much." This candid critique followed our segment on Lewis's Thanksgiving meal giveaway, catching me off guard.

"What do you mean?" I asked.

"You're only showing us the things Ray wants people to see," I heard in response.

To which I replied, "But he does these things whether there's a camera there or not."

The bitter truth hit me like a gut punch. Lewis, who lived his life out loud in every other aspect, had kept silent on this critical chapter of his biography because I'd let him. He engaged his teammates, his community, and his family with passion and charisma. So, yes, he knew what he was doing when he invited our cameras to Harvard. He had wanted to tell his story away from the Ravens' facility—in his own words and in his own way. He was raising his voice and engaging the broader community in the only remaining hidden aspect of his story. He wanted people to see it and hear it, just as he'd done with every other aspect of his life. In retrospect, his conviction was admirable.

The Lewis episode of *A Football Life* earned some of the series' highest ratings ever. The following season (2012), Lewis's last, the Ravens beat San Francisco in Super Bowl XLVII (47), 34–31. He retired on top. As he scaled the podium for the postgame trophy presentation, he spotted me standing next to the steps. He smiled and stuck out his tongue. I gave him a thumbs-up for excelling in his two most accomplished roles: Hall of Fame player and Super Bowl champion.

The Longs

Howie Long (*father, born 1960*)

Defensive End

- Oakland/Los Angeles Raiders (1981-93)

Chris Long (*oldest son, born 1985*)

Defensive End

- St. Louis Rams (2008-15) · New England Patriots (2016)
- Philadelphia Eagles (2017-18)

Kyle Long (*second-oldest son, born 1988*)

Offensive Guard

- Chicago Bears (2013-19)
- Kansas City Chiefs (2021)

Howie Long (Howard on his birth certificate) forever changed professional football.

Officially, Howie entered the Pro Football Hall of Fame (Class of 2000) as a defensive end—more specifically, a *left* defensive end—in Raiders game-day programs. But the Raiders learned by experiment that

Long could pass rush, run-stop, and cause havoc wherever he lined up. Because every NFL team has good pass blockers and lesser ones, the Raiders would isolate Howie on an opponent's weakest link, then turn him loose. The results always favored the Raiders.

But football almost didn't happen for this native Bostonian. Thanks to a loving extended family, Howie eventually made his way to Milton High School in an affluent Boston suburb. As a senior, he achieved Scholastic Coach All-American status. After starting for four years at Villanova University, Howie replaced an injured athlete at the 1980 Blue-Gray Football Classic, where he won defensive MVP honors and attracted the attention of the Super Bowl champion Raiders. Al Davis drafted Howie in the second round (forty-eighth overall selection). His impact was enormous.

By 1983, Long was an All-Pro. "Howie Time" became part of pro football vernacular. As he once described it to NFL Films, "I really just don't like violence . . . but, you know . . . sometimes they hit that switch!" In a regular-season game against Washington, he recorded 5 sacks. In Super Bowl XVIII (18), Howie and the Raiders' defense allowed a single touchdown in a 38–9 trouncing of NFL MVP Joe Theismann's record-setting Washington offense. Over his thirteen-year career, Howie made eight Pro Bowls and won several Defensive Player of the Year titles.

At one point during this stretch, Seattle coach Chuck Knox told NFL Films, "Long might be the most dominant force in defensive football today." Giants coach Bill Parcells added, "We have to do something about this guy, or *he* may destroy what we're trying to do in the game."

I met Howie one summer afternoon in 1987 at the Los Angeles Coliseum. I was directing for NFL Films's syndicated show *This Is the NFL*, and Long had agreed to do lead-ins for a five-part series called *Legendary Linemen*. We shot these segments deep in the bowels of the old stadium, in locker rooms and tunnels. I distinctly remember two things about that day.

First, Howie worked without a teleprompter. He committed our scripts to memory and delivered convincing, air-worthy takes into mirrors or directly at our cameras with relative ease: "We measure many modern athletes in dollar signs. We measure Chuck Bednarik in minutes. Sixty of them. . . ." This particular script went on awhile. Howie nailed it the very first time.

Second, in a conversation between camera setups, I asked him about a remark attributed to him by *Sports Illustrated* writer Paul Zimmerman. The magazine quoted Howie as telling Chicago Bears guard Kurt Becker, "I'm going to get you in the parking lot after the game and beat you up in front of your family." Howie laughed and said that was his favorite threat. Then, he reminisced about his days at Villanova, during which he was the North Collegiate Heavyweight Boxing Champion. I break into a cold sweat just thinking about tangling with Howie in a parking lot.

In 2017, I codirected a series of commercial segments for Campbell's Chunky Soup. One of my favorites took me and NFL Films to Chicago, where we worked with Howie's second-oldest son, Kyle, a three-time Pro Bowl guard for the Bears. By the time Kyle arrived at the field complex where a local high school football team was practicing, I'd set up a teaching-demo situation on trap-blocking techniques. Kyle immediately embraced the idea and went to work, and I couldn't help but remember how Howie had demonstrated the same innate professionalism on set three decades earlier. Like father, like son.

Later that year, I observed Kyle's older brother, Christopher, playing defensive end for the Philadelphia Eagles. I knew that he'd been released by the Rams in 2016, then signed with New England. I knew that in the fourth quarter of Super Bowl LI (51), Atlanta's Jake Long had drawn a flag for holding Chris, a penalty that had canceled Atlanta's game-clinching field-goal opportunity. And I knew that after earning a Super Bowl ring in New England, he'd cast his NFL lot with Philadelphia. I'd heard that Chris had donated his entire 2017 Eagles salary to charity. And I knew that he was Howie's son and Kyle's brother.

My very last football game as a cameraman was Super Bowl LII (52). The Philadelphia Eagles were heavy underdogs against the defending champion New England Patriots. My soundman for the game was a South Jersey native named Mark Ricci. Needless to say, he and I both wanted the Eagles to win. Prior to kickoff, if you would have told me that Tom Brady would pass for 502 yards and lose, I would have guessed that you'd barely survived a lobotomy. When the Patriots took their first lead of the game (33–32) at 9:22 in the fourth quarter, Mark's spirits sagged, but I quickly reminded him, "Hey, New England hasn't stopped the Eagles yet." Sure enough, the Eagles orchestrated a fourteen-play, 75-yard drive to take a 38–33 lead, then forced a fumble, kicked a field goal, and held on for an improbable 41–33 win.

During postgame festivities, Ricci and I made the rounds, shooting individual Eagles players, families, coaches, and anybody who had a stake in Philly's victory. Just before we headed toward the Eagles' locker room, I noticed family patriarch Howie standing next to the platform during the trophy presentation. He was watching his son Chris from a distance, so I sidled up behind him. When Howie sensed my presence and turned around, I was ready: "Proud moment, Dad?" His chiseled features broadened into a smile: "It doesn't get any better than this!"

The Mannings

Archie Manning *(father, born 1949)*

Quarterback

- New Orleans Saints (1971-82) · Houston Oilers (1982-83)
- Minnesota Vikings (1983-84)

Peyton Manning *(second-oldest son, born 1976)*

Quarterback

- Indianapolis Colts (1998-2011) · Denver Broncos (2012-15)

Eli Manning *(youngest son, born 1981)* (inevitable)

Quarterback

- New York Giants (2004-19)

In the spring of 1976, I took an NFL Films crew to New Orleans to do a shoot with Hank Stram, the Saints' newly hired head coach. Saints quarterback Archie Manning just happened to be at the team's facility, rehabbing his surgically repaired shoulder. One thing led to another, and before long, the grand patriarch of the Manning quarterback family was pumping iron on a machine in the background of our shots while

Stram botched one stand-up after another. When Stram finally did an acceptable take, then left for lunch, I thanked Archie profusely for his extreme patience.

In 1987, the Saints finally won more games than they lost and made the NFL playoffs. By then, Archie was doing radio commentary for his former team. Once again, I took a crew to New Orleans, this time to document the team's first-ever playoff game for NFL Films's annual year-end show *Road to the Super Bowl*. Among the many Saint fans I interviewed was Archie.

His children were present during our setup. Eventually, I heard the scuttling of feet. When I looked toward the sound, three heads peered around a corner, one above the other. Archie's eldest son, Cooper (age thirteen), appeared with his two younger siblings, Peyton (eleven) and Eli (about to turn seven). If only we'd captured that image! During the interview, Archie recounted his struggles with the Saints and seemed pleased the team was thriving under general manager Jim Finks and head coach Jim Mora. That weekend, the Saints imploded in their first-ever playoff game, losing to Minnesota, 44–10.

Peyton came into this world destined for the NFL. In a segment Steve Sabol personally directed and I later edited, Peyton introduced himself at about age five in a local evening news sports sound bite. The broadcaster knelt down, positioned his stick microphone under Peyton's chin, and asked, "You gonna be a football player when you grow up?" Right on cue, young Peyton responded, "Ya-huh." That's five-year-old for "Just watch me, dude!"

When his pro career unfolded years later, Peyton's biggest obstacle proved to be Tom Brady, who outplayed Peyton's Colts in head-to-head playoff matchups. The one year Peyton bested Brady in the postseason, the Colts went on to defeat the Chicago Bears in a rain-soaked Super Bowl XLI (41), 29–17. Peyton had finally made good on his childhood promise.

Little brother Eli fared much better against Brady in big games. In Super Bowl XLII (42) and in Super Bowl XLVI (46), Eli engineered fourth-quarter comebacks to defeat Brady's Patriots. In XLII, after the *undefeated* Patriots (18–0) took a 14–10 lead late in the fourth quarter, Giants defensive end Michael Strahan walked toward the Giants offensive linemen and said "17–14 is the final. 17–14, fellas . . . OK? One touchdown, and we are world champions." After I stopped shooting, I announced to my soundman Mark Ricci, "Fat f***ing chance!"

Then, Eli went to work. In the game's climactic moment, he
several Patriots pass rushers, rolled right, then launched a long flutt
that receiver David Tyree pinned against his helmet with one hand
Patriots defenders floundered all around him. I said to Ricci, "Let's
this reaction. It's going to be *huge*!" Moments later, Eli hit wide receiv
Plaxico Burress with the game winner, and the Giants' sideline erupte
with unabashed joy and exaltation. It remains the most animated touchdown reaction I've ever shot. Eli deservedly earned MVP honors.

Four years later, Eli stunned Brady and the Patriots again. Midway through the fourth quarter in Super Bowl XLVI, Eli threw a perfect deep sideline pass to Mario Manningham that broke the Patriots' spirit and led to a go-ahead score and a 21–17 Giants lead. A last-ditch New England effort fell short, and Eli captured his second Super Bowl MVP award.

That same season was Peyton's last in Indy. A neck injury and subsequent surgery and rehab resulted in the Colts releasing him. Hall of Fame quarterback John Elway was now Denver's executive vice president of football operations and general manager, and he lured Peyton to the Broncos. That season, Denver won thirteen games and lost to the eventual Super Bowl champion Ravens in the NFL playoffs. Peyton was named the NFL's Comeback Player of the Year.

As a Bronco, Peyton frequently worked the sidelines and talked strategy with different position groups—something he *never* did in Indy. My sound-camera colleagues and I compared notes on this. His leadership skills and football knowledge were suddenly on full display. In 2013, the Broncos won another thirteen games. Peyton earned his fifth Associated Press MVP award, then beat Brady's Patriots in the AFC Championship Game, 28–16. But in Super Bowl XLVIII (48), Seattle destroyed the Broncos, 43–8. Was it the end of the Manning family QB dynasty?

Following the game, I walked toward the Broncos' Met Life Stadium locker room, hoping to grab an image of Peyton for posterity. There, I ran into Archie and Peyton surrounded by friends and media types. Something told me that America had not seen the last of the Mannings.

In 2015, I codirected an NFL Films production shoot at Newman High School in New Orleans, Peyton and Eli's alma mater. Both quarterbacks participated in the event. In anticipation of the fiftieth Super Bowl, *CBS This Morning* commissioned a series involving the presentation of ceremonial Golden Footballs to Super Bowl champions. That's the day I learned about the newest Manning, a young quarterback called Arch to distinguish him from his grandfather. Later that year, Peyton did just to help Denver beat the Carolina Panthers in Super Bowl 50. He ed Eli's Super Bowl win total, although Eli remains one up on his brother for Super Bowl MVP awards. And young Arch waits in the gs—quietly perfecting and advancing the family's trade.

Jim Marshall *(born 1937)*

Defensive End

- Saskatchewan Roughriders (1959) · Cleveland Browns (1960)
- Minnesota Vikings (1961-79)

Any opinions on the greatest NFL folly of all time, the single-most-embarrassing moment a player ever perpetrated? The biggest boneheaded act in football history? If you didn't answer "Jim Marshall's Wrong Way Run," either (1) you don't know much about pro football, (2) you never saw the play, or (3) you don't remember the insane radio call.

And here's the kicker: Marshall was a stud. He played college football for Woody Hayes at Ohio State. He left school early to play pro football with the Saskatchewan Roughriders of the Canadian Football League. After he spent one season "oot and aboot" in Canada, the league traded him to the NFL's Cleveland Browns. A year later, the Browns allowed the expansion team in Minnesota to claim him. And that's where he stayed and played the remaining nineteen years of his professional career—at an All-Pro level, and some say at a Hall of Fame level. But I digress.

As a Viking, Marshall started in 270 consecutive games, an NFL record for nonkickers that eventually was eclipsed by Brett Favre. May I remind you that Marshall played defensive end? He lined up against the other team's biggest, strongest offensive linemen, yet in nineteen straight NFL seasons, he *never* missed a start. Like I said, the man was a *stud*.

For years, he ranked as the NFL's all-time career leader in fumble recoveries (30), but his infamous "Wrong Way Run" is one recovery he'd rather forget. It happened on October 25, 1964 (Vikings vs. 49ers). I almost died laughing the first time I watched it. The Vikings radio announcer made it worse: "And Marshall is running the *wrong way*! He's running the WRONG WAY! . . . He thinks he's scored a touchdown, but he's scored a safety!" If you've never heard it, seek it out.

A little-known Steve Sabol special titled *Big Game America* (1968) revealed the *real* Jim Marshall. The bold adventurer who damned near froze to death in the Grand Tetons during a winter expedition. Who nearly bled to death after nicking an artery. Who probably would have returned for his twentieth Vikings season if he hadn't crashed his hang glider on the Minnesota prairie. Based on Steve's *Big Game* material, I pitched a segment idea to CBS's *The NFL Today.*

My first sit-down interview with Marshall came shortly thereafter, in the early 1980s, just a few years after his retirement. We met in Rochester, Minnesota. There, I interviewed him in a hotel room before we went out on the town. As I asked him about the "Wrong Way Run," all of his near-death experiences, and his admiration for Teddy Roosevelt, I quickly realized that he was one of the most interesting human beings I'd ever met. And he liked my ambitious plans for the next day's shoot.

That night, we literally could not buy a drink anywhere in Rochester. Marshall was still a vital male in his early forties. Vikings fans and admirers crawled out of the woodwork just to see him. I drank adult beverages until my liver cried for help. When I stumbled back to my hotel, Marshall was just getting started, carrying on until the wee hours. Our call time was set for 7 A.M., sharp.

The next morning, we followed a very chipper Marshall to a wildlife refuge, where I asked him to fry eggs over an open fire while we filmed from the other side of a raging creek. Marshall dutifully did as instructed, allowing me to depict him as an intrepid man of the wild, which in many ways he was. When we finished, Marshall left me with a reading list and some dietary suggestions. I combined Marshall's unique, poetic slant on life with Steve Sabol's vintage *Big Game America* footage to depict a modern-day Zarathustra, for whom pro football was just one of his numerous talents.

CBS Sports loved it, especially the opening sequence where Marshall recited a large portion of Roosevelt's famous "It Is Not the Critic Who Counts" speech, originally delivered at the Sorbonne in Paris on April 30, 1910. A sweeping musical score over footage of Marshall skydiving in summer skies, then snowshoeing through the Grand Tetons gave the feature short exceptional, nonfootball production value. *The NFL Today* folks got much more than they paid for with that one!

So, years later, near the turn of the century, when HBO Sports asked me to revisit Marshall for *Inside the NFL* and to focus exclusively on his "Wrong Way Run," I was reluctant. And so was Jim: "Come on, Bob. . . . My life and career were about a lot more than that singular moment," Marshall told me over the phone. He was disappointed in me, but he did it anyway.

It was about that time that NFL players started comparing notes. Marshall added his name to a legal effort spearheaded by former Rams defensive end Fred Dryer to be compensated for the use of their football images. Marshall was keenly aware of these proceedings. But by now, he was also a good friend who remembered our previous associations fondly. Then came the Vikings' 2001 *Fifty Year Anniversary* film. A pair of NFL Films producers helped me put it together. I took a crew to the Mall of America in Bloomington, Minnesota, to interview Vikings players from five decades flown there by the team to participate in festivities. Several of them, including Marshall, didn't want to sign our standard release form, demanding payment for their time and contributions. I appealed to our memorable night together in Rochester. Jim smiled at me, shook his head in mock disgust, then signed away his rights for the piece, calling both me and Steve Sabol "sons of bitches" while he did.

Few players I met while working for NFL Films brought as much substance and humanity to the table. Nobody was more sincere or forthcoming. And none combined so much consummate athleticism with so many other pursuits and sensibilities. Marshall truly *was* the subject of Roosevelt's well-known oratorical gem. An NFL ironman "who spends himself in a worthy cause; who, at the best, knows, in the end, the triumph of high achievement, and who, at the worst, if he fails, at least he fails while daring greatly, so that his place shall never be with those cold and timid souls who knew neither victory nor defeat." He could quote this from memory.

By the way, the day Marshall returned a football the wrong way, he also forced a fumble that his teammate Alan Page returned for a touchdown. The Vikings won the game, 27–22. So enjoy the "Wrong Way Run" and the radio call that goes with it, but remember that only a man who "dared greatly" could have made such a bold play, and that approach netted him a lengthy, Hall of Fame–caliber career; a bushel full of great stories; and a transcendent life.

Harvey Martin *(1950–2001)* 🏆

Defensive End

- Dallas Cowboys (1973–83)

One of NFL Films's goals is to memorialize the game's great players and ensure the preservation of their achievements. Sometimes, that process has proven to be very complicated. In its obsessive determination to make 2016's Super Bowl 50 the grandest spectator and television event in the history of humankind, the NFL invited all former Super Bowl MVPs to attend the game. Bart Starr and Chuck Howley were introduced via video. Peyton Manning was shown in the Broncos' pregame locker room. And through it all, one former Super Bowl MVP remained *invisible.*

In Super Bowl XII (12), the Dallas Cowboys beat the Denver Broncos, 27–10. The Cowboys' defensive line outplayed Denver's offensive front so decisively that two Dallas pass rushers were named co-MVPs: defensive tackle Randy White and defensive end Harvey Martin. No Super Bowl before or since has recognized *more than one* Most Valuable Player.

Sure enough, as I stood in the hallway outside the Carolina Panthers' locker room at Super Bowl 50, White stopped to say hello. Suddenly, his teammate Harvey Martin came to mind. He had died of pancreatic cancer on Christmas Eve 2001, and I wondered how the league would handle this. It nearly didn't. The stadium announcer introduced Martin by name, but neither the stadium jumbotron nor the game telecast showed an image of the co-MVP of Super Bowl XII.

Nobody was more upset than Harvey Martin's sister, Dr. Mary Martin. Within weeks of Super Bowl 50, Mary began emailing and telephoning her way through the league's Park Avenue headquarters. Eventually, she pleaded her case to a female executive with strong NFL Films connections. They struck a deal: In exchange for Mary's forgiveness, the fine folks at NFL Films would produce a video on her late brother's life and career for her and the extended Martin family's personal consumption. I drew the assignment.

Martin and I had some history. Late in the 1990s, ESPN commissioned NFL Films to produce a *Where Are They Now?* series profiling retired NFL players of note. I produced all of them, and Martin ranked as one of that series' most intriguing subjects. Yes, the Hall-of-Fame-caliber pass rusher's résumé contained a few not-so-good moments: a series of restaurant failures that led to bankruptcy, some drug and alcohol abuse that resulted in jail time and eight months (on probation) in a court-ordered rehabilitation program.

"People always talk about hitting rock bottom. . . . I know where that is!" Martin once told me.

But his post-NFL life had its good times. He worked as a sportscaster for Dallas's NBC affiliate. He grappled in *WrestleMania 2.* He played the lead role of Applegate in a dinner-theater version of *Damn Yankees.* And he dabbled in TV commercial production. When I took my crew to Dallas,

Martin reenacted that work for my cameras—from storyboard sketches, blocking, and principal photography through final postproduction. My segment on Martin ranks as one of my personal all-time favorite pieces. But on its airdate, ESPN dropped it to make room for a live interview with NFL commissioner Paul Tagliabue. Once again, Martin got screwed!

"No need to apologize, Bob. Not your fault. You did everything you could to make it happen," he said via telephone the next morning. But I knew that he was disappointed, and so was I. So, when I relayed all this to Mary during our introductory phone call in the spring of 2016, she seemed amused by the irony. I assured her that I knew her brother's story and would do it justice. She pledged full cooperation on her end. Both of us eventually delivered. I documented an elite pass rusher's career, culminating with his MVP performance on football's biggest stage—a Super Bowl. I sprinkled in tidbits from his dinner-theater performance, still photos of his sportscasting and wrestling experiences, and a montage of Martin directing and starring in his Tex-Mex restaurant commercial, the only "official" Harvey Martin Production.

Mary put together a massive gathering at a suburban Dallas home involving what appeared to be Martin's entire extended family. Every person in attendance showed up wearing coats, shirts, pants, and outfits in Cowboys blue and white. They brought every piece of Martin memorabilia they owned. I interviewed Mary by herself, followed by Martin's children, siblings, and relatives. Then, I assembled all of them on a giant spiral staircase for a family photo. The stills, awards, and trophies took several additional production hours to arrange and shoot. I worked harder that day than I've worked at Super Bowls, but Mary expected no less, and her brother's life story deserved everything we did.

To this day, Mary serves as the executive director of the Harvey Martin Dream Foundation, a nonprofit organization she founded after Martin's death to "perpetuate Harvey's memory and serve as an advocate for high school students with the greatest needs." As a direct result of her efforts, numerous marginal, deserving Texas high school students have received the educational mentoring and vital financial assistance necessary to allow them to pursue college diplomas and live more fulfilling lives. I hope that my film has helped advance her cause. It certainly contains some fascinating context regarding her brother's life and career that only an older sister would know:

"Growing up, I used to beat up kids who messed with Harvey!" Mary recounted candidly in our interview. Turns out that young Harvey avoided confrontations. Mary also confirmed that their father guilted him into playing high school football: “Harvey overheard my father say, ‘My son doesn’t want to play any sports. Matter of fact, I don’t know what he wants to do.’”

Long-time Dallas general manager Tex Schramm reaped the results of their dad’s subtle coaxing. “One of the first *great* pass rushers,” Schramm called Martin. The evidence supports Schramm’s claim. During the Cowboys’ fourteen-game 1977 regular season, Martin recorded 23 sacks, “unofficially” the highest single-season sack total in league history. (The NFL didn’t recognize sacks as an official statistic until 1982.) The NFL record book lists Michael Strahan’s 22.5 sacks during the NFL’s 2001 sixteen-game schedule and T. J. Watt’s 22.5 sacks during the NFL’s 2021 seventeen-game schedule as the “official” league record, but do the math: Who deserves the record? Once again, the late Harvey Martin doesn’t get his due. But his sister and I know the *real* story.

Joe Montana (*born 1956*)

Quarterback

- San Francisco 49ers (1979-92) · Kansas City Chiefs (1993-94)

During the summer of 1995, I spent a morning working with Joe Montana one on one in a San Francisco hotel suite. Numerous encounters, including this one, had demonstrated to me that Montana was recognizable around the world for his career’s iconic moments. On this occasion, I discovered that his memories of grade school were just as sharp. As two former western Pennsylvania quarterbacks—with totally different levels of accomplishment, of course—we compared notes on our offenses, playbooks, and best memories. His eyes lit up as he relived a game against Monessen High School, which had cemented his eventual scholarship offer from Notre Dame. Amazing how ingrained those high school “Glory Days” still are, regardless of age.

NFL game programs listed Montana as six feet two inches tall and 210 pounds. Both numbers seemed inflated. Most of his peers possessed stronger throwing arms, but his poise under pressure and ability to rally teams to victory, traits he exhibited at Notre Dame, manifested themselves in spectacular fashion in the NFL. His franchise-making moment, the one everybody remembers, occurred on January 10, 1982, during the 1981 NFC Championship Game against the Dallas Cowboys. Trailing by 6 points late in the game with a Super Bowl berth on the line, Montana rolled away from pressure, then tossed up a pass to wide receiver Dwight Clark, who leapt high over Dallas cornerback Everson Walls to make "The Catch." My friend and colleague Bob Smith captured the moment for posterity. In that instant, an NFL dynasty was born. By decade's end, Montana's team had won four Super Bowls.

In Super Bowl XXIII (23), Montana enjoyed his finest championship moment, another common memory for his fans. Trailing Cincinnati 16–13 with 3:18 left in the fourth quarter, Montana stood calmly in the 49ers' offensive huddle and made a celebrity sighting. Turning to rookie offensive tackle Harris Barton, Montana said, "Hey, look, there's John Candy." Barton looked where Montana was staring, then turned back toward his quarterback in disbelief: "We're trying to win a Super Bowl, are you nuts?" Montana just smiled. He was loose. Eleven plays later, Montana hit John Taylor for the game winner with 34 ticks left on the clock, yet for whatever reasons, Jerry Rice won MVP honors.

The following year, Montana threw 5 touchdown passes in San Francisco's 55–10 win in Super Bowl XXIV (24)—earning his third MVP nod. Near game's end, I watched 49ers running back Roger Craig hatch his "three-peat" notion. No team had ever won three Lombardi Trophies in succession, but on January 20, 1991, Montana's 61-yard TD pass to Taylor gave the 49ers a 13–6 fourth-quarter lead over the New York Giants in the NFC title game. A "three-peat" looked likely. Then came the most vivid history-changing moment I've ever witnessed or shot.

With 9:42 left in the game, Montana abandoned the pocket and rolled right. When he set his feet to throw, Giants defensive end Leonard Marshall leveled him. I've never captured a more brutal hit. My sound-speed shot became the NFL Films's official visual record of the event. Montana missed nearly two full seasons recovering from the impact and subsequent related injuries. When Steve Young took over and excelled as San Francisco's quarterback, Montana requested a trade.

Surprisingly, not until he moved to Kansas City had I ever worked close enough to Montana to hear him on the sidelines. In 1993, I shot several Chiefs games, during which Montana, head coach Marty Schottenheimer, and Kansas City coaches gathered in front of me to discuss crucial play calls. During these conversations, Montana's voice was always the most respected. Not surprisingly, in his first Kansas City season, he took the Chiefs to the AFC Championship Game.

The following preseason, at a 1994 American Bowl event in Tokyo, Japan, the NFL convinced Montana to do an autograph appearance at a Tokyo department store. My assistant, the late Mike Villanova, and I represented NFL Films. As you might expect, Montana traveled with a personal bodyguard. Following the appearance portion of the event, Montana, the bodyguard, Villanova, and I piled into a waiting elevator. Just before the door closed, an eager Japanese male teenager squeezed in to join us. He stood there gawking wide-eyed at the American football legend, but Montana's protector had a plan. While Montana humored the adoring young man, his bodyguard hit a floor button during our descent. When the doors opened unexpectedly, the bodyguard shoved the teenager out of the elevator with maximum force. I should have kept my camera running.

In April 1995, Montana announced his retirement from pro football. When I learned that NBC had hired him to work as an analyst on the network's Sunday pregame show, I told a colleague, "They must have offered him a king's ransom." By 1995, nobody really could argue against the idea that Montana had succeeded Johnny Unitas as the G.O.A.T. (Greatest Of All Time) quarterback. But as a studio analyst? His former teammate Matt Millen once told NFL Films, "Montana has the personality of a stone." So, NBC turned to NFL Films for help, and that's how and why I met Joe in a San Francisco hotel suite in 1995.

I was asked to produce a segment on Montana's famous Super Bowl XXIII (23) game-winning drive. NBC arranged for me to interview him, his head coach Bill Walsh, and anybody else I thought mattered. I shot him on a green screen for use in the definitive account of his most historic game-winning possession. On the appointed day at the appointed hour, he knocked on the door. As I ushered him in, I noticed a bellhop standing down the hall behind a shrub, staring at both of us.

Joe Montana and I bonded. I walked him through every play call and outcome. He recounted the drive in amazing detail. By the time we finished, a handful of well-wishers stood silently in the hallway, awaiting Montana's departure, and a veritable throng of folks stood outside in the parking lot. "They're not here to see me," I said, as I shut the door behind him. They most certainly weren't there to reminisce about Pittsburgh high school football, either.

I knew that bellhop looked suspicious!

Ray Nitschke *(1936–98)*

Middle Linebacker

- Green Bay Packers (1958–72)

In 1967, when I was fourteen years old, I sent off for a poster of Green Bay Packers middle linebacker Ray Nitschke, which I then taped to the ceiling above my bed. Two years later, the aging Packers dynasty came to my hometown. On Sunday, I bought a ticket and watched Green Bay beat the Steelers, 28–14. Afterward, I stood outside Pitt Stadium for nearly an hour to see my idol in person. I held Nitschke's Coke can while he autographed my beloved poster. Four decades in the company of NFL players and coaches have cured me of hero worship. I've met and worked with dozens of all-time greats—but I still wish my mother hadn't thrown away my poster when I went to college.

Why Nitschke? Because he was *bad-ass*! His Packers teammate and Hall of Fame offensive tackle Forrest Gregg once told me, "When we lined up against our offense in live team drills and Ray got those big forearms in your face, you knew it was time to scrimmage, mister!" In a preseason prime-time telecast, Nitschke tackled Dallas tight end Pettis Norman so viciously that the 220-pound receiver staggered back to the Cowboys' huddle, *quite literally* looking out through his helmet's ear-hole. Yet when CBS analyst Tom Brookshier called Nitschke "an animal" during a 1960s CBS postgame interview, he became visibly upset.

Nitschke's childhood was less than ideal. Orphaned prior to his high school graduation in a Chicago suburb, Nitschke barreled toward adulthood full of anger. He fought anybody who crossed him and struggled academically. Football saved his life. He played double duty as a quarterback and safety in high school. He dreamed of leading a Big Ten team to the Rose Bowl. But at the University of Illinois, when injuries depleted the team's starting offensive backfield, head coach Ray Eliot converted the quarterback/safety to fullback/linebacker. By the end of Nitschke's senior season, he ranked among the best collegiate linebackers in America. The lowly Green Bay Packers selected him in the third round of the 1958 NFL Draft.

Flash forward to Green Bay in the early 1980s: I traveled there with CBS analyst Irv Cross to produce a "Legends of the Game" segment for *The NFL Today*. My concept called for Cross to do a stand-up at a local print shop while a Packers newsletter rolled off the press behind him. I asked him to allude to the "mild-mannered sportswriter" who contributed to this edition.

At Nitschke's residence, I sat Ray down in front of an old Remington typewriter and filmed him pecking away at the keys with his two monstrous index fingers. After several rehearsals, Nitschke (as Clark Kent) ripped out the page, removed his horn-rimmed glasses, then stared deadpan into the camera. When I proudly announced, "That's a wrap," Nitschke settled into his true self. With little warning, he put Irv Cross in a headlock from which he could not escape—and trust me, he was trying. This went on for some time. At one point, Irv looked toward me and the crew for help. I wasn't sure what to do, but I certainly wasn't packing kryptonite.

Was I concerned? Hell, yes! Floorboards were shaking. And my poster-boy hero was enjoying himself immensely. In postproduction, I added John Williams's famous Oscar-nominated film score to my money-shot sequence to reveal Green Bay's "Superman!" The montage of hard-hitting Nitschke plays that followed was worthy of both the DC Comics hero and one of pro football's all-time great defenders. The Monday morning after it aired, *The NFL Today*'s producer called me to celebrate my "vision and great use of contemporary music." Sorry, Irv, but it was all worth it.

Nitschke treated NFL ball carriers much worse than he did Irv Cross. In fifteen seasons as Green Bay's defensive leader, he collected five NFL

Championship and two Super Bowl rings. When *Sporting News* magazine listed its all-time one hundred greatest NFL players, Nitschke—a linebacker—came in at #18. In 1978, he was enshrined in the Pro Football Hall of Fame. Once he became a member, he began making a speech at the hall's annual Saturday luncheon that preceded each season's induction ceremonies, a members-only event for guys with gold jackets. Nitschke's impassioned message to new members welcoming them to "the greatest team of them all" brought tears to many eyes.

In September 1997, on a flight from Somewhere, USA, into Green Bay, Nitschke showed up next to me in the first-class cabin. We reminisced about his Superman portrayal. I asked about his three adopted children, now fully grown. I bragged about my son, Daniel, an excellent eight-year-old baseball player growing up in his mother's home. Suddenly, Nitschke grew concerned about my absence in Dan's day-to-day life. I assured him that I coached all Danny's baseball teams, that I took custody visits seriously, and that I would never be an absentee father.

Nitschke, an orphan with his own adopted children, wasn't satisfied. While I took a nap, he dug out a piece of tablet paper and wrote the following:

> To Danny Angelo,
>
> "A Real Star," Good luck always. Study hard. Play hard. And never, NEVER give up. Love you, God bless.
>
> Dad's friend from Green Bay,
>
> Ray Nitschke

What struck me the most was Nitschke's beautiful penmanship. Compared to my scribble, his strokes looked like calligraphy. Not bad for an angry young man raised by older brothers. For a street corner and schoolyard pugilist who lost his sophomore year of athletic eligibility due to poor behavior and worse grades. For a guy who aspired to quarterback a Rose Bowl win but wound up manhandling NFL ball carriers (and Irv Cross) for fifteen seasons. Danny's mother framed it, then hung it in Dan's bedroom—just like the poster I used to have. "Like father, like son."

I didn't know it then, but I would never see my high-school hero again. The following spring, Ray died of a heart attack in Venice, Florida. He was just sixty-one years old. The annual luncheon welcoming new members to the Hall of Fame now bears Nitschke's name, as well it should.

Chuck Noll *(1932–2014)*

Guard and Linebacker

- Cleveland Browns (1953-59)

Assistant Coach

- Los Angeles/San Diego Chargers (1960-65) - Baltimore Colts (1966-68)

Head Coach

- Pittsburgh Steelers (1969-91)

I watched him emerge from the dormitory and approach from a distance. Immediately, a kaleidoscope of butterflies fluttered about in my stomach. I waved to make certain that he saw where I was waiting.

I'd witnessed how difficult he could be to interview. Chuck Noll was famously reserved, and I had reason to be intimidated. I'd turned my camera his way numerous times with few positive results. But on this August 1979 day at the Pittsburgh Steelers' training camp (at St. Vincent's College, in Latrobe, Pennsylvania), I would have to address him face to face with no buffer between us. As I stood to shake his hand, mine was sweating.

So began my first personal encounter with the head coach and architect of the 1970s Pittsburgh Steeler dynasty. Noll sat down on the bench across from me and waited for me to begin. Now, I was pouring sweat. Some people's reserve comes from defensiveness, and others' comes from knowing where they stand and having nothing to prove. Noll's was the latter. I ran through my list of questions regarding the Steelers' chances of winning an unprecedented fourth Super Bowl in six seasons. He answered thoughtfully, carefully, and politely. He was not going to give Houston Oilers head coach Bum Phillips, a potential Super Bowl rival, any bulletin-board material. During our first film change, I mentioned Sarge Wilkins, a 1937 graduate of Neville, my Pittsburgh-area high school, who had played with Cleveland Browns great Marion Motley at the legendary Great Lakes Naval Training Center during World War II.

"How old are you?" Noll asked me. "Twenty-six," I replied. Noll smiled broadly. When we finished the interview, Noll reminisced about his own twenties, playing pro football for the Browns alongside Motley, Otto Graham, and one of the greatest football teams of all time prior to his Steelers. That year, they won their fourth Lombardi Trophy in six years, a record that may someday be equaled but will *never* be broken. Since that time, I've met and worked with most of Noll's starters. At last count, ten of them were members of the Pro Football Hall of Fame, and several more should be. They all love to share stories about their soft-spoken mentor. Some of them sound the same no matter who tells them. One in particular fascinated me.

On the morning of December 23, 1974, Noll arrived for work angry. The day before, Noll's Steelers had dispatched the Buffalo Bills in the divisional round of the AFC Playoffs, 32–14. The day before that, the Oakland Raiders had rallied to defeat the two-time defending Super Bowl champion Miami Dolphins, 28–26. Here is how Noll's players remember the Steelers' team meeting on that fateful Monday morning:

ANDY RUSSELL (linebacker): Chuck came into the room . . . and he ordinarily would be calm, cool, and unemotional . . . but something was bothering him. . . . You could tell he was *hot*!

MEL BLOUNT (Hall of Fame cornerback): He said . . . , "Those Raiders think they won the Super Bowl."

JOE GREENE (Hall of Fame defensive tackle): And he said, "Fellas, I've got news for you. The Super Bowl is two weeks away, and the best damned team in pro football is sitting right here in this room!"

JON KOLB (offensive tackle): This man believes this. . . . He really believes we are the best team.

FRANCO HARRIS (Hall of Fame fullback): Yeah, you know what? We *are* the greatest team in football.

These are actual quotations I collected while interviewing Noll's players about this meeting over many months. Strung together, they provided the narrative for an "NFL Storybook" segment I produced for an episode of HBO's *Inside the NFL* that aired during the 2000 season. And it gets better:

DWIGHT WHITE (defensive end): Chuck was always a tight-lipped person . . . , but this time, he got on the wagon with us—and that's all we needed.

GREENE: To go into the biggest game of your life knowing you're going to win, knowing they [the Raiders] didn't have a chance . . . how can you match that?

RUSSELL: That game . . . was the best game the Pittsburgh Steelers ever played!

JOHN STALLWORTH (Hall of Fame wide receiver): And Chuck's statement was the key to the changing of the mindset . . . that the forty-five players in this room *were* the best damn team in football!

HARRIS: This guy [Chuck] knew it . . . then, he let us know it. And the rest is history!

In the three years I produced "NFL Storybooks" for HBO, no segment garnered more praise than this one. Few segments made a stronger impression, because TV audiences are far more inclined to believe people who actually lived through events as opposed to a narrator's script. Noll's players had come together for him before, and they came together for him again to tell the story better than any voiceover ever could have.

One day much later that season, my office phone rang: "This is Joe Greene from the Arizona Cardinals. . . ." (Greene was now an assistant coach.) "Is this Bob Angelo?"

"Mean Joe" thanked me for sending him a VHS of the segment, calling it "one of the best things [he'd] ever seen."

Curt Gowdy, who narrated the segment and had questioned my sparse script, called to remark, "Now I understand why you had so little for me to say. . . . Those Steelers said it all."

As Noll himself said on camera regarding his famous team meeting, "There was a little bit of excitement . . . one of those 'Amen, brother' moments. . . . They felt they were a team of destiny."

At Super Bowl XL (40), Bill Cowher's Pittsburgh Steelers beat the Seattle Seahawks, 21–10. During pregame, I wandered into a corridor that contained a private escalator moving VIPs up toward their reserved seats. While I was setting up a shot, I noticed Noll riding the stairs toward his destination. Several years earlier, I'd sent him several copies of the segment.

He nodded his head in quiet acknowledgment and waved. No words were necessary. No sweat!

Terrell Owens *(born 1973)*

Wide Receiver

- San Francisco 49ers (1996-2003) · Philadelphia Eagles (2004-05)
- Dallas Cowboys (2006-08) · Buffalo Bills (2009) · Cincinnati Bengals (2010)
- Seattle Seahawks (2012)

Terrell Owens generated a lot of hate for someone who did his job as well as any wide receiver of his era, someone whose teams were always better *with* him than without him. He sought attention, it's true, but he also paid for it.

In the early 2000s, ABC Sports commissioned NFL Films to produce a weekly series called *Seven Days to Monday.* Each weekly episode ran three to four minutes at halftime during *Monday Night Football.* Episodes focused on an individual player's or coach's preparation for that week's game. Participants agreed to at least one extended interview, a practice wiring, and several off-field events as conditions for our commitment. With these terms in place, I signed on to spend an entire work week with Owens (aka T. O.) in San Francisco. ESPN's Suzy Kolber was also competing for his time, as were national and beat writers covering the 49ers. Good luck to me, right?

Guess what? Owens couldn't have been more professional. If I scheduled an interview for 4:30, he showed up ready to go at 4:25. He wore a wireless microphone at practice without incident. He invited us into his home. He allowed us to shoot his private workout with his very own personal trainer (more on this later), who flew in from Atlanta for the occasion. In short, Owens proved to be the perfect subject. His only request was that we pronounce his first name correctly.

I'm not disputing T. O.'s reputation as a troublemaker. In a 2000 game in Dallas, Owens scored a touchdown, then sprinted to midfield to dance and celebrate on the Dallas Cowboys' star—*twice*! The second time resulted in a brawl. San Francisco head coach Steve Mariucci suspended him for a week. Owens interpreted that punishment as an act of betrayal. I'm not sure whether he ever forgave Mariucci.

Later that same season, in Jerry Rice's final Candlestick Park appearance as a 49er, Owens had the audacity to catch an NFL single-game record *20* passes in a 17–0 San Francisco win. Incredibly, sportswriters and 49er loyalists took issue. How dare the young upstart upstage Rice, NFL royalty?! Perhaps Owens should have dropped Jeff Garcia's passes intentionally in deference?

Then there were Owens's much-ballyhooed touchdown celebrations. The Sharpie tucked in his sock used to autograph the football he carried across the goal line, then handed to his own financial advisor, standing nearby in the front row. Grabbing a 49ers cheerleader's pom-poms, then helping her lead the 49ers faithful in raucous applause. Hey, the guy made people laugh during the NFL's dreaded "No Fun League" period, but by 2003, the 49ers sucked, and the Bay Area was sick of Owens.

So, he joined Andy Reid's Philadelphia Eagles and, not surprisingly, contributed mightily to their 2004 NFC Championship run. I shot one of the games the Birds lost that year, a November road game against Pittsburgh. I witnessed a sideline disagreement between Owens and Eagles quarterback Donovan McNabb. It started with the two men standing together. As Owens vented his frustrations, McNabb started moving away until he had totally distanced himself from the rant. I used my zoom to keep McNabb on one side of the frame and Owens on the other. Owens kept making his points over the deafening Pittsburgh crowd, until the quarterback and the pass catcher were no longer within earshot. As Rod Stewart observed, "Every Picture Tells a Story."

A month and a half later, on December 19, 2004, Cowboys safety Roy Williams pulled Owens down by his horse collar, spraining Owens's ankle and breaking his fibula, prompting an NFL rule change. Eagles trainers gave Owens little chance of rehabbing in time for the postseason.

But when Super Bowl XXXIX (39) arrived and the Eagles squared off against the New England Patriots for the Lombardi Trophy, Owens was there, catching 9 passes for 122 yards, rolling up big YAC (Yards After the Catch) while steamrolling wide-eyed Patriots defenders in the process.

A medical miracle, you ask? The heart of a champion is more like it. Owens single-handedly kept Philly's offense competitive that day. As I watched, I hearkened back to my week with him in San Francisco. I remembered how his personal trainer had steered him through one of the most physically demanding workouts I'd ever seen. I had shot every rep on every device, just waiting for Owens to puke his insides out. The NFL editors who clipped and cut it had called it some of the most intense weight-room footage they'd ever seen. Yes, the troublemaker had a work ethic. So, when Owens showed up against New England, I was not surprised. After the Eagles lost, I followed the team up the tunnel toward their locker room. Owens leaned against a corridor wall, shaking hands and offering condolences to his teammates.

Which would explain why the Dallas Cowboys forgave Owens his previous trespasses and signed him to a three-year, $25 million deal just four days after his Eagles release, on March 18, 2006. T. O. spent three seasons in Dallas, catching more passes, scoring more touchdowns, and adding new wrinkles to his celebratory repertoire—this time, depositing the ball into the supersize Salvation Army bucket on Thanksgiving Day in Texas Stadium. In 2007, Owens was leading the league in pass-receiving yards when he suffered a high ankle sprain. As I predicted, Owens returned for the postseason, catching a TD pass in Dallas's 21–17 playoff game loss to New York. Then, in the postgame press conference, he broke down in tears.

Lots of people offered manifold opinions on that moment. Here's mine: After years of incredible individual production, Owens once again overcame personal injury to return *to help his team win.* With Tony Romo at the helm, the Cowboys finished 13–3 and earned a first-round playoff bye. Then, they fell apart against the Giants, a team they'd beaten twice during the regular season.

Was he "locker-room poison," as many insisted? Six different NFL teams (and an Arena League franchise) paid him to catch passes. Bill Parcells (who signed him to the Cowboys in 2006) made a career out of signing "winners." Owens presently ranks second all time in career touchdown catches and receiving yards. The McNabb-era Eagles did not advance to a Super Bowl until Owens arrived. In 2005, Owens asked for a new contract. The Eagles suspended him, then won just six of sixteen games.

Nope, Owens's last chance at a Super Bowl ring slipped away that sad day against the Giants. He wept because he wanted more than Hall of Fame recognition—for himself as well as for the teams that embraced his skill set, his fiery spirit, and his superlative inner strength. The NFL needs more players with T. O.'s attributes.

Duane Charles "Bill" Parcells *(born 1941)*

Head Coach

- New York Giants (1983-90) · New England Patriots (1993-96)
- New York Jets (1997-99) · Dallas Cowboys (2003-06)

No NFL head coach I've ever known worked harder to cultivate a "tough-guy" image than Bill Parcells—a genuine enigma. Network close-ups routinely captured him venting at his players, quarterback Phil Simms in particular. Yet he'd wear wireless microphones during regular-season games for NFL Films long before the league made such cooperation semi-mandatory. He would challenge and confront our cameramen angrily on the sidelines or in his own locker room, but he'd also swap stories for hours with Steve Sabol.

An excerpt from his book *Parcells: A Football Life* recounts an incident with his high school basketball coach and mentor, Mickey Corcoran. After a difficult defeat, the fifteen-year-old Parcells said, "Coach, there are no moral victories. Winning is all that counts." Once, when Giants beat writers questioned him at a news conference, he responded, "You see? That's why sometimes I call you guys 'Commies.' There it is right there—subversive from within."

Projecting strength is essential when dealing with Lawrence Taylor or Phil Simms. But it fueled Parcells's dark side when it came to "Commies."

In the late 1990s, the NFL Owners Broadcast Committee officially guaranteed NFL Films the right to use "boom microphones, specifically in team bench areas." Before that, Parcells had relished intimidating soundmen who would lower their boom poles into position to capture "media assets." He was even tougher on their cameramen.

Yet we still were tasked with capturing Parcells getting doused with Gatorade after Giants Super Bowl victories, which happened twice during his tenure: Super Bowl XXI (21), a 39–20 win over Denver, the Giants' first NFL title since 1956; then again in Super Bowl XXV (25), a 20–19 win over Buffalo that would have gone the other way had the Bills' Scott Norwood not pushed his game-winning, 47-yard field-goal attempt "wide right." I truly harbored no ill will toward Parcells, but when he retired after that Super Bowl, I hoped I'd never see him again. Alas, in 1993, New England Patriots owner Robert Kraft hired Parcells to coach the Patriots. By 1996, the Patriots made the AFC Championship Game. And Steve Sabol had an assignment for me: "Ange, we're doing Super Bowl pregame segments for Fox Sports called 'Super Bowl Diaries,' and I want you to do the AFC side." This meant that if the Patriots beat Jacksonville in the AFC title game on January 12, 1997, I would remain on location first in New England and then in New Orleans (site of Super Bowl XXXI [31]) for two weeks in close company with Parcells. By now, Parcells's former quarterback and sometimes whipping boy Simms was working in television and would show up regularly at NFL Films. Just hours after Steve had apprised me of my impending *Mission: Impossible*, Simms knocked on my office door. "Steve sent me down here to talk to you about Bill Parcells," he said. "I'm all ears, quarterback," I replied, full of self-pity.

For the next fifteen minutes, Simms offered me some of the best free advice I've ever received. To paraphrase: "Don't let Bill bully you. Do not show weakness. Because if you let him push you around, he will." Steve later told me that he'd spoken with Parcells about my crew's possible presence in Foxboro. Parcells had promised "cooperation—to a certain point." Between Parcells's words and Simms's admonition lay some uncharted and potentially fatal production terrain.

That Sunday, I rooted for Jacksonville; New England won, 20–6. After the game, my four crew companions and I drove to the Providence, Rhode Island, Marriott, where we would live or die for the next week. I barely slept that night. On Monday morning, January 13, 1997, we set out for old Foxboro Stadium, an aging relic better suited for monster-truck rallies than network TV production work. Patriots media relations folks ushered us to an empty locker room deep in the bowels of the building. And there we waited—patiently, all day long, with no human contact!

Finally, as the clock approached 5 P.M., Parcells strolled in to find us. He seemed surprised: "You guys been down here all day?" he asked. "That's what you told your folks to do with us, Coach, you flaming asshole!" I thought to myself. Then, I played my passive-aggressive card: "Your PR people said you'd get to us by the end of the day." I could see that he was moved by our quiet obedience. He laid out his plan, which included access to several players as well as some team practices and meeting events. We left that day quietly optimistic about the rest of the week.

Then came Wednesday morning's team meeting. Afterward, one of my player subjects told me that Parcells had banned involvement with all media in New Orleans—which meant that my "Super Bowl Diaries" show would be out of business by the weekend. So, I called Parcells on it. His face turned red as he stepped into my personal space: "What are you trying to do here, take over my football team?" I never broke eye contact: "This is *not* what you promised Steve Sabol." He glowered at me in silence for an eternity. Heeding Simms's warning, I refused to back down or even look away from Parcells's intimidating stare. Finally: "Wait right here!"

When he returned, my two player subjects walked dutifully behind him. "What I said in this morning's meeting about not working with the media in New Orleans . . . it doesn't apply to these guys, OK?" I showed no emotion and said nothing. Parcells smirked and stormed off.

The following mid-week, outside the New Orleans Superdome, Parcells passed me on his way to his team bus. He circled back and asked, "You getting everything you need down here, Bob?"

In his 2013 Hall of Fame acceptance speech, Parcells described the sanctity of the locker room this way: "If you're willing to help, come on in. If you're not, then get the heck out of here." In the world according to Parcells, I suppose a "Commie" would have turned tail and run. Thanks again for the advice, Phil Simms.

Following his team's 35–31 loss to Green Bay in Super Bowl XXXI (31), Parcells retired again, but not before offering the media this quotable tidbit on coaching: "They want you to cook the dinner, at least they ought to let you shop for some of the groceries, OK?"

His power trips did not keep him from enshrinement in the Pro Football Hall of Fame. After all, in the Gospel according to fifteen-year-old Parcells, "Winning is all that counts." He did that often enough.

Sean Payton *(born 1963)* 🏆

Assistant Coach and Coordinating Positions

- Philadelphia Eagles (1997-98) · New York Giants (1999-2002)
- Dallas Cowboys (2003-05)

Head Coach

- New Orleans Saints (2006-21) · Denver Broncos (2023-Present)

Webster's Dictionary defines *karma* as "the effect of any act, religious or otherwise; the law of cause and effect; inevitable retribution."

I mention this in advance of sharing my personal stories involving Sean Payton, the long-time, Super Bowl–winning head coach of the New Orleans Saints from 2006 through 2021. I'll say this as well: He is my least favorite person, alive or dead, in the National Football League. I can't think of a close second.

Without a doubt, Payton ranks as one of the finest offensive minds in NFL history. A former high school, college, and pro passer, Payton worked his way through various college coaching jobs before joining the Philadelphia Eagles staff (1997–98), then that of the New York Giants (1999). He coordinated the Giants' offense from 2000–02 but lost his play-calling responsibilities to head coach Jim Fassel late in the season. The Giants went on to win the NFC Championship and play in Super Bowl XXXV (35). Despite the personal setback, Payton landed a job with Bill Parcells as the Cowboys assistant head coach and quarterback coach from 2003–05.

In 2006, the New Orleans Saints named Payton their head coach. Soon thereafter, Payton signed free-agent passer Drew Brees. I asked Payton why he had acquired the former San Diego Charger, and he explained (paraphrasing), "He's been a winner at every level." Under Payton's tutelage, Brees climbed to the top of the NFL record book for quarterbacks in nearly every major statistical category. The Saints became annual and legitimate Super Bowl contenders.

But working on the Saints' sideline offered me a different perspective on Payton. During pregame activities, Saints public relations directors often sought out NFL Films sound cameramen (like myself) to remind us of Payton's game-day transformation—this despite a 1997 NFL Broadcast Committee resolution specifically giving NFL Films crews the right "to use boom microphones in bench areas."

Payton saved his very best for a New Orleans home game. As I focused on Payton and others getting ready to respond to a Saints touchdown, a New Orleans policeman grabbed me by the arm and escorted me away from my position. I went off on the cop. I screamed that I was doing my job, that I was allowed to do my job, and that he should "keep [his] hands off me!" In hindsight, it was probably not my best-ever sideline decision, but I was beyond pissed off. Incredibly, the city cop backed off, turned toward the Saints assistant public relations director standing nearby, then lifted his palms toward the sky, as if to say, "I gave it my best shot." I saw *red*.

The NFL's head of security Milt Ahlerich was in the Superdome that day. I mentioned to him during pregame that Payton often tried to intimidate sound cameramen (like myself), especially at home games. So, I sought him out and told him what had just happened. I pointed out the cop, the PR person, and, of course, the head coach.

Turns out that Payton and the New Orleans Saints *were* hiding something. On March 21, 2012, NFL commissioner Roger Goodell suspended Payton for the entire 2012 NFL season. After a league investigation, the NFL concluded that the Saints were operating a "bounty program." In short, the Saints were pooling money, then rewarding players for "knocking out" opponents. Some of the terminology I heard later included *cart-offs*, with different payouts for different degrees of injury caused. I truly hope that one of my sound bites helped seal Payton's fate.

Sadly, the NFL reinstated both Payton and his defensive coordinator, Gregg Williams, the alleged ringleader of the whole thing. Even worse, Williams played a prominent role in a future *Hard Knocks* season, while Payton (and Brees) continued to make history as well as alter it.

For example, a Saints pass rusher sprained Brett Favre's ankle in the Superdome during the 2009 NFC Championship. An accident? Not likely. The result: Favre moaning in agony on the Vikings' sideline while trainers worked furiously on his injury. Lesser men would have been *carted off* to the locker room to return on crutches, but Favre soldiered on, setting the Vikings up with a chance to win with two minutes left in the game. Unfortunately, Favre rolled right on a gimpy leg, then threw across his body for an interception. Payton's Saints won the overtime coin toss, beat the Vikes, 31–28, then went on to capture the Lombardi Trophy.

But, just maybe, "the effect of some acts" lingers in the cosmos. In a 2017 playoff rematch between the Vikings and Saints, a last-second Hail Mary pass and a botched open-field tackle allowed Stefon Diggs to hustle down a vacated sideline, resulting in an improbable 29–24 Vikings victory—the only such last-play-in-regulation walk-off playoff game win *ever.*

In 2018, perhaps the worst non–pass interference call in the history of mankind prevented the Saints from icing a win against the Los Angeles Rams. In overtime, Greg Zuerlein kicked a 57-yard field goal, and Payton once again was denied a Super Bowl appearance.

In the 2019 NFC Wild Card game, an overtime bomb from Kirk Cousins to Adam Thielen set up a fade route touchdown pass to Kyle Rudolph—and Payton's Saints missed out on another Super Bowl appearance. In the 2020 postseason, Brees suffered an injury against Tom Brady and Tampa Bay. The Bucs went on to defeat the Chiefs, 31–9, in Super Bowl LV (55). In Payton's final New Orleans season in 2021, the team missed the playoffs—and Payton called it quits.

As you'll recall, one of *Webster*'s *karma* definitions is "inevitable retribution," another way of saying, "What goes around, comes around." Couldn't happen to a nicer guy.

Adrian Peterson (*born 1985*) (🛡 inevitable)

Running Back

- Minnesota Vikings (2007-16) · New Orleans Saints and Arizona Cardinals (2017)
- Washington Commanders (2018-19) · Detroit Lions (2020)
- Tennessee Titans and Seattle Seahawks (2021)

The first time we met, Adrian Peterson got me good! The year was 2007. I was working in the Vikings' locker room after a Minnesota home victory. When head coach Brad Childress had finished addressing the team, Vikings media relations executive Bob Hagan asked me whether I'd ever met Peterson. Nope. So he walked me over, introduced us, then stepped back to watch. I lowered my camera and extended my right hand to the NFL rookie running-back sensation.

Peterson nearly crushed it. And all the while, he smiled as if he wasn't even trying. My fingers and knuckles hurt for weeks. Later, I learned he'd done the same to an NFL Films colleague, a bigger stronger guy who had nearly dropped to his knees while making Peterson's acquaintance.

So, I wasn't surprised that he tore through NFL defenses for 1,341 rushing yards and easily won the Associated Press Rookie of the Year Award. Obviously, it wasn't just his handshake that was formidable. In his second season, in 2008, Peterson led the NFL in rushing, the first of three times he would do so. The Vikings won the NFC North title and advanced to the playoffs for the first time since 2000. And once again, in another postgame locker-room victory celebration, I absentmindedly slid my fingers into Peterson's vice grip without preparing myself. Same result!

I often described Peterson to friends and colleagues this way: "He's made of different materials than the rest of us." In 2011, when a pair of torn ligaments prevented him from rushing for 1,000 yards for a fifth straight time, he began his rehab. Just eight months later, he validated my "different materials" claim, starting on opening day in 2012 for the Vikings.

By Week 16, he'd rushed for 1,898 yards. On the season's final weekend, Minnesota hosted the division-leading Green Bay Packers in a game they had to win to qualify for the playoffs. I was shooting sound. In the third quarter, on a second down and 27, Peterson picked up 28 and then later capped the drive with a touchdown reception. Late in the fourth quarter, with 2:54 remaining, the game tied at 34, and the capacity crowd chanting "M-V-P," the Vikes took over at their own 28-yard line. When they crossed midfield, the entire Vikings' defense gathered around me near the end of the bench area to watch the offense operate. The scoreboard I framed over their shoulders tracked Peterson's progress toward Eric Dickerson's 1984 NFL single-season rushing record of 2,105 yards. At first, 2,060. Then, 2,064. Then, a timeout, with 24 seconds remaining in regulation.

The Vikings had advanced to the Packers' 37. During a timeout, I did the math. If Peterson could break one for a TD, not only would the Vikings make the playoffs; but Peterson would set a new single-season rushing record on the same play, an NFL "Mega-Moment." He damned near did it! On second down and 10, Peterson hit the hole, broke it outside to the left, then began running through Packers defensive backs on his way toward the end zone. A shoestring tackle by Green Bay safety Morgan Burnett tripped him up close to the 10-yard line. Sonofa—!

A field goal would secure the victory. A turnover was not an option. Head coach Leslie Frazier did the right thing: He sent out placekicker Blair Walsh to kick the game winner. And Peterson ended the season with

2,097 official rushing yards, 8 yards shy of Dickerson's all-time single-season record. He never once complained. In fact, I whined about it more than anybody else. But this time, when I offered him my congratulations in the postgame locker room, I shoved my right hand so far into his that even Superman couldn't have caused me any discomfort.

Peterson played four more seasons in Minnesota. His 2014 season ended abruptly due to indictment on child-abuse charges over his choice to discipline his son with a "switch" (standing vinelike plant with the leaves removed). Peterson calmly explained that was how his father had disciplined him, but his explanation did not move the powers that were, and the NFL barred Peterson from all team activities. Prior to his planned return in Week 11, the league suspended him for the remainder of the 2011 season. But when people predicted his demise, I said, "No way he goes out like that!"

The following season, Peterson rushed for 1,485 yards and won his third NFL rushing title, once again lifting the Vikings into the postseason. It marked his final hurrah in Minnesota.

In 2016, torn knee ligaments again ended his season early, this time in Week 3. In 2017, he spent a month with the Saints and two with the Cardinals. I ran into him late that year in Arizona after a Cardinals win. When he spotted me across the locker room, he smiled broadly. I made my way to his side and offered my hand. Although he probably didn't even know my name, he recognized me as somebody who'd been around him for his entire career. He shook my hand the way he always did—like Superman. When we parted company, I knew that it would be the final time I would see him in person—I was retiring in February 2018, and I fully expected Peterson to join me on the sidelines of working life. What more did the man need to prove?

So, imagine my delight the following year, when he started showing up weekly on the NFL RedZone channel as a member of Washington, where he posted yet another 1,000-yard rushing season. Like I said, "Different materials!"

So, what will be Peterson's legacy?

For starters, he's the fourth leading rusher of all time, with no active player even close. Had he not lost nearly two complete seasons to injuries and a suspension, he might easily rank second, trailing only Emmitt Smith. His body of work shows shiftiness, flat-out speed, and pure power. In 2012 alone, he recorded more than 1,000 of his 2,097 total rushing yards *after* initial contact by defenders. Think about that for just a moment! Only the most narrow-minded electors will vote against his inevitable enshrinement in the Pro Football Hall of Fame.

Finally, there's that legendary handshake. I never asked him who advised him to do that or why he made it standard operating procedure. I'm just glad I finally started looking out for it.

Q-Ratings (NFL Broadcasters and Media Personalities)

John Facenda *(1913–84)*

- WCAU-TV (CBS) Evening News Anchor (1948-73)
- NFL Films Narrator (1964-83)

If you watched NFL Films programming in the sixties, you remember John Facenda, aka "The Voice of God." His rich, pleasing baritone contained the slightest hint of a "stage British" accent, ironic for a Philadelphia-born gentleman of Italian descent. NBC's Bob Costas called Facenda's voice "one of the most remarkable instruments in the history of broadcasting." For decades, Facenda anchored WCAU-TV's evening newscast. His nightly signoff, "Have a nice night tonight and a good day tomorrow. Goodnight all," still echoes in the souls of Philadelphians. Because I grew up in Pittsburgh, I've only heard these things from friends and colleagues.

My earliest exposure to Facenda dates back to my first high school football camp in late August 1966. One night after dinner, our coach strung up an NFL Films production on a 16mm projector. Facenda's opening line stated, "In the NFL, there are many stars . . . but only *one* Superman!" A montage of player close-ups ended with LA Rams defensive end David "Deacon" Jones. Wow! I felt goosebumps and gladiator courage all at once.

So, in the summer of 1975, when I walked into the NFL Films recording studio and saw Facenda sitting behind the glass, rehearsing a colleague's script, I could barely contain my hero worship. Months later, I directed my very first Facenda narration. Fellow producers advised me to write less, not more. They explained that Facenda disliked "dirty copy": handwritten revisions over typed scripts. And they encouraged me to spell out difficult names phonetically, just in case. Per my twenty-two-year-old confidence, I did none of the above.

"Bobby, you should have had this script retyped . . ." were among the first eloquent words out of his mouth. When I asked him to speed up a line because his natural pace would have extended past the highlight into a subsequent talking head, he replied politely, "Perhaps you should have written less copy." His candid observations were in no way mean-spirited or nasty—they were simply "right." Lessons learned.

Later that year, the veteran producers invited me to a private, closed-door, male-only screening of a Facenda outtakes tape. The lights dimmed, and the "Voice of God" permeated the silence. Incredible as this may seem, Facenda could not pronounce certain simple names. One in particular haunted him: Hank Stram. That's right, *Stram*. Facenda mangled the name beyond belief multiple times, and after each attempt, he politely and audibly encouraged himself: "Come on, John, get this right" or "Dammit, John, this is an easy one." Apparently, one day his frustrations came to a boil, resulting in this closing line in Facenda's top-secret outtakes tape: "This script has done for filmmaking what pantyhose has done for [BEEP BEEP]!"

My jaw hit the floor. My colleagues could barely contain their amusement. I realized that somebody must have put him up to this—no way in hell would this honorable, well-spoken gentleman ever say anything so raunchy and ribald without a helluva lot of coaxing. Eventually, I learned that he did the line on the condition that it would be part of every rookie producer's professional education. Yet coming from Facenda's golden vocal cords, even raw profanity exhibited an air of eloquence and distinction. His voice was that good!

Phyllis George *(1949–2020)*

- CBS Sports (1975-77, 1980-84) • CBS Morning News (1985)

In 1975, the year I began working at NFL Films, CBS Sports launched a brand-new version of its Sunday pro football pregame show called *The NFL Today*. The original three-person, on-air cast featured Brent Musburger, a Chicago-based, sports-TV anchor, and Irv Cross, an extremely intelligent but inexperienced TV person who had played in the NFL at a high level of excellence for eight seasons (1961–68). Rounding out the trio was a former Miss America, Phyllis George.

Media critics openly wondered why CBS Sports would hire a beauty queen to work on its hard-core football show. Since NFL Films's official creation in 1965, the company had provided hours of game footage and prepackaged segments for CBS's numerous variations of its Sunday pregame show. Not surprisingly, that relationship continued with George. My colleague Louis Schmidt produced most of her segments during her two stints with CBS. Every so often, he would direct material that other folks would edit. Starting in 1976, sometimes "other folks" included me.

One morning in 1977, my supervisor, John Hentz, walked into my office and said, "You're going to Denver today. . . . You're working with Phyllis George." Turns out Schmidt was sick in bed, and I was the nearest warm body with location production skills. So, off I went to Colorado. I outlined my segment on the flight, wrote stand-ups, prepared questions, and reviewed my notes on Craig Morton, the born-again Broncos quarterback who was leading Denver to stunning victories. My cameraman had shot most of George's pieces before and would be familiar to her. I would not.

At Stapleton Airport, Phyllis greeted the crew warmly. I could see that she was looking for Louis Schmidt, not a twenty-four-year-old kid from Pittsburgh, aka me! I introduced myself. She was totally underwhelmed and a bit confused, but I assured her that I'd mapped things out nicely. I presented my scripts and questions to her so she could review them en route to the Broncos' team facility. Her spirits lifted. I laid out my plan for the segment. She seemed satisfied. And as we walked through the airport, I realized that people were staring and pointing at her. I felt empowered just being in her presence. Amazing how contagious celebrity can be.

In later years, I ran into Phyllis at the fancy New York City wedding of NFL commissioner Pete Rozelle's stepdaughter Jeanne Cooke, where I was one of the groomsmen. She introduced me to her then-husband John Y. Brown, the one-time owner of Kentucky Fried Chicken and a former governor of Kentucky. He shook my hand unnecessarily hard, as if trying to prove something.

We reminisced about her best segments. When I mentioned Roger Staubach, she smiled. Basically, Staubach was normally quite boring, but Phyllis got him to say, "I enjoy sex as much as Joe Namath, but I only do it with one girl, my wife . . . but it's still fun!" Her good looks and radiant smile disarmed her interview subjects—even Captain America. She affected people in an extremely positive way.

I also remembered a not-so-good moment involving LA Rams QB and former Rhodes Scholar Pat Haden. Schmidt's question included the word *epitome*, as in "You are the epitome of an overachieving blah, blah, blah. . . ." When she asked it, she pronounced it as *EP-uh-tome.* Oops!

The unofficial "First Lady of Television Sports" died on May 14, 2020, of complications from a rare blood cancer called polycythemia vera. I called Lou Schmidt to commiserate, feeling a wave of nostalgia coupled with sadness. No matter what else, Phyllis George was the *epitome* of a classy lady.

Curt Gowdy *(1919–2006)*

- Boston Red Sox (1951-66) • NBC Sports (1955-60, 1965-78)
- ABC Sports AFL Football (1960-61) • CBS Sports (1979-80)
- ABC: Olympic Coverage • "American Sportsman" (1965-86)

Curt Gowdy's broadcasting résumé was impressive. My first recollection of Gowdy dates back to 1960, when he did play by play for the brand-new American Football League on ABC Sports. Four decades later, Gowdy narrated segments I produced for HBO Sports's *Inside the NFL*. The show's producers dubbed them "NFL Storybooks" (1999–2001). When they suggested that Gowdy do my narrations, I was delighted, for I truly wanted to work with the broadcasting legend in person.

But I didn't always appreciate Gowdy. In my opinion, he favored the original eight AFL teams over the NFL teams that had subsumed them in the 1970 merger. He seemed to admire the Oakland Raiders, especially when they were playing my hometown Pittsburgh Steelers. When Oakland defeated the two-time defending champion Super Bowl Miami Dolphins in the 1974 AFC playoffs, Gowdy and Don Meredith called the

Raiders' winning touchdown pass from Ken Stabler to Clarence Davis one of the most famous sports broadcasting moments of all time. In an ironic twist, Gowdy's Raiders references inspired Chuck Noll to speak to his team in a way he never had before—launching the Pittsburgh Steelers 1970s dynasty. (See this book's entry on Noll.)

During NBC's broadcast of Super Bowl XIII (13) between Pittsburgh and Dallas, Gowdy continually referred to the Terrible Towels being twirled by Pittsburgh fans as "Dirty Towels." Steelers fans did not take kindly to the insinuations. I harbored a professional grudge until I met Curt Gowdy and worked with him. In just minutes, all was forgiven.

I personally admired his versatility, range, and experience. A Wyoming native, he authored a book titled *Cowboy at the Mike*. But when he arrived at a Boston sound studio to narrate my "NFL Storybooks," he was eighty years old, and I couldn't figure out why I was hearing unusual clicking sounds layered beneath the finely crafted language in my scripts. Even worse, I quickly ran out of phony reasons to ask for retakes. Finally, the audio engineer told me matter-of-factly that Gowdy's dentures sometimes rattled in his head. No extra charge!

But guess what? Gowdy's voice still resonated with the sports fan in me. His immediately recognizable tone imparted significance to the biggest live television events and the shortest segments. Whether millions were watching or thousands were listening, Gowdy gave the images he was describing stature and meaning. When he died in 2006, I retrieved the "NFL Storybooks" still active in my edit system and watched them again—just to feel good! I barely noticed Gowdy's dentures clicking in the background.

Harry Kalas *(1936–2009)*

- Houston Astros Play-by-Play Announcer (1965-70)
- Philadelphia Phillies Play-by-Play Announcer (1971-2009)
- Westwood One Radio · Mutual Broadcasting · CBS Radio
- Notre Dame Football Play-by-Play Announcer
- NFL Films Narrator and Show Host (1975-2009)

First and foremost, Harry Kalas was the voice of the Philadelphia Phillies. He began narrating shows and segments for NFL Films in 1975, the same year I was hired. I enjoyed picking his brain about Bob Prince, the long-time lead announcer of my hometown Pittsburgh Pirates. I once confided to Kalas that I had aspired to be a baseball announcer. He never shared my confidence, and we always had that in common.

He once told a roomful of NFL Films producers that I was the best writer in the company. Even I didn't believe that, although I did appreciate his vote of confidence. For years, we collaborated on *NFL Game of the Week* shows and *Inside the NFL* segments for HBO. In 1980, I inherited the Philadelphia Phillies highlight film from another NFL Films producer. That year, for the first time ever, the Phillies played in and *won* a World Series, beating the Kansas City Royals in six games.

In those days, Major League Baseball prohibited local TV and radio stations from broadcasting the so-called Fall Classic, so as not to compete with the national broadcast. So, Harry agreed to record a simulated "live call" of Tug McGraw's final pitch and strikeout—one time! No retakes. No bells and whistles. It was a thing of beauty. I opened my highlight film with it and brought tears to the eyes of thousands of Philadelphians. Kalas's powerful and emotional recreation will live on forever, as if he actually did it during the moment, and I cherish the small role I played in it.

In 1986, Steve Sabol asked me to perform a face-lift on NFL Films's long-running but absurdly out-of-date syndicated show *This Is the NFL*—known internally by the acronym *TINFL*. He wanted it to look and sound like *Entertainment Tonight*, a fast-paced, half-hour magazine show that used modern graphics to introduce segments on TV, movies, and entertainers. I wasn't certain that NFL Films owned enough up-to-date video technology and know-how to pull this off, so I studied *ET* and our edit rooms for weeks before presenting Steve with my master plan.

In the end, we commissioned a new high-tech set, lit it with every light on our sound stage, hired a big-time video editor from a New York post-production house, paid an Ohio-based graphics firm to generate a shiny show opening—and then paired Steve Sabol with Harry Kalas to co-anchor our weekly program. People who'd grown accustomed to our primitive, low-tech studio look couldn't believe that NFL Films had entered the "modern video era." The additional cash Harry raked in for all the extra work resulted in an annual postseason event at his favorite suburban Philadelphia hangout, where everybody associated with *TINFL* would eat, drink, and celebrate the season's end—while Kalas tipped each and every member of the waitstaff with $100 bills. The entire company looked forward to the event that became known simply as "Harry's Party."

Those close to Harry knew that he could access large blocks of Phillies tickets. One night, I used a few to take my wife and several other folks to a game. Our seats were just below the TV and radio booths. At one point prior to the first pitch, he spotted me walking down toward the field and started calling out to me: "Ange!" People started staring at Kalas and then down at me. Somehow, I remained oblivious to it all. When I returned, my wife pointed up at the broadcast booth and said, "Harry wants to see you."

Naturally, by the time I made my way up there, Harry was off eating his pregame meal. As I returned to my seat, I could feel the eyes of everybody within earshot of all this watching me. "We work together sometimes," I told several of the curious. Knowing Kalas made me very conspicuous. People wouldn't stop staring at me. Amazing how well-known and popular he had become in Philadelphia.

In 2003, I convinced ESPN to give me a shot at directing some college baseball. They assigned me the Super Regional series between North Carolina State and the Miami Hurricanes in Coral Gables. I had *never* directed a live sports event before. What had I gotten myself into?

So, I asked Harry for an introduction to the Phillies' technical broadcast team. He hooked me up with one of the Phillies' two primary TV directors, J. R. Aguila. Eventually, I sat in the control room during a pair of home-game telecasts and studied Aguila's well-rehearsed and flawless live-TV technique. Then, it was my turn in Coral Gables—and the technical director announced, "Thirty seconds to air!"

I almost asked him, "Who are you talking to?" Then, I realized that he was talking to me! What had I done?

Somehow, I survived. I compiled a "Best Sequences" tape that I sent to Aguila, who said "Not bad for your first attempt." Later that summer, I saw Harry at NFL Films. I told him that I didn't sleep the night before the first telecast or the second. Without judgment, he said sympathetically, "Ange . . . live TV is an entirely different animal." From that day forward, I never looked at him quite the same again.

In April 2009, my wife and I were cleaning our Wildwood, New Jersey, shore home when her brother called with sad news: Harry Kalas was dead. Fittingly, he took his last breath in the press box at Nationals Park in Washington, D.C., where he was prepping to do another baseball game.

Above all else, "Harry the K" was the voice of the Philadelphia Phillies. Rest in peace my dear friend and colleague. There will never be another one like you.

Alex Karras (*1935–2012*)

· Detroit Lions Defensive Tackle (1958–62, 1964–70) · ABC Monday Night Football Analyst (1974–76) · Numerous Feature Film Roles in *Paper Lion, Blazing Saddles, M*A*S*H, Babe, Centennial, Victor/Victoria, Against All Odds,* and others · Costarred with Susan Clark and Emmanuel Lewis in ABC Sitcom *Webster* (1983–87)

During his *Monday Night Football* debut, Alex Karras took one look at the steam rising from Raiders defensive lineman Otis Sistrunk's bald head, then announced, "There's Otis Sistrunk, from the University of Mars!"

ABC Sports knew what they were getting when they hired Karras. Back in 1966, author George Plimpton had recognized Karras's keen wit and penchant for pranks during the writing of his tell-all pro football training-camp book *Paper Lion*. When Hollywood turned the book into a 1968 feature film, Alan Alda portrayed Plimpton, and Karras played himself, his first foray into acting. In Mel Brooks's 1974 classic old West comedy *Blazing Saddles*, Karras gained national notoriety as Mongo, a big dumb thug who rides into town on a bull, then sucker punches a horse, knocking it out cold. When a local sheriff questions Mongo's motives, Karras responds, "Don't know. . . . Mongo only pawn in game of life." The character Karras created remains the stuff of pop-culture legend.

Or, as Karras once told me, "They had this idea I was a ruffian. This rough, tough character. And I played that role. When you get dubbed that role, you might as well play that role."

By the time I took Irv Cross and an NFL Films crew to Karras's Paramount Studio offices in the early 1980s, he was married to fellow actor Susan Clark and working to secure the lead role in a film about Glenn "Pop" Warner, the former college football coach and innovator whose name is still associated with competitive youth football. Despite his résumé, Karras didn't get the role. To the best of my knowledge, the film was never produced. Somebody *will* eventually make that movie.

Karras warmed up noticeably when I advised him that he was one of the stars on my electric football team. His mood brightened even more when his wife popped in to chat business. But it all turned to poop when I insisted that Cross ask him about his 1963 NFL suspension for gambling—after all, it was part of his story. Karras finally lightened things by recounting how, after his return to football in 1964, he refused to call a coin toss, telling the referee, "I'm sorry, sir . . . I'm not permitted to gamble."

I don't remember anything about the final segment except Irv Cross's stand-up. Our camera was set up across the street from Paramount Pictures. The sun was not shining on the Paramount sign, and Karras agreed to do his introductory walk for our cameras just once. Fortunately, Irv nailed his stand-up on the first take. When I contacted Karras after the segment aired, he and Clark's personal assistant told me about a new prime-time TV project the couple might soon be doing together, a sitcom called *Webster*. I wished them both good luck.

Bottom line, Karras played pro football at a Hall of Fame level, finally attaining the honor as part of the fifteen-person Centennial Slate Class of 2020. Lined up beside Roger Brown, the duo anchored a Lions defense that might have dominated the early 1960s had it not been for Vince Lombardi and his Green Bay Packers. He certainly dominated my electric football field. And in the end, the self-declared ruffian proved to be a pretty damned good actor.

Andrea Kremer *(born 1959)*

- NFL Films Producer/Director/Editor/Writer/Talent (1984–1989)
- ESPN Correspondent (1989–2006)
- Sideline Commentator for NBC's *Sunday Night Football*
- NFL Network Chief Correspondent
- HBO's *Real Sports with Bryant Gumbel* Correspondent
- Analyst on Amazon Prime Video's *Thursday Night Football*
- Co-host of CBS Sports's *We Need to Talk*

No one has watched Andrea Kremer's rise with more pride than I have. In an industry that could have pigeon-holed her as "the female sports reporter," her own chops and instincts made her the highly respected female sports journalist of substance.

On a visit to her hometown of Philadelphia, Andrea once mentioned my name on Ray Didinger's popular WIP-FM Radio show. When asked about her path to the 2018 Pete Rozelle Radio-Television Award presented each year for "longtime exceptional contributions to radio and television in professional football," she thanked me and a couple other former NFL Films folks for helping her advance her career.

I first met her in 1984, the year Steve Sabol and Bob Ryan hired her to be the first female producer to work at NFL Films. We became friends almost immediately. I respected her diligence and work ethic. What she didn't already know about the game of football, she wanted to learn. When it came to players and teams, she arrived as well-versed as anybody. She brought with her a newspaper-writing background and endless ambition. And most importantly, at heart, she was a true *journalist* with a knack for storytelling, a trait that serves her well to this day.

In 1986, Steve asked me to take over and remodel *This Is the NFL* (aka *TINFL*), a weekly syndicated show that NFL Films had been producing since the Mesozoic Period. He wanted a new and improved show that looked and felt like *Entertainment Tonight*. Unfortunately, back then, NFL Films's video capabilities weren't quite prime-time caliber. What we did possess was a stable of capable producers—Andrea among them. By then, I'd discovered her other professional assets: her willingness to work long, hard hours; her innate sense of pacing; her dogged research style; her openness to criticism; her recall; her intelligence; and much more!

None of those remarkable qualities made *TINFL* a ratings success. Although long-time NFL Films aficionados noticed the modern graphics and the slick new format, our airtimes in most local markets were less than ideal. Audiences liked the content when they happened to stumble upon the show, but it's tough to build a weekly following with a mere mention in *TV Guide* and piss-poor time clearances. It was during the November sweeps period that I got an idea. Eventually, I mentioned it to her.

"How would you like to be talent on next year's *TINFL*?" Together, Andrea and I worked out the details, and at some point in 1987, Steve gave us permission to do a screen test. I set it all up. Everything I wanted her to do involved simulated situations: an on-camera interview, a stand-up lead-in, a reading off the teleprompter—stuff like that. We shot it all on NFL Films's tiny little forty-by-forty-feet sound stage. I'm pretty sure that we brought in a makeup person. I sat with Andrea in the green room until she was ready to go, then walked back to the control room.

The room was packed with curious NFL Films employees. Some were well-wishers. Some were there to witness the spectacle. Many of the non-producer NFL Films female employees seemed downright hostile. I sat down in the director's chair, opened my line to Andrea's ear, and counted her down to her first screen test. I definitely did *not* mention the mixed audience gathered around me.

She did well enough to earn Steve Sabol's approval, and she became *TINFL*'s official field reporter for the 1987 NFL season. I directed her first-ever segment, a piece on New York Giants nose tackle Jim Burt, a New Jersey resident just up the turnpike from NFL Films. Not sure where we got it, but we borrowed a convertible sports car for her stand-up. We both laugh about this today.

During her first season, I directed several of her segments and watched her confidence grow with each new production. By her second *TINFL* season in 1988, she was doing weekly on-camera lead-ins to her segments. Our graphics department designed a background specifically for her. But when our ratings didn't budge, Steve soured on our whole *TINFL* experiment and took back control of his weekly show. In 1989, I moved on to a season-long *Where Are They Now?* series for ESPN—and Andrea hired an agent, then joined ESPN.

She spent her first year with the company living in Chicago. One Saturday night before a Bears game, I joined her for dinner at Pizzeria Uno. I'd never seen her more alive. She'd survived the high school cheerleading competitions on which she'd cut her teeth for the network and was now working as ESPN's Midwestern correspondent. The meatier the segment, the more she rose to the challenge. In 1994, the network relocated her to Los Angeles. By then, she was a regular on ESPN's *SportsCenter* as well as across all the network's synergistic platforms. When an old-school, fellow NFL Films employee remarked to me, "Great, now I can't watch *SportsCenter* anymore," I literally felt sorry for him. I thought back to the crowd who had gathered in the NFL Films control room to watch her audition, and I laughed out loud. NFL Films's loss was ESPN's gain.

These days, Andrea is her own brand. She appears regularly on HBO's *Real Sports with Bryant Gumbel.* Her interview skills remain razor sharp. Her storytelling talents have always served her well. Her journalistic integrity is beyond reproach.

Way to be, AK. I thought you might be destined for bigger and better things—and you knew it.

"Dandy" Don Meredith *(1938–2010)*

- Dallas Cowboys Quarterback (1960–68)
- *Monday Night Football* Commentator (1970–73, 1977–84)
- NBC Football Commentator (1974–76)
- TV and Motion Picture Actor (1973–2002)

In 2017, my final full season shooting football games for NFL Films, I met Michael Meredith at a Dallas Cowboys home game.

Michael is an actor, a filmmaker—and son to "Dandy" Don Meredith. He described his *First Cowboys* project to me, a documentary reliving the formative years of the Dallas Cowboys. I wished him luck. I'm pretty sure that I told him that I'd once worked with his father at the Los Angeles Coliseum. The elder Meredith had proven to be an able actor, too, and a better sport than I could have hoped for. But pregame conversations evaporate over time unless captured on film or video. In fact, my memories of working with his father aren't that clear either.

The year was definitely 1976. Retired Dallas Cowboys quarterback Don Meredith was working with Curt Gowdy on NBC Sports's top NFL broadcast team. Bill Fitts, producer of NBC Sports's football pregame show *GrandStand*, truly liked a Halloween Day segment I had just produced for his show, so he requested me for a project involving Meredith. It included a location shoot at the Los Angeles Coliseum. I was twenty-three years old and excited beyond belief.

Just a decade earlier, I had been an aimless high school student rooting against Meredith and his Dallas Cowboys in both of their NFL Championship Game appearances against Green Bay (1966 and 1967). Vince Lombardi's team won both games, then went on to win Super Bowls I (1) and II (2)—although back then, the events were still called NFL-AFL Championship Games. Now, I was producing pregame segments for a major network television sports operation. I couldn't believe my good fortune.

Explaining the project over long distance, Fitts said that he wanted Meredith to appear in costume as "Father Time." He wanted me to walk Meredith in and among the marble columns at the top of the Coliseum while Meredith talked about the trials and tribulations of aging quarterbacks. If memory serves, Fitts suggested that I profile Earl Morrall, Billy Kilmer, and Joe Namath. He left the rest of the treatment and execution up to me. By the time my plane landed in LA, I had outlined and written all of it. Selling the concept to Meredith was my next hurdle.

On shoot day, the lighting truck, costume people, and makeup artist all arrived before Meredith. When he did appear, he could not have been more agreeable to a young gun depicting him as an old man. I mean, I still had zits! Yet he sat in his makeup chair and listened to my ideas and shooting schedule with keen interest. I waited for the inevitable litany of critiques and changes, but it never came. Near the end of the preproduction process, the makeup artist fit a long gray beard over Meredith's face—and I laughed out loud.

"This isn't supposed to be funny, Bob. It's tough out there for veteran quarterbacks," he said in an affected tone with a mischievous smile. "Just trying to get into character."

I knew it was going to be a great day.

For several hours, Meredith limped along on his prop cane amid the "ancient" backdrops, lamenting how the advancing years "were robbing these once great specimens of their powers," or whatever tripe I had written. By the time we were ready to record pure voiceover, Meredith and I were clicking. Reading my line "lame ducks and wobblers," referring to Kilmer's passes, Meredith noted with a smile, "Billy sure knows how to do that." He was especially impressed that I mentioned the rocking chair that Morrall kept in the Dolphins' locker room.

"Pretty sure somebody 'presented' that to Earl as a suggestion," Meredith said.

The segment aired on *GrandStand* later that season, possibly on Thanksgiving Day. I honestly don't remember. I do recall Fitts telling my boss, "This is an Emmy-caliber segment." I did not win one, but I did make a friend for life. From that day forward, I could not walk past Dandy Don on a pro football field without Meredith stroking the invisible beard hanging from his chin.

This is the story I hope that I told Michael Meredith that night in Dallas. But again, in the excitement of pregame warm-ups, much is forgotten.

Jack Whitaker *(1924–2019)*

Announcer/Commentator/Field Reporter

- WCAU-TV Philadelphia (began in 1950) · CBS Sports (1962–81)
- *The NFL Today* Commentary and Location Work
- Hosted *CBS Sports Spectacular* (began in 1961) · ABC Sports (1982–93)

In 1945, Jack Whitaker took an artillery shell on the beach at Normandy. He survived to become the most eloquent and accomplished sports broadcaster I've ever known. Great colleagues make their peers up their game. Whitaker did that for me.

I worked with Whitaker several times in 1981, his final season as part of the CBS Sports award-winning and trend-setting pregame show *The NFL Today*. I was producing a collection of segments called "Legends of the Game." On our very first collaboration, I learned that Whitaker would not accept my "mailing it in."

Our subject was Lance Alworth, the first original AFL player to be elected to the Pro Football Hall of Fame. One of the questions I wrote for Whitaker began, "Some considered you to be too small and too slow to play professional football. . . ." He asked the question, and Alworth looked puzzled. Later, Whitaker said to me, "I'm pretty sure Lance Alworth was pretty damned fast. . . . If we're going to work together, do your homework before you write your questions, please!"

On our next trip, we visited Norm Van Brocklin at his Georgia pecan farm. I had learned everything I could about the Hall of Fame quarterback and two-time head coach, but when it came time to record my stand-up, Whitaker said, "Let me work on this a little bit." His words put butterflies in my stomach—his on-camera essays were becoming legendary. And CBS Sports executives told me that he wrote his own material, much the way Eric Sevareid did when doing commentaries alongside Walter Cronkite on the *CBS Evening News*. I pondered what might happen next.

When I caught up with Whitaker, he was sitting on a tractor in the middle of a field. "Ready when you are!" he said. We placed the camera, turned on his microphone, and I hollered, "Action!" What followed was a brilliant piece of oratory linking Van Brocklin's farm and his NFL career to General Sherman's march through Georgia. There was no need for a retake.

Our most memorable excursion took us to old Municipal Stadium in Bloomington, Minnesota, the original home of the Vikings. Here was an opportunity. Not only did I research the old ball park's vaunted visual history; I devised a stand-up that would earn Whitaker's respect. The skies cooperated, filling with ominous gray clouds just as we arrived to shoot. I borrowed a football from the Vikings, handed Whitaker my script, then asked him whether he could catch a pass. He smiled and asked, "Can you really pull this off?"

You betcha! The next-to-last shot in the edited segment features the low end-zone angle of Drew Pearson's famous 1975 game-winning reception of Roger Staubach's desperation heave. To all fans of NFL football, it's known simply as the "Hail Mary." Only this time, the ball Pearson throws into the stands doesn't just fly over the top of our camera—it lands in the hands of Whitaker, sitting alone in the deserted end-zone seats. As the music abruptly ends, Whitaker stands, walks down the steps toward the camera, then says goodbye to the grand old ballpark.

At the airport, Whitaker pulled out his newly minted CBS corporate American Express card and announced, "Whatdya say we break this thing in right?" The drinking lamp was lit—as was the entire crew by takeoff. Whitaker lifted his glass to me, smiled, and said, "Great job today, guys!" Vindication.

Quarterbacks

George Blanda *(1927–2010)*

- Chicago Bears (1949-58) - Baltimore Colts (1950) - Houston Oilers (1960-66) - Oakland Raiders (1967-75)

Age isn't known for making athletes better, but George Blanda knew better.

Near the turn of the century, I interviewed Blanda for an "NFL Storybook" segment that aired on HBO Sports's *Inside the NFL*. It revisited a miraculous stretch of games in 1970 during which the forty-three-year-old Blanda had passed and kicked the Raiders to four straight come-from-behind wins and one tie to keep the Raiders atop the AFC Western Division.

I'd heard that Blanda could be a tough interview, but I refused to believe the rumors. How could one of seven children sired by a Slovak coal miner from western Pennsylvania not be a stand-up guy? So, I told him about my mother's southeastern European roots and my own western Pennsylvania football experiences. I also mentioned that Curt Gowdy would narrate the finished segment. Soon, we were swapping stories like family.

Regarding his 1970 heroics, Blanda told me, "It gave people in the middle age group some hope that they can accomplish anything they want to if they want it hard enough . . . but I thought I was twenty-one." These weren't the words of a difficult interview subject. And he wasn't finished: "You're not over the hill because of age—a number. . . . The fact is, you get better."

I applauded the Associated Press for naming him the Male Athlete of the Year—at age forty-three. Kind of like Tom Brady, just a half century earlier. As the Raiders' legendary radio announcer Bill King said when Blanda's 53-yard field goal beat the Cleveland Browns in overtime in the middle of that five-game streak, "George Blanda has just been elected King of the World!"

OK by me.

Terry Bradshaw *(born 1948)*

- Pittsburgh Steelers (1970–83)

When the Pittsburgh Steelers selected Louisiana Tech quarterback Terry Bradshaw with the first overall pick in the 1970 NFL Draft, pro football pundits predicted big things for him.

In a world built on relationships, first impressions go a long way, and Bradshaw had a long memory. I ended up on the right side of that combination, while Chuck Noll wasn't so lucky. Many people forget that Pittsburgh's strong-armed savior was no overnight sensation. In 1974, Steelers head coach Noll benched a healthy Bradshaw and named Joe Gilliam the team's opening-day starter. Later, Terry Hanratty took over the position. Not until October did Bradshaw settle back in as Pittsburgh's quarterback. By then, his relationship with Noll had suffered irreparable damage.

The 1974 Steelers beat the Minnesota Vikings, 16–6, in Super Bowl IX (9). The Steelers' defense allowed zero points, and Franco Harris won the game's MVP award. Bradshaw completed 9 passes for 96 yards and a touchdown. *Sports Illustrated*'s Dan Jenkins described the Steelers as "the only team to reach the playoffs without a quarterback"—harsh, even by today's standards.

By 1975, I was working for NFL Films. That Steelers team lost only two regular-season games. For the first time in his career, Bradshaw threw more touchdowns than interceptions and was much less of a liability. So, when he took off running against Baltimore in the first round of the AFC Playoffs, got hit hard and flipped, landed oddly on one leg, and came up limping badly, the air emptied out of my parents' living room. We all stood and cheered when he trotted back out for the second half with no apparent ill effects. The Steelers powered through the Colts, survived an AFC Championship ice game against the Oakland Raiders, and then beat Dallas in Super Bowl X (10), 21–17. Bradshaw was knocked out of the game by Larry Cole just after launching a 64-yard TD pass to Lynn Swann, a touchdown that would stand as Pittsburgh's eventual margin of victory.

My first personal encounter with Bradshaw took place early in Pittsburgh's 1978 season. That team won its first seven games, and Bradshaw enjoyed his best-ever passing year. Future Hall of Fame receivers Swann and John Stallworth caught everything Bradshaw tossed up, and Harris could still leave an entire defense in his wake. During their undefeated start, I took CBS Sports's Jayne Kennedy to Bradshaw's apartment to do a piece for *The NFL Today*.

I don't remember the details, but a Steelers official accompanied us to the dwelling Bradshaw shared with JoJo Starbuck and some very young puppies. I noticed an acoustic guitar propped up in the corner, so I wrote a "Steelers Song" for Kennedy and Bradshaw to sing. While my crew lit an interview set and Kennedy entertained the doggies, I wrote a little ditty to the classic tune of "Oh, Susanna." All I remember is the final chorus line: "When the weather gets cold, the black and gold . . . are gonna be . . . Super Bowl . . . bound!"

When Bradshaw arrived home from practice and I presented my plan, he bought in. He and Kennedy began rehearsing. Needless to say, CBS Sports loved it. Surprisingly, Bradshaw and Kennedy sounded pretty good together, and he strummed the necessary three chords flawlessly. After that, Bradshaw kind of recognized me on football fields—kind of. That year, 1978, Pittsburgh won the third of four Super Bowls they would win over six seasons, and Bradshaw won the first of back-to-back Super Bowl MVP awards. His promise was now fully realized.

But his relationship with Noll remained strained. At a 1979 preseason game, before I started shooting a sound camera, I shot Bradshaw exiting the field after throwing a touchdown pass. Noll met him as he jogged past on his way toward the bench.

"What play was that?" Noll asked. "Touchdown," Bradshaw replied. Their relationship had achieved that level of strain. No wonder Noll never liked boom microphones and sound cameras around. Good thing for Noll I was *not* shooting sound yet that day. Pittsburgh writers would have had a field day interpreting *that* sound bite.

Tom Brady *(born 1977)* (🛡 inevitable) 🏆

- New England Patriots (2000-19) · Tampa Bay Buccaneers (2020-Present)

NFL Films vice-presidential types kept me away from Bill Belichick and his security staff for most of the years Tom Brady played in New England. When I did shoot a Patriots game, I usually shot the other team. When I had to work the Patriots' bench, I never once got a usable sound bite involving Brady. To this day, I root against Belichick passionately.

As for Brady, for years I stuck to my guns and insisted that Joe Montana was the G.O.A.T. (Greatest Of All Time) quarterback. My reasoning was simple: Montana played in an era when big hits on quarterbacks were an integral part of winning football games. During Brady's NFL tenure, any defender who breathed hard on a passer in the pocket seemed to draw a flag—in particular, *Cry Brady*, my nickname for Tom Terrific.

Two games changed my mind about Brady forever. The first was Super Bowl LI (51). As per NFL Films's executive order, I shot sound of the Atlanta Falcons and their sideline. At one point midway through the third quarter, the Falcons led, 28–3. A Brady touchdown pass (and a missed point after touchdown) and a Steve Gostkowski field goal later, the Falcons' lead shrank to 16 points. And the Falcons' defensive players were studying the scoreboard after every play. I could hear their minds working: "If Brady scores another touchdown and gets the 2-point conversion . . . then does it again before that clock runs out . . . ?" Guess what, Atlanta? You lose! In fact, you already have. He's way over there on his own sideline, but he's also right here in your heads, taunting all of you, undermining your confidence, sparking mini-insurrections between players and position coaches. His mere presence on the field was tearing the Atlanta Falcons' defense apart right before my eyes. Wow!

The other game that changed my mind about Brady was Super Bowl LV (55). Tampa Bay bought every available skill player of note, then delivered them to Brady's offensive huddle. The Bucs manhandled the defending champion Kansas City Chiefs, 31–9. Forty-three-year-old Brady threw 3 touchdown passes in the game. Can you say, "Greatest Of All Time"? Congrats, Mr. Brady. You idolized Montana growing up. Now, you've surpassed him.

Brett Favre *(born 1969)*

- Atlanta Falcons (1991) · Green Bay Packers (1992-2007) · New York Jets (2008)
- Minnesota Vikings (2009-10)

People have gotten a lot more bothered debating Brett Favre's legacy than Favre ever seemed to get playing football, despite the injuries he overcame and the many years he played.

Favre's best statistical season took place in Minnesota in 2009, the year he turned forty. He remains the only player to win three consecutive Associated Press NFL Most Valuable Player Awards (1995–97). He started in

297 consecutive regular season games over 19 seasons (321 counting playoff games), a quarterback durability record that likely will stand forever.

And it all started so badly.

In 1991, Atlanta Falcons head coach Jerry Glanville did not want his team to use a second-round draft selection (the thirty-third overall pick) on Favre. He branded him "Mississippi" after Favre's home state and said, "It would take a plane crash for me to put him in a game." Of the four drop backs Favre made in his one-year Atlanta career, two resulted in interceptions and a third in a sack.

His marriage with Green Bay head coach Mike Holmgren made him a Hall of Famer. I observed one of Holmgren's now-famous "First Fifteen Play Calls of the Game" meetings prior to a Packers preseason contest in Madison, Wisconsin, in the late 1990s. As former Eagles head coach and longtime Packers backup quarterback Doug Pederson and several aspiring young signal callers listened intently, Holmgren listed the selected plays Green Bay's offense would run to start the game. I felt privileged to watch Holmgren in action. Favre fought off boredom.

During pregame warm-ups, Favre strummed his air guitar and sang along to the country and western tunes being piped into the stadium over the PA system. He wore a wire for the occasion. His absolute refusal to be bothered by the upcoming full-contact event intrigued me. Nothing fazed the guy. Perhaps that's why he played through a first-degree shoulder separation, a torn right bicep, a broken left thumb, and who knows how many concussions.

I worked around Favre for many years, but my closest interactions came during his first season in Minnesota. Vikings head coach Brad Childress downplayed Favre's signing and arrival. In truth, Childress's introduction of Favre to local media seemed downright disrespectful. Fortunately for the Vikings, Favre again wasn't fazed. The spectacular season he put together would have resulted in a Vikings Super Bowl appearance if the Saints hadn't deliberately and severely sprained Favre's ankle.

In a pattern later exposed in the "Bountygate" scandal, the injury took place on January 24, 2010, during the 2009 NFC Championship Game in New Orleans between the Saints and the Vikings. After the injury, I shot Favre writhing in pain on the Vikings' sideline trainers' table. I captured the moment from two different angles and stood close enough to hear Favre's groaning sounds. I could not believe that Favre then returned to the game and damned near led the Vikings to a storybook fourth-quarter win and a berth in Super Bowl XLIV (44). Perhaps someday Childress and then-Vikings running backs coach Eric Bieniemy will explain how and why the comeback failed. Trust me, there's a story there.

Say what you will about Favre's 302 career interceptions, the most by any quarterback ever, not to mention his off-field shenanigans. But when he played, he started every week, finished most of those starts, and won way more games than he lost. Win or lose, he had fun playing football, and he made it fun to watch. His first-ballot Hall of Fame induction says it all.

Dan Marino *(born 1961)*

- Miami Dolphins (1983-99)

Few NFL passers have ever put together better seasons than Dan Marino's 1984 assault on the NFL record book.

Following his Pro Bowl rookie season, in 1984, Marino threw an NFL record 48 TD passes, a single-season mark finally bested by Peyton Manning's 49 two decades later, in 2004. Marino's record of 5,084 passing yards in a season lasted until Drew Brees threw for 5,476 in 2011. The Dolphins won fourteen of sixteen regular-season games and then blew out Seattle and Pittsburgh in the postseason, setting up a much-anticipated matchup between Marino's Dolphins and Joe Montana's San Francisco 49ers in Super Bowl XIX (19).

Trailing 7–3 in the first quarter, Marino orchestrated a beautiful six-play, 70-yard drive, hitting five straight throws that concluded with a Super Bowl touchdown toss to tight end Dan Johnson. The play came right at me, and I thought to myself, "I got the signature shot of Dan Marino's first-ever touchdown pass—surely, the first of many." Turns out, he would never throw another in a Super Bowl.

Overall in that game, the 49ers sacked Marino four times, intercepted him twice, and allowed just a pair of field goals the rest of the way. San Francisco won convincingly, 38–16. Montana won his second Super Bowl MVP award, then appeared with Marino in a beautifully directed and edited Coca-Cola commercial, two western Pennsylvania quarterbacks with seemingly bright futures. But while both made the Pro Football Hall of Fame, Marino's remaining sixteen NFL seasons resulted in just eight postseason appearances. Only twice did the Dolphins qualify for the AFC Championship Game, losing once to the 1985 Patriots (pre–Tom Brady), 13–5, and the second time to Jim Kelly's 1992 Buffalo Bills, 29–10.

Back in those days, I personally admired Marino. On November 24, 1985, he made the vaunted, record-setting Chicago Bears defense appear quite ordinary on *Monday Night Football*, decisively beating Mike Ditka's previously unbeaten team, 38–24. He frustrated Bears pass rushers all night with his vision, lateral movement, and legendary quick release. Chicago never lost again en route to a 46–10 demolition of the New England Patriots in Super Bowl XX (20).

At the Meadowlands, on September 21, 1986, I shot an epic battle between Marino and New York Jets quarterback Ken O'Brien. Back on NFL Draft Day in 1983, when O'Brien was selected before him in the first round, Marino famously (and allegedly) asked his agent, "Who's that?" On this September afternoon, O'Brien answered definitively. The two quarterbacks combined for nearly 900 net passing yards. Marino threw six touchdown passes in the game, yet Miami lost in overtime, 51–45.

My most vivid recollection of that game is of Miami facing a third-and-long at some point in the first half. With the crowd roaring at a deafening decibel level, Marino looked over the Jets' defense and decided to audible. Seriously? I lowered my camera and waited for the delay of game penalty. Somehow, Marino communicated his intentions to his teammates. He took the snap, then threw a laser beam over the middle for a first down. Again, I lowered my camera and looked at Marino, this time thinking, "The play-by-play sheet will not reflect that you audibled to that particular play—and that's a damned shame, because I'm standing here wondering, 'How in the hell did you pull that off?'"

But despite prolific passing seasons and record-setting statistics, Marino played in only one Super Bowl and contributed mightily to his team's disappointing finishes. When he retired, he transitioned into sports broadcasting. That's when I discovered Marino's dark side.

Around the turn of the century, I produced segments called "NFL Storybooks" for HBO's weekly studio highlights show *Inside the NFL*. The show's producer would travel from New York to NFL Films's Mount Laurel, New Jersey, offices to screen my rough cuts. Once they were approved, legendary broadcaster Curt Gowdy would narrate them at a Boston sound studio convenient to his residence. According to the producer, when these segments were rolled into the show during HBO's live-to-tape studio sessions, the announcers on set would cease their conversations, put down their cell phones, and enjoy the historical subject matter. But after two successful seasons with Gowdy, HBO's execs decided to give the voiceover task to Marino, their newest on-air talent.

Marino would record them weekly, by telephone, whenever he was available. OK, I could accept those terms—the man was busy. What pissed me off thoroughly was Marino's attitude during our recording sessions, as if he were doing me some gigantic favor. The fact is, his quintessential Pittsburgh accent sounded amateurish, and his elocution was piss-poor. I preferred hearing Gowdy's dentures rattling around in his head to Marino's lackluster intonation and parochial monotone. Yet when I dared ask Marino to do a retake, I could hear him bristling. In retrospect, I should have advised him where to insert his condescending tone and uninspired reads.

Toward the end of my career, I occasionally encountered Marino on a football field or the Miami sideline. Eventually, I learned to avoid him completely.

Roger Staubach (*born 1942*)

- Dallas Cowboys (1969-79)

Roger Staubach was the star-spangled quarterback of "America's Team." He ranks as one of the finest human beings I've ever met . . . and one of the most boring interviews I've ever done—except for one tantalizing tidbit.

During a conversation about running quarterbacks, out of the blue in what amounted to an aside, he said, "I could have run for 1,000 yards . . . if Coach Landry would have let me." Wow! This was *gold*. But when I asked him to say it again in straight-forward fashion, he danced around it for a good long while, and I got nothing

As thoughtful as Staubach was in interview situations, he rarely delivered definitive declarations. I refer to this as "Beating around the Bush Syndrome." He rated 10 out of 10 in that category. But as the NFL Films producer who wrote and edited the Staubach episode of *A Football Life* said to me, "If that's the worst you can say about the guy, you're really not saying much." After all, he won a Heisman Trophy at the Naval Academy; served his country during the Vietnam War; engineered a slew of come-from-behind, fourth-quarter NFL victories; led the Cowboys to their first and second Super Bowl wins (VI [6] and XII [12]); ran the football as well as many pure running backs; and in 2018 received the Presidential Medal of Freedom, bestowed by presidents to Americans who have made "an especially meritorious contribution to the security or national interests of the United States, world peace, cultural or other significant public or private endeavors."

He's basically a gold-studded, All-American treasure. Just a little boring is all!

John Randle *(born 1967)*

Defensive Tackle and End

- Minnesota Vikings (1990-2000) • Seattle Seahawks (2001-03)

John Randle is my favorite NFL player and *friend* of all time, period!

He was that rarest of commodities: a defensive tackle who could rush quarterbacks. Like Bob Lilly and Alan Page before him, Randle's interior pass rush disrupted offensive game plans. In 1997, he became the first interior lineman to lead the NFL in sacks. At one point in his career, he was the highest-paid defensive player in history. For these achievements, he was voted into the Hall of Fame in 2010, his second year of eligibility. Yet he almost never played in the NFL.

"I didn't think an undrafted free agent could get into the hall," he told me during his six-hour *A Football Life* interview. "A lot of people wouldn't believe my story if it didn't happen. You couldn't write that script." Allow me to summarize: Randle grew up sleeping in the same bed with two older brothers in a twenty-by-twenty-feet shack in the east Texas town of Mumford. His single mother made $23 a week. His home lacked running water: "We didn't have a bathroom. We had to go to the outhouse. It had a single seat. Some people had a double-hole outhouse. . . . That was *big* time!"

His older brother Ervin played linebacker for the Tampa Bay Bucs. Randle played for tiny Trinity Community College and then Texas A&M Kingsville. When no NFL team drafted him, his brother arranged a tryout in Tampa, but the Bucs and Atlanta passed on signing him. Noting his weight of just over 240 pounds, coaches deemed him "too small to play defensive lineman in the NFL." But Minnesota defensive coordinator Floyd Peters promised him, "If you can make 250 pounds, I'll sign you."

So, John went to a hardware store and bought a heavy chain belt that he wore under his sweatpants. At weigh-in, Randle tipped the scales at 251 pounds. He was now a Viking. As a 1990 rookie, he earned his salary on special teams. In 1991, he started in eight games and recorded 9.5 sacks. In 1992, new head coach Dennis Green and defensive coordinator Tony Dungy made Randle a Vikings starter. Then, defensive line coach John Teerlinck went to work on Randle's technique.

"He came to me and said, 'I want to be a really good player,'" Teerlinck told me for Randle's episode of *A Football Life*. "His exact words were . . . , 'I wanna have nice stuff . . . and my mom told me if you wanna have nice stuff, you're gonna have to really work hard.'"

No problem. As Randle told me, "Back home, I would be out chopping cotton for $2 an hour. And we're getting paid for this [football]? This is *easy*!"

At a Vikings summer practice in Mankato, Minnesota, I wired Teerlinck while he coached the Vikings' defensive line. After the team's first period, I approached him and asked, "Is he always . . . ?"

Teerlinck finished my sentence for me: "Number 93? Yep. Randle's got one speed . . . full!"

Randle mastered every pass-rush technique Teerlinck taught him. He worked on them tirelessly in dining halls, shopping malls, and airport lines. He even invented and perfected one of his own: a straight arm shiver with one arm followed in rapid succession by a parrying motion with his other. Randle proudly called it the "Jab Olé!"

"We'd be walking into hotels, and John would . . . 'Olé!' [a teammate or a hotel guest]," Dungy remembered. "I'm sure people were saying . . . , 'What's wrong with this guy?'"

And Randle's game included an added dimension: "I saw myself as the small dog in the group," he explained. "Being a small dog, you gotta have a big bark. So, I started talking."

Films wired Randle five times during his career. Trust me, *nobody* in NFL history spewed a better line of trash talk than John. Among my favorites: "Regulators, mount up." And "Big dogs are in the HOUSE!" And, of course, to an opposing lineman, "I'll kick your whole family's ass!" Each and every new Randle wiring was more impactful and entertaining than the one before.

Brett Favre told us this story about Randle and Packers center Frank Winters: "He'd come up to the line and say . . . , 'Hey Frankie, how's Elita and Aubrey and Alexa doing?' And Frank would come back to the huddle and ask me . . . , 'How's he know my wife and two girls?'"

TEERLINCK: Believe it or not, he was *not* crazy. There was a method to his madness.

DUNGY: Everybody hears the motor mouth and all the crazy stuff . . . which overshadows what he did play after play after play after play!

FAVRE: I hated playing against John Randle. . . . We never overlooked him. . . . This guy was a tremendous player and game changer. . . . One on one, he'd beat the guy every time.

Favre would know: Nobody sacked him more times in his career than Randle. And nobody in his path was safe. His well-conceived brand of psychological warfare made linemen lose focus, running backs fumble footballs, and quarterbacks lose their minds. In Tampa Bay, Randle so infuriated Bucs passer Trent Dilfer that Dilfer attacked him after a sack. It marks probably the only time in NFL history that a passer was thrown out of a game for punching a pass *rusher.*

"When you beat an offensive lineman, you take his soul," Randle said to me with a big, broad smile. "Sacks are better than sex. 'Sack-cess' is forever!" In fourteen NFL seasons, Randle recorded 137.5 sacks, ranking tenth of all time. He's the only *interior* linemen in the bunch. Not bad for an undersized young man whose backup career option was garbage man.

"I used to see the garbage men working. . . . They work for the city, got city benefits . . . ," Randle recalled vividly. "That's gonna be my job. I'm gonna be a garbage man. Start working about six, be done by noon, drink some cold beers. . . . Got it made in the shade."

Today, there's a bustling restaurant in downtown Minneapolis called "Randle's." In it, there's a replica of his Hall of Fame bust. And Randle's suburban mansion is full of really "nice stuff."

"I have definitely lived the American Dream," Randle says modestly. "I'm living it right now." Nobody deserves his "Sack-cess" more.

Andy Reid *(born 1958)* (🛡 inevitable) 🏆

Head Coach

- Philadelphia Eagles (1999-2012) • Kansas City Chiefs (2013-Present)

Hall of Fame head coach and creator of the "West Coast Offense" Bill Walsh spawned a slew of future head coaches who went on to advance his forward-thinking offensive-play designs and strategies, putting quarterbacks in position to win. Mike Holmgren was one of his best.

In 1992, Holmgren became head coach of the Green Bay Packers. Almost immediately, he hired an offensive assistant from the college ranks who'd never risen above assistant coach status, a round-faced, soft-spoken, former Brigham Young offensive tackle named Andy Reid. While working on the Packers' sideline in 1997, I listened to Reid discussing coverages with Green Bay quarterback Brett Favre. I appreciated his attention to detail and the scope of his passing-game knowledge. Reid saw me and my camera, glanced up at my soundman's boom microphone hanging over both their heads, then continued coaching—usually a sign of supreme confidence.

In January 1999, the Philadelphia Eagles hired Reid (on Holmgren's advice) to be their new head coach. Almost immediately, Reid volunteered to be part of one of NFL Films's *Six Days to Sunday* productions. I was not surprised. Most coaches don't want cameras around their football teams for an entire work week, the standard *Six Days* format. They consider production crews to be "needless distractions" that undermine a team's single-minded focus on game preparations. But this former offensive lineman exuded quiet confidence. At an initial preproduction meeting, Reid pulled a five-inch thick, unbound collection of single pages off a shelf, shuffled down to a random page, then allowed me to read what the Eagles would be doing during the last week of September at 1:20 P.M. in preparation for a Sunday road game against the New York Giants. I was totally impressed by his organization—and, of course, his confidence.

When that week actually arrived, the Eagles stood 0–3 and had suffered a shutout to the Bills the Sunday before. But on Monday morning, my crew and I showed up to begin *Six Days* of behind-the-scenes work with Andy's Eagles. I walked to the front of the team's meeting room, camera in hand, waiting for Reid to arrive. Several players pointed out exactly where I should stand. When Reid entered, he marched directly toward my position: "Would you mind getting the heck out of my way, please?" The room erupted in laughter. I'd been set up—not a good start.

But things quickly improved. Our access was unlimited. Cooperation from the top down allowed us to shoot meetings, wire players and Reid at practice, and visit players at home during evening hours. By design, multiple crews showed up on Wednesday and Thursday, the NFL's two busiest practice days. Rookie quarterback Donovan McNabb strolled through the locker room, mugging for cameras while wearing nothing but his jock strap. By week's end, I'd made arrangements with Reid to do a Saturday "ride along" while he drove to his son Garrett's high school football game. That morning, I wired Reid, then rode with him from Veterans Stadium to Garrett's high school in a Philadelphia suburb. I shot Andy walking through the crowd toward his wife, Tammy, who was waiting in the bleachers. I heard her ask about me. Reid replied, "He's part of the family now."

"Well he's not part of *our* family," Tammy shot back. Ouch for me.

By 2001, Reid's offensive wisdom and patience had turned McNabb from a wandering jock into a promising passer who would lead the Eagles to four consecutive NFC Championship Games. The 2004 team advanced to Super Bowl XXXIX (39) to play the Patriots. I worked on the Eagles' sideline that day. In a scoreless first quarter, I remember three successive plays during an eleven-play Eagles drive that altered Reid's life and his career trajectory. On first down and goal at the Patriots' 8-yard line, Mike Vrabel sacked McNabb for a 16-yard loss. On second down and goal, Patriots defensive back Asante Samuel intercepted McNabb's errant pass and returned the ball across midfield. But a Patriot penalty gave Philadelphia a fresh set of downs and new life at New England's 19-yard line. Surely, McNabb would make good on the opportunity.

But on the very next play, McNabb failed to look off Patriots safety Rodney Harrison, eyeballed his intended receiver all the way, then floated a ball into Harrison's hands. As McNabb jogged toward Reid on the sideline, he was actually laughing. "What's so funny?" Reid asked. And in that instant, I realized that McNabb was immune to Reid's detailed instruction and would never win a championship—and that Reid had hitched his coaching wagon to a flamed-out star.

Reid coached the Eagles for eight more seasons. He worked wonders with Jeff Garcia, filling in for the injured McNabb in 2006 and winning five straight games plus a surprise Wild Card playoff victory over the Giants. Minus McNabb in 2010, Philly finished 10–6 and upset Dallas in the postseason, Reid's final playoff win with the Eagles. By now, Philadelphia's sports writers were growing increasingly weary of Reid's pat response at post-loss press conferences: "I need to do a better job coaching them." In August 2012, after a lengthy battle with drugs and addiction, Andy's son Garrett died suddenly while working at the Eagles' summer training camp. The Eagles finished the season with a record of 4–12, then fired Reid. I feared for the coach's emotional well-being.

Just two weeks later, Reid became the new head coach of the Kansas City Chiefs. In 2013, Reid and quarterback Alex Smith began a run of five straight winning seasons, followed by four more postseason failures. In 2018, Reid installed young phenom Patrick Mahomes at the quarterback position. Here was a young passer who benefitted from Reid's attention to detail and thorough preparation. Andy created offensive designs tailored to Mahomes's unique skill set and worked with him weekly. In his first season as a starter, Mahomes was named the NFL's Offensive Player of the Year, and the Chiefs advanced to the AFC Championship Game. In 2019, the Chiefs beat San Francisco in Super Bowl LIV (54), 31–20, winning their first NFL Championship in half a century. In 2023, Reid and Mahomes won another, a 38–35 victory over Andy's old team, the Philadelphia Eagles, in Super Bowl LVII (57).

Suddenly, Reid ranked as one of football's greatest offensive innovators. Eleven former Reid assistants have become NFL head coaches. Four more wins will make Reid the league's fourth-winningest head coach, trailing only Don Shula, Bill Belichick, and George Halas. These things did *not* happen overnight. They resulted from years of focus and dedication. From dozens of game days, breaking down coverage schemes while sound crews listened! From years of putting passers willing to learn in positions to win. Congratulations, Andy. Your dogged perseverance has cemented your rightful place in the Pro Football Hall of Fame.

The Rooneys

Art Rooney Sr. (*father, 1901–88*)

Founder, Chairman, and Owner

- Pittsburgh Steelers (1933-88)

Dan Rooney (*son, 1932–2017*)

General Manager, President, and Owner

- Pittsburgh Steelers (1969-2016)

Of all the pictures hanging beneath magnets on my home refrigerator, only one is work-related: It's a photo of me and Art Rooney Sr., standing in his Three Rivers Stadium office. The picture dates back to the early 1980s. Art dated back to the turn of the twentieth century.

Arthur J. Rooney was a Pittsburgh legend. In 1918, he won the Amateur Athletic Union welterweight title before trying out for the U.S. Olympics team. He moved on to minor league baseball, eventually taking over as player-manager for the Wheeling Stogies, a team my father claims to have played for briefly while Art ran the show. Eventually, in 1933, he purchased the city's NFL franchise with $2,500 allegedly won at a racetrack. He named his team the "Pirates." In 1942, Art changed that name to the "Steelers." His players rewarded his investment with the first non-losing season in franchise history. Not until 1972 did the Pittsburgh Steelers win a division championship.

In 1978, I was producing Jayne Kennedy for CBS Sports's *The NFL Today*. The Steelers set us up to interview Art in his legendary stadium office, surrounded by forty-five years' worth of his favorite and most-cherished memorabilia. When we began, Kennedy dutifully ran through my list of prepared questions, and I sat there listening rather than producing. The interview went well—or so I presumed, until I received a phone call the next day from Steelers publicist and Art's confidant Ed Kiely. "Bob, why did you ask Art about buying the Steelers with racetrack winnings?" Because I learned about it in my research. . . . Because my dad told me the story when I was a kid. . . . Because everybody in Pittsburgh repeated and loved the story, true or not!

"What kind of piece are you doing here? You told us this was going to be positive." I assured Kiely that I harbored no ill will toward "the Chief." Fact is, I was honored to be sitting in Art's presence, and I had put that question at the top of Kennedy's list as a warm-up to start things off on a lighter note. In all likelihood, I had no place for Art's honest answer in the segment anyway. Good relations were restored, and CBS and the Steelers liked my final version.

Early on, I knew Art's oldest son Dan only by sight. For many years, he sat on the NFL Owners Board of Directors for NFL Films. He visited Steve Sabol at our Philadelphia production facility only when problems arose. In 1978, the year Pittsburgh won its third Super Bowl, I inherited the team's annual highlight film, which I called *Return of the Champions*. The Steelers invited me to the official premiere. I took my parents to the event, and Dan and his father congratulated me on a job well done. All three Pittsburgh TV stations covered it for their evening news shows.

That same year, I started screening the Steelers highlight film for my Neville Island hometown friends, Steelers fans all. It became an annual event. In the mid-1980s, KDKA-TV (Pittsburgh's CBS affiliate) dispatched a sports reporter named Steve Talbot to cover the event. His segment aired that night and lasted well over a minute on the station's eleven o'clock newscast. Dan must have seen it. From that day forward, following the official team premiere of my highlight film, Dan would ask me, "So, Bob, when's your Neville Island premiere?"

Like his beloved father, Dan was Pittsburgh personified. In the 1980s, his patience and ability as a solution finder and consensus maker helped the NFL and its Players Association work through two major labor wars. Eventually, he joined the eight-man Management Council Executive Committee, NFL owners' highest-ranking group. Yet he never walked by me without stopping to say, "Hello"—even when he, a Republican, was President Barack Obama's ambassador to Ireland.

During this period, I took a crew to the Steelers' Three Rivers Stadium offices to do interviews for various NFL Films shows. Art saw me roaming the hallways and invited me and several of my closest Neville Island friends (who were tagging along) to stop by for a visit. He wanted to know their names, what they did for a living, and from what distant shores their ancestors hailed. As the son of immigrants, Art took a true interest in "monikers and nationalities," to quote his exact words. As I listened to him talk about his family's racetrack interests, my now-departed friend David Hufnagle took the picture that still survives on my refrigerator.

For many years, I used Steelers media passes to get my father into NFL games. The upstairs box where our cameramen worked looked into the Steelers' owners' box. My dad delighted in timing his bathroom trips so that he would run into Art in a stadium corridor. When Art died in 1988 of complications from a stroke, my dad mourned along with the entire greater Pittsburgh region. Upon Art's passing, I started calling Dan "Mr. Rooney," but he would have none of it. When the Steelers played in Super Bowls, I shot sound on their sidelines. I wiped tears from my eyes the day Dallas beat Pittsburgh in Super Bowl XXX (30), 27–17. Dan was standing right next to me. At Super Bowl XL (40), I openly celebrated the Steelers' 21–10 win over Seattle. Again, Dan bore witness. In the closing seconds of Super Bowl XLIII (43), I rejoiced when the Steelers shut down Kurt Warner's desperate comeback bid in a 27–23 Pittsburgh win.

But my most personal moment with Dan occurred during the pregame of Super Bowl XLV (45). By then, back problems were causing him great discomfort. He called me from a distance, then edged toward me as best he could. When media folks approached, he waved them away: "Please, guys, this is private!" Then, he told me in simple language that a writer had skewed his words to make it appear that he objected to Ed Sabol's election to the Pro Football Hall of Fame: "Tell Steve [Sabol] that I never said those things and that writer misrepresented me. Will you do that for me, Bob?" Why wouldn't I?

These days, Dan's son Arthur Rooney II runs the Pittsburgh Steelers. He has Dan's warm, sensitive eyes and his grandfather's conviction. He's a Rooney. In Pittsburgh, what else matters?

The Sharpe Brothers

Sterling Sharpe *(born 1965)*

Wide Receiver

- Green Bay Packers (1988–94)

Shannon Sharpe *(born 1968)* 

Tight End

- Denver Broncos (1990–99, 2002–03) · Baltimore Ravens (2000–01)

I met Sterling Sharpe first. The date was November 4, 1990. The Packers were playing the San Francisco 49ers in Milwaukee's County Stadium. I'd been warned that Sterling might not like a camera in his face during pregame, so I approached him with my wide-angle lens and camped out in front of him. Moments later, he covered my lens with one of his hands. I had only myself to blame.

I met Shannon Sharpe nearly five years later. The date was October 8, 1995. Shannon's Broncos were slaughtering the New England Patriots in old Foxboro Stadium. I was shooting sound behind the Broncos' bench when Shannon got an idea. As I approached, he picked up a bench telephone: "I'm calling the president. . . . Mr. President . . . we need the National Guard. . . . We need as many men as you can spare because we are killing the Patriots. . . . Send the National Guard, please . . . emergency!" He hung up and addressed the fans: "They're coming. . . . Help is on the way."

Because the whole thing appeared staged, NFL Films did not name it Sound Bite of the Year, but it provided me with the perfect icebreaker for a far-more-extended exposure to Shannon six years later: a month-and-a-half long project shooting the Baltimore Ravens' 2001 summer camp for a series that HBO Sports was calling *Hard Knocks*. I produced and directed the first two seasons.

During rookie hazing at lunch, when first-round draft pick and tight end Todd Heap disclosed his $2 million-plus signing bonus, Shannon fell off his chair, choking in mock disbelief. It made for some entertaining television. But Tony Siragusa and his ongoing antics dominated the first episode. The morning after it aired, I walked onto the practice field and heard a distant summons.

"Yo, Bob . . . Bob Angelo . . . get down here!" With these words, Shannon asked me to join him and two good friends near the extreme rear of the Ravens' calisthenic formation. When I arrived, Sharpe, Rod Woodson, and Ray Lewis got right to the point: "So, what's up with all of Tony's airtime?" they asked, pretty much in unison.

"Because you guys act like our cameras are coated with player repellent!" I replied. My hard line worked. When Siragusa barricaded the doors to the tight ends' meeting hut one night, stranding them all inside for hours, Shannon responded by "stealing" Siragusa's SUV and parking it at a nearby shopping mall. Eventually, Siragusa negotiated its return in Shannon's room, with multiple cameras rolling. HBO viewers savored every juvenile moment. Woodson and Lewis invited me to their homes during off days and stopped walking away from our cameras. Eventually, my entire crew of two-dozen-plus became invisible to them.

Shannon's brother Sterling was on his way to the Hall of Fame until a freak injury in 1994 ended his playing career at its peak. ESPN hired Sterling to do analysis. Suddenly, the famously reticent pass catcher found his voice. The immediacy of Sunday afternoons had prepared him well for the challenges of live television, and Sterling excelled. He knew the game, established and then cultivated contacts with every NFL team, and soon elevated himself to the top of the studio analyst heap. He spoke loudly and exuded confidence. He *knew* how to do TV. Thankfully, he started teaching me.

In 2003, NFL Films made me the producer of an Xs and Os show on the league's brand-new NFL Network. My show *Playbook* debuted on November 4, 2003. Sterling joined former players Glenn Parker and Solomon Wilcots as my on-camera talent. All versions of these hour-long, weekly shows were produced live-to-tape, which essentially means "prerecorded." At peak capacity, we were shooting three one-hour shows on a single Thursday afternoon.

Unfortunately, I was learning my job on the fly. To that point, most of my NFL Films career was spent as a film producer. Television involves control rooms and talent and makeup artists and rundowns and packaged segments and a whole host of other things with which I'd had very little actual hands-on experience. My TV naivete was not lost on Sterling. From the very beginning, he challenged many of my core beliefs, methods, and techniques. In retrospect, I'm glad he did.

Eventually, I learned how to collaborate rather than dictate. Yes, TV audiences loved NFL Films footage, but viewers also respected "talking heads," especially if their words rang true. Great sound bites and spectacular slow motion can hypnotize, but blunt player assessments by analysts with hard-earned credentials leave a mark, such as on the day in 2004 when Sterling referred to the Eagles' starting wide receivers James Thrash and Todd Pinkston as "Trash and Stinkston."

One afternoon at NFL Films, Sterling overheard me discussing fundraising for my son's baseball travel team. "Put me down for a thousand dollars," he said. Later that week, I called him at his South Carolina home to make certain that he was serious. He seemed insulted that I asked.

Had Sterling played two more seasons, he would have been part of the 1996 Packers' Super Bowl XXXI (31) victory over the New England Patriots. Shannon played fourteen full seasons and retired as the all-time leader among tight ends in every major statistical category. Along the way, he played on three winning Super Bowl teams and was inducted into the Pro Football Hall of Fame in 2011.

In retirement, he followed his brother into television, first as an analyst for CBS's *The NFL Today* and then as a cohost on ESPN's *Skip and Shannon: Undisputed.*

Sterling often called Shannon "the best tight end in pro football history." Shannon looked up to and admired his older sibling. In an ultimate show of respect—and a genuine demonstration of brotherly love—Shannon gave Sterling the first of his three Super Bowl rings.

I'm proud to call both my friends.

Tony Siragusa *(1967–2022)* 🏆

Defensive Tackle

· Indianapolis Colts (1990–96) · Baltimore Ravens (1997–2001)

I'm not certain that the premiere season of *Hard Knocks* would have succeeded enough to become an annual HBO television event without the participation of the late Tony Siragusa, aka "Goose."

Yes, NFL Films paid Siragusa, Shannon Sharpe, and several other participants an "honorarium" for their involvement. But, as Tony told me three weeks into the project, "Bob . . . that money ran out a long time ago." Still, the undrafted, veteran defensive tackle provided TV audiences a steady stream of one-liners and observations for the duration of the show's seven-week shoot, despite several visits to hospitals in two different states. And it all started with this: "When I came into this league, I got a $1,000 signing bonus . . . not $12 million. . . . All these guys drafted first round, they come in with their nice new cars . . . don't park 'em near me, cause you're gonna have dents all over the side of your cars."

He refused to submit to daily weigh-ins. Instead, he recruited a rookie to post numbers for both himself and teammate Rob Burnett. He lambasted my white crew socks before the first practice: "Bob, roll those things down. . . . You dress like an old man. . . . I'm losing respect for you." One night after meetings, he dragged all the rookie defensive linemen to a Westminster, Maryland, watering hole named Johansson's Pub for a little karaoke. He warned the Black players, "If I were you guys, I wouldn't rap in this place, you might get killed. . . . Lots of rednecks around here."

One night, he locked the tight ends in their meeting room. Future Hall of Famer Sharpe was one of his victims. Our *Hard Knocks* crews showed up as a perplexed, female security guard dutifully reported for our camera's benefit, "Their door was barricaded with a table."

The shots from inside the cabin of Sharpe trying to break out were priceless. When teammates eventually freed the captives, player development director Earnest Byner declared, "It's all fun and games until somebody get they eye poked out."

To which Sharpe added, "I don't give a f*** about no fat-ass Goose." He vowed revenge. Intrigue was in the air.

Several days later, an ever-alert *Hard Knocks* crew caught up with Sharpe as he got behind the wheel of Siragusa's vehicle. Who knows how he procured the key? "This is my good buddy Goose's truck. . . . Told you

I'd get him back," Sharpe told our cameras. When Siragusa discovered that his SUV was MIA—and his own room key no longer worked—he knew where to begin his investigation. Soon, opposite each other in Shannon's room, they negotiated terms of surrender.

Sharpe: "You humiliated me on national television and I want restitution. . . . I want you to say, 'Shannon, I apologize.'"

After many half-truths and considerable back-and-forth banter, Goose came clean: "Alright, I locked you in the damned room. . . . I apologize, and I promise I'm done effing with you for the rest of this camp." (It should be noted that he crossed his fingers while making this promise.)

Sharpe returned Siragusa's keys and got his "restitution," and America got its first-ever look at the pranks that grown men perpetrate when they're locked away in rooms miles from their homes and families and are force-fed a steady diet of football. That week, a Los Angeles sports columnist described *Hard Knocks* as "a seminal moment in television sports history." And Goose's candid observations continued.

To a rookie whom Siragusa nicknamed "Fish": "Did you weigh me in today?" To a teammate getting taped: "Look at those toes. It's like he's been kicking cannonballs." To me, during an interview: "When I think of meetings, I think of nap time. Give me a bottle with a nipple on it." And so on.

But Tony's best material poured forth during his two hospital visits. The first occurred when an exam revealed bone spurs aggravating the soft tissue in one of his knees. Our crews arrived as he was being prepped for arthroscopic surgery. Siragusa showed us his two knees: "This one I marked 'YES' and the other 'NO.'" Sure enough, our cameraman revealed Siragusa's two knees, inscribed in Sharpie. When a nurse asked him what he'd like to drink when he woke up, Goose replied, "A great big vanilla milkshake."

"Only clear liquids," she said, to which Siragusa countered, "How about vodka? That's clear."

Then, there was the matter of Siragusa's pregnant wife, Kathy. While Siragusa was convalescing from his surgery, Kathy went into labor at Overlook Hospital in Summit, New Jersey. Eventually, the two welcomed Ava Kathleen Siragusa (7 lbs. 12 oz.) to the world. One of my crews joined the couple in Kathy's hospital room. Siragusa couldn't resist. Beaming at his wife, he observed, "Does it look like she had a baby four hours ago? Some of those women over there . . . picking their babies up . . . they had their babies yesterday . . . and they look like they got hit by a truck!"

Finally, Siragusa went one up on Sharpe. During one of the later episodes, Sharpe questioned whether Siragusa's wife really *was* pregnant and about to give birth. As Siragusa exited Overlook Hospital, he turned to our camera and said, "Maybe Shannon Sharpe will believe me now. We had a baby." Then, Goose flipped Sharpe off on national television.

Tony returned to action for the 2001 regular season, his final year in the NFL. The Ravens won ten games and qualified for the postseason. But after a Wild Card win over Miami, 20–3, they lost in Pittsburgh, 27–10. Their back-to-back Super Bowl dream ended. In 2004, Goose joined Fox Sports as the first and only "on-field analyst" working NFL games, which he did for twelve seasons. I ran into him at a Super Bowl in New Orleans. He secured a table that night for me and five guests of my choosing at Emeril Lagasse's original restaurant in the Warehouse District. I was not surprised that a six-foot-three-inch, 340-pound Italian would have such connections. Franco Harris and Lydell Mitchell sat at the table next to mine. U.S. Women's Soccer star and former NFL Films show host Brandi Chastain waved from across the room. Thanks again, Goose.

While researching this book, I read that Siragusa has worked as a spokesman for Depends for Men, designed for "men who leak a little . . . to guard their manhood with man-style protection."

Face it, football fans, the man had a way with words. When he died in his sleep in June 2022 at the age of fifty-five, I read one glowing tribute after another from friends, teammates, opponents, and well-wishers. I stand by my first paragraph. Without Goose's quick-witted candor and impactful presence, *Hard Knocks* would have been far less interesting, and future editions might have never happened. RIP, Tony. You were a great, big, wonderful, totally entertaining human being! There should be more like you.

Otis Sistrunk *(born 1946)* 🏆

Defensive Tackle

- Oakland Raiders (1972-78)

Otis Sistrunk followed a largely untraveled path to professional football.

After graduating from William Spencer High School in Columbus, Georgia (Class of 1964), Sistrunk enlisted in the U.S. Marines. Following his discharge, he doubled as a Milwaukee meat-packing specialist and a semipro football player for the West Allis (Wisconsin) Racers. Two years later, he cast his fate with the Norfolk Neptunes of the Continental Football League. There, a Rams scout spotted him. One year later, in 1972, the Oakland Raiders signed this big bald man to a contract.

Sistrunk began shaving his head long before it became fashionable. During a 1974 *Monday Night Football* telecast, an ABC cameraman shot the back of Sistrunk's head. Cool air temperatures and perspiration conspired to create "steam" that billowed from Sistrunk's alien-looking dome. ABC analyst Alex Karras couldn't resist. Modifying the team's media-guide entry listing Sistrunk's "U.S. Mars" service (U.S. Marines), he said, "There's Otis Sistrunk from the University of Mars!"

Over a seven-year NFL career, Sistrunk made a Pro Bowl and tormented quarterbacks on a weekly basis. When the 1976 Raiders beat the Minnesota Vikings in Super Bowl XI (11), Sistrunk became the first player with zero college experience to become a Super Bowl champion. Advertisers took notice of his unique alpha-male presence. In a famous Miller Lite beer spot, several Raiders discuss the brew's virtues while playing pool in a tavern. One of them eventually says, "Your turn, Otis." Sistrunk rips the table from its moorings and tilts it so all the balls drain into a corner pocket. The Raiders' opponents say, "Hey, you cheated!" In unison, Sistrunk and the Raiders reply, "So?"

After football, Sistrunk gravitated toward professional wrestling. In 1981, he and Michael Hayes won the National Wrestling Alliance Georgia Tag Team Championship. But when Sistrunk's football earnings began to dwindle, the Martian found his way back to the military, taking a job at Fort Benning in his hometown of Columbus, Georgia. That's where I made his acquaintance.

I was producing a *Where Are They Now?* segment for ESPN. After shooting Sistrunk at work on the base, I asked him to join me for dinner. He chose the restaurant. In an extremely large dining room surrounded by locals, as women and their male companions stared at Sistrunk from a distance, he leaned forward and offered me some of the most profound wisdom I've ever heard: "Bob, guys hates to admit it, but if they wants to make it with chicks, they gots to tell 'em lies!"

My mouth fell open. I sat there flabbergasted at his frankness. Finally, I asked, "Otis, would you mind if I wrote that down?" And I did, with a pen I borrowed from our waiter, on one of the restaurant's paper napkins. I stashed it away and later rediscovered it in a drawer at NFL Films, the day I packed up for retirement.

He still shaves his head, even in retirement. And why wouldn't he? Some guys prefer a look less conventional and a career path less traveled. Especially "My Favorite Martian."

Emmitt Smith *(born 1969)*

Running Back

- Dallas Cowboys (1990-2002) · Arizona Cardinals (2003-04)

One Sunday morning, October 27, 2002, I met Emmitt Smith at the Dallas Fort Worth International Airport Marriott. Together, we would ride in his car to Texas Stadium.

I sat in the passenger seat, filming Smith while he drove. I interviewed him and filmed the entire event for posterity. I don't recall the specifics of our conversation. Most likely, I allowed him to set the stage for this particular day's inevitable events; he needed just 92 yards to surpass Walter Payton's career total of 16,726 yards to become the NFL's all-time career rushing leader. It was a moment Emmitt had been working toward his entire life, his personal NFL goal.

Workers at security checkpoints and parking lot entrances wished him well. I kept checking my equipment to make sure that my exposure was right and my settings were correct—there would be no "take 2" for any of this. By the time he walked into the Cowboys' locker room, I'd already shot two roles of film. I was pretty sure I'd documented the trip fairly well.

Then, I studied my options for Smith's much-anticipated game-time entrance. I realized that the descent down the narrow stadium walkway to the stadium floor would be a jam-packed cluster. Every credentialed cameraman would want to capture the moment. So, when Smith emerged from the locker room, I fell in *behind* him. With my wide-angle lens mounted, I walked him down to the stadium porthole. A sea of cameramen moved backward down that same porthole in *front* of Emmitt, their Nikons and Sony video cameras adding a surreal historical dimension to my *tracking* sound shot. Dallas's #22 was pushing the masses. I'm still proud of my improvisation.

In the end, the Seattle Seahawks beat the Dallas Cowboys that day, 17–14. But early in the fourth quarter, Smith ran for 11 yards to surpass Payton's all-time mark. During the ensuing media mayhem, Daryl "Moose" Johnston—Smith's lead blocker for most of his career—walked into an emotional man-hug with Emmitt, close enough for my benefit. I nearly broke into tears listening to them celebrate one another. In hindsight, it was one of my most memorable days as an NFL Films cameraman.

If you've followed football through the years, you've heard alcohol-fueled loudmouths proclaim, "Hell, I could have rushed for a thousand yards behind that Cowboys line." Indeed, Dallas's offensive front during their three Super Bowl seasons (1992–95) was extremely large, nasty, and effective. At five feet nine inches, Smith was difficult to spot behind those guys. At 210 pounds and with a low center of gravity, Smith was even tougher to tackle. Trust me, he *lost* very few yards over his fifteen-year career. Unlike many big play backs, he rarely moved in reverse.

But Emmitt's most salient quality was *character*. In 1993, the defending Super Bowl champion Cowboys needed a win over the Giants in the Meadowlands on the season's final Sunday just to repeat as NFC Eastern Division champions. In the second quarter, Smith took off on a 45-yard sprint that ended with a very hard tackle. He suffered a shoulder separation on the play.

As Cowboys trainers worked to determine the degree of Smith's injury and assess his chances of return, I knew in my soul that he'd be back. When he did rejoin the offensive huddle, a hush fell over Giants Stadium. New York's chances of winning evaporated. In a performance for the ages, Emmitt handled the ball sixteen more times over the final quarters, despite an injury that would have sidelined most mortals. The Cowboys won the game, clinched the NFC East, earned a two-week bye, and secured home-field advantage on their way to back-to-back Super Bowl victories.

With all due deference to Dallas's stout offensive-line play, with acknowledgment to his fellow "Triplets" Troy Aikman and Michael Irvin, without Smith, the Dallas Cowboys would *not* have won three Super Bowls in four seasons (1992, 1993, and 1995). Their entire system was built around Smith's ability to gain yards on the ground, break initial tackle attempts, keep the team out of second-and-long situations, and minimize opponent possessions while exhausting the game clock. In fourteen Cowboys seasons, he averaged 312 carries each year. That's an insane share of the workload. Entire defenses would wither and wane before Emmitt. That's *character*.

In 2002, his final Cowboys season, I produced and directed the second season of HBO Sports's *Hard Knocks*. The Cowboys proved to be willing and cooperative subjects. Early on, I seized the opportunity to wire Emmitt at practices and interview him as often as possible. When he told me that his father was a bus driver, I asked the transportation crew chief whether Smith could drive one of the team buses from San Antonio's Alamo Dome back to the teams' Center City hotel dormitory. Without checking with Smith, I assured the driver that he knew what he was doing.

Sure enough, Emmitt performed flawlessly. We covered the occasion with multiple cameras. HBO Sports loved it. Soon thereafter, Smith took the whole transportation theme to a higher level. He invited me and my crew to fly in a private jet he'd rented to travel home from a late preseason game. Later, he lambasted me and my NFL Films colleagues for not using nearly as much footage as we should have. I told him that I didn't control the editing process, but he didn't want to hear it. He wanted to see more bang for his buck.

At some point during the early 2000s, I took a crew to a tribute for Payton, Chicago's late, great Hall of Fame running back. Smith strode to the podium, worked his way through the first few minutes of his speech, then broke into tears. I don't remember anything after that. In retrospect, Smith's words no longer mattered. When he finished his speech, Payton's oldest son, Jarrett, embraced Smith as if the Cowboys' star actually *was* his deceased father. The adoring crowd stood and applauded while wiping away tears.

Indeed, Emmitt had set out to succeed Payton as the NFL's leading rusher. Payton knew in his heart that someday, somebody would eclipse his record. Sports at all levels often produce bittersweet moments such as this, but I'd never witnessed one so powerful in person.

Jarrett couldn't have been happier about his father's successor, and I couldn't have been happier to witness this special moment in all their lives.

Like I said, *character*!

Jim Taylor *(1935–2018)*

Fullback

- Green Bay Packers (1958-66) · New Orleans Saints (1967)

I can't quite remember when or where I first read the following observation, but I *do* recall that it went something like this: "He'd trample his mother for a yard!"

Perhaps in a *Sport Magazine* article. Or maybe in the scratch-off comic area on the back of a Topps football card (circa 1962). Either way, at a very tender and impressionable age, I wanted to know more about Green Bay Packers fullback Jim Taylor, the "trampler" in question.

Taylor was Vince Lombardi's fullback during Green Bay's golden years. He put together five consecutive 1,000-yard rushing seasons (1960–64), the first NFL player to do so. In 1962, Taylor led the entire NFL in rushing yards, the *only* season from 1957 through 1965 that Cleveland all-time great Jim Brown did *not*! For his efforts, Taylor was named the league's MVP.

No other Packers running back is remotely close to Taylor's 81 career rushing touchdowns. One could argue that Lombardi developed and perfected his "Power Sweep" with Taylor's size and skill set in mind. Taylor and Paul Hornung in the Packers' backfield with three Hall of Fame blockers in front of them (center Jim Ringo, guard Jerry Kramer, and guard/tackle Forrest Gregg) dominated most of the defenses they faced in the early 1960s. Not many teams had the sideline-to-sideline pursuit capability to contain them, but the New York Giants did.

My earliest Taylor recollection dates back to the 1962 NFL Championship Game (Packers vs. Giants, on December 30). Green Bay and New York were playing on TV before more than sixty-four thousand fans in Yankee Stadium. The air temperature peaked at seventeen degrees. Gale-force winds were blowing. One sustained gust blew an NBC camera off a platform. Who knows what the wind chill measured? Frigid, even on TV!

No matter. The Packers arrived as defending NFL champions. One year earlier, Green Bay had beaten New York, 37–0, at Lambeau Field. This time, the Giants' proud defense vowed to be ready. Although I was only nine years old, I remember the adults around me admiring Taylor's toughness as Giants middle linebacker Sam Huff piled on him, play after play. Taylor and Huff seemed to be on the verge of a fistfight most of the afternoon. I wasn't sure who to root for. Late in the second quarter, Taylor burst through a hole and ran untouched through the Giants for a 7-yard touchdown—and the room exploded in cheers. Turns out my dad's side of the family felt the same way I did. In the end, Green Bay prevailed, 16–7, winning a second-consecutive NFL title. I liked Taylor, and my hometown team sucked at the time, so I went rogue.

As the decade progressed and the Steelers kept losing, I became an unabashed Packers fan. If and when Pittsburgh's CBS affiliate televised Lombardi's team, my family's old black-and-white Magnavox was tuned to KDKA Channel 2. I still get chills when I recall Ray Scott's succinct play-by-play style: "Taylor . . . behind Kramer's block . . . touchdown, Packers!" It was music to my young adoring ears.

In 1965, Green Bay beat Cleveland, 23–12, Lombardi's third NFL Championship in five seasons. In 1966, the Packers hung on to defeat Dallas for yet another NFL title. Then, in a brand-new event retroactively rebranded as Super Bowl I, Green Bay thrashed the Kansas City Chiefs, 35–10. Taylor scored the game's first-ever rushing TD on a vintage 14-yard power sweep. I leaped from my chair while my parents sat in silence. By then, they'd grown weary of my strange allegiance to this meat-packing, toilet paper–manufacturing town somewhere in northern Wisconsin.

Flash forward to the early 1980s. I was producing segments with Irv Cross for CBS Sports's *The NFL Today* called "Legends of the Game," and my upcoming subject was none other than Jim Taylor, now retired in Baton Rouge, Louisiana, the site of his college football heroics at LSU. All I remember about Irv's interview is Taylor's response when asked about Sam Huff and that 1962 NFL Championship game that I watched with my extended family during Christmas vacation. Apparently, despite the day-long beating he took, when Taylor scored the frigid game's only touchdown, he offered Huff the football with a suggestion of where he might put it. That's when I remembered Taylor's football card and that whole "trample his mother for a yard" thing. The man still had moxie.

As the afternoon progressed, I learned why Taylor (now at least fifty years old) appeared to be in peak physical condition: He'd developed an avid interest in tennis. Irv was a dedicated jogger. During camera breaks, as the two shared notes about their respective fitness regimens, I casually mentioned that I'd been playing lots of tennis myself that summer. Immediately, Taylor challenged me to a match after the interview. Can't say "no" to a man who'd "trample his mother for a yard!" So, when we wrapped, I found myself walking with my crew a safe distance behind Irv and Taylor, toting one of his extra tennis racquets. As we approached a vacant local court, I blurted out to my crew, "We'll be out of here as soon as I kick Taylor's ass."

Lombardi's fullback stopped in his tracks. He and Irv both stopped and turned in unison to face me. Apparently my voice carries. Ever want to become invisible? In the awkward quiet that ensued, I suddenly remembered Bugs Bunny once saying, "Think fast, Rabbit!" So, I mentioned the "footwork and racquet preparation" Taylor had described earlier that afternoon and said that I was looking forward to seeing them. Anything to lighten the mood!

As we prepped to play, I recalled Taylor's earlier response when Irv had asked him to recount his pithy conversation with Huff following his touchdown in the 1962 NFL Championship—something like "Why don't you shove this football where the sun doesn't shine, Mr. Huff!"

I wondered what adventures lay ahead.

Turns out, Taylor's "footwork and racquet preparation" were excellent. For a man roughly two decades my senior, he played winning tennis, outlasting me in a surprisingly long best-of-five match, 3–2. Considering the alternatives, I was *very* glad to shake hands afterward. The Hall of Fame fullback smiled, squeezed my fingers, looked me in the eye, and asked, "So what happened to that ass-kicking you promised?"

Touché! The "Trampler" and I made nice.

Duane Thomas (aka "The Sphinx") *(born 1947)* 🏆

Running Back

- Dallas Cowboys (1970-71, 1976) · San Diego Chargers (1972)
- Washington Commanders (1973-74) · The Hawaiians (1975)
- British Columbia Lions (1977) · Green Bay Packers (1979)

> Of all sad words of tongue or pen, the saddest are these:
> "It might have been."
> —John Greenleaf Whittier

Born and raised in Dallas, Texas, Duane Thomas played college football at West Texas State University. The Cowboys selected him with the twenty-third overall pick in the 1970 NFL Draft. In his rookie season, Thomas led the team in rushing and earned NFL Rookie of the Year honors. The Cowboys advanced to Super Bowl V (5) to play the Baltimore Colts. In that game, often called the Blunder Bowl, the two teams combined for 6 interceptions and 5 lost fumbles. In the end, Baltimore's Jim O'Brien kicked a field goal as time expired. The Colts prevailed, 16–13.

The most critical of the game's 11 turnovers was a Thomas fumble. It happened in the third quarter at the Baltimore 1-yard line. A Cowboys touchdown there would have given Dallas a hard-earned lead. The rookie runner was crushed. On the bench, Thomas lamented to teammates, "I lost the game for us." Perhaps that's when "the Great Cosmos" began to close in.

In an article written by Gary Cartwright for *Texas Monthly* titled "The Lonely Blues of Duane Thomas" (February 1973), Thomas describes "the Great Cosmos" thusly: "It's a trap White people pull on Black people. Once you get caught . . . you never get out." Thomas's fumble left him vulnerable to the predictable but relentless fury of a largely White media machine that held him responsible. After Super Bowl V, Thomas disappeared for six months. When he resurfaced, he confronted a *Dallas Times Herald* writer: "Hey, I read that fumble was the play that lost the game. I didn't know that I was the one who was expected to win it." Adding to his woes was Dallas's refusal to renegotiate his three-year-long rookie contract. As "the Great Cosmos" foretold: "Once you get caught . . . you never get out."

So began Thomas's period of total silence, during which he became "the Sphinx." For months, he refused interviews, ignored his teammates, and sat mute at team meetings, once turning his chair toward the wall rather than answer a question. In August 1971, the frustrated Cowboys tried to trade Thomas to the New England Patriots. NFL commissioner Pete Rozelle voided the deal, so Thomas returned to Dallas for the 1971 season and played at an All-Pro level. He led the league in rushing touchdowns, and Dallas advanced to Super Bowl VI (6). Against Don Shula's youthful Miami Dolphins, Thomas rushed for 95 yards and scored a key touchdown. The Cowboys won the game, 24–3, Dallas's first Super Bowl victory. By nearly all accounts, Thomas was the consensus choice for the game's Most Valuable Player award. But staff at *Sport Magazine* (the award's presenter) questioned how Thomas might behave at the banquet ceremony in New York. To cover their asses, they announced Roger Staubach as the winner.

The epic event that football fans remember about this game occurred during the postgame locker-room interviews. While the great Jim Brown stood behind Thomas, offering moral support, CBS analyst Tom Brookshier asked, "Duane, you do things with speed, but you never hurry . . . a lot like the great Jim Brown. . . . You never hurry into a hole, you take your time, make a spin, yet you still outrun people. Are you that fast, are you that quick, would you say?" I felt butterflies in my stomach as I awaited Thomas's response, his first words in months.

"Evidently," said the Sphinx.

Flash forward a decade or so. Sometime in the mid-1980s, Steve Sabol asked me to do NFL Films's first-ever interview with Thomas. It was scheduled to take place in a Dallas hotel during the off-season. This time, Thomas showed up with former AFL star Abner Haynes, who grew up in the same Dallas ghetto as Duane. After some awkward handshakes and introductions, Thomas sat down in front of me, and I asked my first question. He talked nonstop for eleven minutes—I know this because a four-hundred-foot roll of film rolling at sound speed through a 16mm camera runs just over eleven minutes. He did the same thing with our second roll. Two problems: (1) He didn't address either question and (2) I couldn't understand anything he was saying. No exaggeration—Thomas's interview was stream-of-consciousness rambling, long-winded nonsense. He was not concerned with being understood. As Cartwright wrote, "You couldn't *interview* Thomas, but you could *talk* with him." I turned toward Haynes for help. He shrugged his shoulders.

This scenario went on for nearly three hours. I kept returning to the questions Steve had identified as the most important. I kept pressing, Thomas kept talking, and nothing emerged that could be distilled from the cosmic level it came from. When I called the office to report the results, the best I could say was "He certainly didn't hold back." My final question was a setup. In postproduction, NFL Films dubbed Steve Sabol's voice over my own. In that segment, we hear Sabol ask Thomas, "Would it be safe to say that Duane Thomas let his performance speak for itself?"

On cue, Thomas leans forward in his chair, then replies, "Evidently."

Here's my hack analysis: Duane Thomas believed that he'd given the Cowboys far more value than his rookie contract had paid him. Although he felt crippling guilt over his Super Bowl V (5) fumble, he still equated respect with a new contract and more money. Factor in Jim Brown's presence, and you've got the makings of racial protest. Enter "the Great Cosmos," "a trap White people pull on Black people." During his "silent period," he could maintain control over the situation. But to what end? Money? Respect? Something more cosmic? I don't think that Thomas ever knew or decided. Critics attributed his recalcitrance, disrespect, and descent to drugs, mental illness, whatever—and his descent came quickly. "The Great Cosmos" kept turning. Traded by the Cowboys to the Chargers in August 1972, Thomas sat out the entire season. In Washington (1973–74), he totaled 442 rushing yards over two years. Then came stints with the Hawaiians in the short-lived World Football League (1975), a return to Dallas (1976), a visit with the British Columbia Lions in the Canadian Football League (1977), and a final misfire in Green Bay (1979).

Circa 2010, Thomas appeared in an episode of the NFL Films series *America's Game*, recalling Super Bowl VI. Narrator Martin Sheen detailed "the season-long soap opera" Thomas had cultivated, referring to him as a "crisis waiting to happen."

Hall of Fame defensive tackle Bob Lilly said simply, "I just can't tell people enough how good he was. . . . I hated to see a person waste a Hall of Fame career. . . . I expected [him] to be the next Jim Brown." So did everybody.

As Whittier wrote, "Of all sad words of tongue or pen, the saddest are these: 'It might have been.'"

Johnny Unitas *(1933–2002)*

Quarterback

- Pittsburgh Steelers (1955) · Baltimore Colts (1956-72)
- San Diego Chargers (1973)

If you're my age (over seventy) and you collected Topps NFL football cards as a kid, you know that Johnny Unitas's card bore the number *1*. As a kid, I assumed that it was the bubblegum company's rating of Johnny U's NFL standing, but then I noticed that his Baltimore Colts teammate Alan Ameche's card was number *2*. The rest of the Colts continued on from *3*. The Topps Cards *Checklist* confirmed all this.

But in the early 1960s, my first theory could have been right. Sure, Jim Brown was active, as were Paul Hornung, Y. A. Tittle, Frank Gifford, and dozens of other future Hall of Famers. But Unitas's card seemed special. To find it while fanning through the package meant that a kid's collection suddenly had status. And I swear, Topps issued fewer Unitas and Brown cards than those of all the lesser-known players, although I have no actual evidence of conspiracy.

Everybody who knows NFL history knows his story. Selected by the Pittsburgh Steelers—his hometown team—in the ninth round of the 1955 NFL Draft, Unitas was cut during summer camp. So, he worked a construction job to support his family while playing semipro football with the Bloomfield Rams. The Rams paid him a whopping $6 per game.

In 1956, the Baltimore Colts invited him for a tryout, much to the dismay of Paul Brown, the Hall of Fame coach of the Cleveland Browns, who'd just lost Otto Graham to retirement and was turning over rocks looking for a replacement. Somehow, Unitas made the Colts' final roster. Two weeks into the regular season, Baltimore's starting quarterback, George Shaw, was injured, and Unitas took the field. His first pro pass was intercepted by the Chicago Bears and returned for a touchdown. His next offensive snap resulted in a fumble that the Bears recovered. But Unitas persevered, leading the hapless Colts to wins over the Green Bay Packers and Paul Brown's Cleveland Browns.

In 1957, Unitas settled into the starting quarterback role. His 2,550 passing yards and 24 touchdown passes were both NFL highs. A future Hall of Fame pass catcher named Raymond Berry led the NFL in receiving yards. And the Colts' 7–5 record was the best in the team's young history. By 1958, Unitas and Berry's daily, post-practice pass-and-catch drills had given them exceptional game-day chemistry. Their timing and execution were the envy of the NFL. Former Rookie of the Year (1956) and future Hall of Famer Lenny Moore was developing into one of the most versatile running backs in the sport. And the Colts' defense was filling holes and growing teeth.

With Unitas at the helm, the Colts won the NFL's Western Division, then traveled to New York to play the Giants for the NFL Championship. League historians have nicknamed this contest "the Greatest Game Ever Played." Seventeen participants from this game (coaches and players) are now enshrined in the Hall of Fame. It took place during Christmas break, and although it was blacked out in New York, a record forty-five million people watched the game on TV. Unitas executed a perfect two-minute drill to bring on sudden-death overtime, a new wrinkle just implemented.

Unitas drove the Colts the length of the field before Ameche ran them to a 23–17 win. It remains a contest rich in drama, history, and mystique.

In the early 1980s, I traveled to Unitas's suburban Baltimore home to ask him all about it. Just making this interview happen was an achievement. In the early 1980s, Unitas and NFL Films were feuding over his image rights. Like many retired players from earlier eras, Unitas wanted to be compensated when NFL Films used his image in shows and segments. The NFL, of which NFL Films is an independent subsidiary, refused to venture there. Fortunately, our talent coordinator mentioned that the subject of my segment was Unitas's friend and former teammate Raymond Berry. So, Unitas relented, and a date was set.

Sitting down with Johnny U to discuss Berry was one of the highlights of my first decade with NFL Films. His recall of the 1958 championship game was perfect. He walked me through every meaningful moment in both the Colts' two-minute drive that set up the game-tying field goal, then the game-winning overtime possession that won it. He offered particular insights on Berry's five catches during those two drives, things that only a gutsy quarterback and his favorite pass catcher would know about. I felt privileged to be in Unitas's presence.

As we spoke, I could tell that he liked me. I mentioned my working-class upbringing in Pittsburgh, always a favorite with a fellow Steel City resident, and I mentioned that my mother hailed from southeastern Europe, knowing that Unitas's parents had migrated from Lithuania in Europe's Baltic region. And, of course, I mentioned my delight when I acquired his Topps football card.

By the interview's end, I'd made up my mind to do something I'd done only two other times while working for NFL Films. Twice, I'd chased former athletes through airports for autographs: once in Detroit for hockey Hall of Famer Gordie Howe's and the other in Atlanta for Muhammad Ali's. The day I interviewed Unitas, I was a thirty-plus-year-old married man.

"John, would it be possible to get your autograph?" I asked. "Certainly, Bob," said Unitas.

At that point, I heard, "Me, too." And "Me as well." And "I'll take one." My camera operator was in his fifties. My soundman was approaching fifty. The assistant cameraman was forty-five-plus. The room erupted in relieved laughter. Unitas pulled out production stills and autographed each one per our personal requests. My son, Daniel, gets mine when I'm cremated—and not a moment before.

After the Colts abandoned Baltimore and fled to Indianapolis, Unitas boycotted most Colts events forever. He asked the Pro Football Hall of Fame to remove his display unless it referred to him as a "Baltimore Colt." (To date, the hall has not complied.) Unitas donated his collection of Colts memorabilia to the Babe Ruth Museum in Baltimore. Only after the Cleveland Browns left Lake Erie, moved to Maryland, then changed their name to the Baltimore Ravens did Unitas attend a pro football game in his adopted city. He would stand stoically at the Ravens' 30-yard line and allow cameramen to shoot his profile. The one and only time I did swear Unitas winked at me. Although I was then approaching fifty, as giddy.

I thought about his football card. I remembered watching "the Greatest Game Ever Played" on my family's old black-and-white Magnavox during Christmas break. Topps got it right. Johnny U was #1.

Norm Van Brocklin *(1926–83)*

Quarterback

- Los Angeles Rams (1949-57) · Philadelphia Eagles (1958-60)

Head Coach

- Minnesota Vikings (1961-66) · Atlanta Falcons (1968-74)

In June 1975, as part of my initial NFL Films training, the company made me screen selected films and feature shorts. One mic'd-up special made a lasting impression: Atlanta Falcons head coach Norm Van Brocklin wired for sound in a game played on October 13, 1968.

Seems that the Dutchman (Van Brocklin's nickname) paced NFL sidelines, chain-smoking cigarettes while admonishing his players' shortcomings. My most vivid recollection involved running back Harmon Wages, a free spirit who years later would describe his ex-girlfriend-turned-network-show-host Deborah Norville as "Darth Vader's sister." The sound bite: "You don't go back into the game until I tell you to . . . understand, Harmon?" By now, coach and player were standing nose to nose on the sideline. "You're in the big leagues now . . . you understand? So, let's start growing up."

Coaches *do* speak like this to their players. My high school coach dressed me down all the time, but rarely in full view of the entire team during a game, accompanied by physical intimidation. Turns out that

Van Brocklin was famously hot-tempered. He also was a Hall of Fame quarterback with two NFL championships on his résumé. In 1950, he earned "co-starter" status on the Los Angeles Rams alongside future Hall of Fame passer Bob Waterfield. The Rams scored an astounding 466 points in a twelve-game schedule, averaging 38.8 points per game—*still* the all-time NFL single-season points-per-game record. Waterfield and Van Brocklin ranked first and second in passer ratings.

The following season, on October 28, 1951, in a game against the New York Yanks that Waterfield missed due to injury, Van Brocklin passed for 554 yards. Seven decades later, *that* NFL single-game record for passing yardage also still stands. In that year's NFL Championship against the Cleveland Browns, Van Brocklin's 73-yard touchdown pass to Tom Fears sealed a 24–17 Rams victory. In 1960, Van Brocklin's final pro season and his third as Philadelphia's starting quarterback, he led the Eagles to a 17–13 win over the Green Bay Packers. For the record, this was the one and only playoff loss on Vince Lombardi's Hall of Fame coaching résumé.

So, in 1981, when Van Brocklin's name appeared on my research list for a CBS Sports "Legends of the Game" feature, I was excited about meeting him in person. On the other hand, I was concerned how the segment might turn out. Without a doubt, Van Brocklin was an exceptional football player. But as a head coach for thirteen seasons with two different NFL teams, he was pretty much an abject failure: three winning seasons with *zero* postseason appearances, truly one of the *worst* NFL head-coaching performances on record!

I was happy to learn that Jack Whitaker would be my talent. The Philadelphia native, whose TV career had blossomed at the city's CBS affiliate, WCAU, actually knew Van Brocklin. I welcomed his help.

So, off we went to a pecan farm in Social Circle, Georgia, a historic crossroads community east of Atlanta. We did the interview outside to take advantage of the rural backdrop. Comfortable with Whitaker, surrounded by his home's bucolic charm, Van Brocklin enjoyed recounting his exploits with the high-scoring Rams. He and Whitaker shared their reminiscences about the 1960 Eagles. But when discussing his coaching career, he really didn't have many good things to say about himself or his players. And as Whitaker methodically pushed through my list of questions, Van Brocklin's mood darkened noticeably. Nevertheless, he addressed every last one of them.

When we finished the interview, my veteran talent set out to select the perfect backdrop for his stand-up, and Van Brocklin fixed his eagle-eyed gaze on me.

"So, what's your role in all this?"

I explained that I would clip the interview, assemble selections in the order in which I intended to use them, intercut game action, integrate and edit music, then, finally, write Whitaker's narration before the segment entered final postproduction.

"Ever play football, Bob?" Van Brocklin wondered.

When I admitted to being a high school quarterback, his entire manner became far more accepting. I described the limited offense we ran and the handful of play-action passes that dominated our repertoire.

"We invented most of that stuff in Los Angeles. And I bet your receivers weren't as good as mine," he remarked.

No, Norm, I didn't have Hall of Famers Tom Fears and Elroy "Crazylegs" Hirsch in my huddle. When we left, Van Brocklin gave each of us our very own bag of pecans. At the airport, while we all toasted our interviewee, Whitaker shared his favorite stories, such as the time the Falcons lost a game on a field goal kicked by a soccer-style kicker born outside the United States. "They oughta change the goddamn immigration laws in this country," Whitaker quoted Van Brocklin as saying, referencing the foreign-born soccer-stylists who were showing up on NFL teams in the mid-1960s.

Little did we know that the cantankerous two-team NFL champion would die of a heart attack at the age of fifty-seven, less than a year later, which brings me to Whitaker's favorite Van Brocklin story—and mine, too, now.

As his health declined and Norm needed brain surgery to remove a tumor, the ever-irascible Van Brocklin offered up the perfect ex post facto explanation: "It [actually] was a brain transplant. They gave me a sportswriter's brain to make sure I got one that hadn't been used." The Dutchman. A true original.

Dick Vermeil *(born 1936)*

Head Coach

- Philadelphia Eagles (1976–82) · St. Louis Rams (1997–99)
- Kansas City Chiefs (2001–05)

By his own admission, Dick Vermeil was a hard-working, emotional man. In 1975, his UCLA Bruins earned a trip to the Rose Bowl. There, they upset the undefeated Ohio State Buckeyes to win the National Championship, but not before UCLA players threatened to strike over Vermeil's two-a-day practice schedule in preparation for the game, a harbinger of things to come.

Soon thereafter, Philadelphia hired Vermeil to work his magic with the Eagles. Owner Leonard Tose's team hadn't appeared in the NFL postseason for nearly two decades. Vermeil posted a sign above the locker room door that read "Nobody ever drowned in sweat." Then, he changed the culture of a losing organization by working them harder than they'd ever worked before. By his third season, the Eagles had qualified for the playoffs, due in no small measure to the famous "Miracle at the Meadowlands" of November 19, 1978: a fumble recovery returned for a touchdown by Herman Edwards that beat the NY Giants on the game's final play. The Giants could have won had they just snapped the ball, then fallen on it. Vermeil attributed the victory to his team's new work ethic.

On the season's final Sunday, the Eagles beat the Giants again, 20–3, to clinch an NFC Wild Card berth. In the postgame locker room, as players celebrated around him, Vermeil walked into the embrace of team owner Tose. Sobbing with joy, Vermeil (accidentally) turned toward Steve Sabol's sound camera, then said, "That one's for you, Boss. That one's for you." An instant NFL Films classic, one of the most emotional images the studio ever recorded—especially after our mixers edited out Tose's on-camera response, something like "We showed those c***-s*****s."

Two years later, in 1980, Vermeil led the Eagles to their first conference championship since 1960 and advanced to Super Bowl XV (15). Along the way, he proudly wore his joy and emotions on his sleeve. A few folks at NFL Films wondered whether he might crack. I personally witnessed one of his locker-room outpourings. I observed the coach's "open-heart" policy that engendered quivering lips and moist eyes all around. I realized that this guy was on to something. Hard work was not just about toughness—sometimes it was about *tough love.*

Then came the Super Bowl. Eagles linebacker John Bunting later said, "Our week of practice was brutal. We basically went back to training camp." During the game, Vermeil was mic'd-up. "We're all looking a little bit tight. . . . We look exhausted. . . . It's because of nerves. We need to relax a little bit," he lamented. Oakland shellacked the Eagles, 27–10. Two years later, at age forty-six, Vermeil bade Philadelphia a tearful farewell: "Right now, I'm gonna take my own advice and step down out of coaching. . . . I'm emotionally burned out. . . . I'm my own worst enemy. . . . I'm far too intense. . . . I don't mean I'm about to go off my rocker, but I'm burned out." So ended Vermeil's first incarnation as an NFL head coach.

For the next fourteen years, he worked as a game analyst, first for CBS (1983–87), then for ABC (1988–96). He turned down at least one head-coaching offer every year. But when the chance to resurrect the struggling St. Louis Rams came along, Dick could not resist, despite some pressing concerns: Could a sixty-year-old guy who'd been away from the game for a couple of generations still coach? Would he make the same mistakes? Would "all work and no play" make the Rams dull boys?

I caught up with Vermeil at his 1998 Rams training camp. We wired him, then followed him around during morning practice. We could barely keep up. Energy was never Vermeil's issue. The fact is, his lengthy padded practices were hard on his players and production crews. And at each of his coaching stops, Vermeil worked no sudden miracles. In fact, in Vermeil's first two years, the St. Louis Rams floundered. As reserve quarterback Kurt Warner noted in the NFL Films *America's Game* series, "It got ugly in '98. We called a players-only meeting. We were going to have a coup. Guys were saying, 'We're not going out to practice.'"

But the Rams stayed the course. They brought back former assistant Mike Martz to run the offense. They acquired quarterback Trent Green and running back Marshall Faulk in trades. They drafted wide receiver and future Hall of Famer Torry Holt, who won 1999 NFL Rookie of the Year honors. And they allowed veteran players to air their grievances. Vermeil, the toughest of taskmasters, listened, acknowledged, and adapted. Even when Green suffered a season-ending knee injury in the preseason that caused Vermeil to tear up at a news conference, he maintained his razor focus on the team's future.

"You get emotional, it hurts," he said. "But we are not going to use Trent Green as an excuse for losing. We're gonna rally around Kurt Warner, and we'll play good football." Talk about a classic understatement. Warner played MVP football as "the Greatest Show on Turf" was born. The Rams finished the season 13–3, then fought their way to Super Bowl XXXIV (34). Leading by 7 points with one play left, Rams linebacker Mike Jones tackled Titans receiver Kevin Dyson 1 yard short of the end zone. The Rams won, 23–16. Vermeil's "tough-love" approach was vindicated. As usual, Vermeil was mic'd up during the game.

"That's it, we won it, WOO HOO! That's the game, it's over!" No tears of joy this time, just pure, unadulterated bliss. Soon, Vermeil's two young grandchildren were riding his shoulders while his wireless microphone captured the magic: "We won the Super Bowl. . . . Didn't we win the Super Bowl?" he asked the little tykes rhetorically. "Give 'em a thumbs-up!" His grandkids acknowledged our cameras. Later that week, Vermeil retired again.

In 2001, the Kansas City Chiefs came calling, luring Vermeil into his third NFL head-coaching job. And again, the pundits wondered out loud whether Vermeil would be up to the challenge. By 2003, the Chiefs had won their first nine games. Vermeil appeared poised to become the first and *only* coach in league history to take three different teams to Super Bowls—but it didn't happen. In 2005, Vermeil announced his retirement plans in advance of the season. In Vermeil's final NFL game, NFL Films wired him one last time to capture his emotions. He did not disappoint.

"It's alright to cry," Vermeil told wide receiver Dante Hall as they hugged and sobbed during pregame warm-up. Later, Hall told NFL Films, "I felt like I was losing my dad all over again."

In the end, Vermeil's strategy combining hard work and tough love won hearts and championships.

Bill Walsh *(1931–2007)*

Head Coach

- San Francisco 49ers (1979-88)

One of the unlikeliest developments of my NFL Films career was becoming a personal friend of Hall of Fame head coach Bill Walsh—on a first-name basis, no less. It's exciting to know a genius, especially when they hate being called such. But when he was bothered by a problem that needed solving, you could tell that his mind was on a different level.

I barely knew Walsh before he became the head coach of the San Francisco 49ers in 1979. A former high school running back, Walsh transitioned to quarterback at his first college (San Mateo), then tight end and defensive end at his second (San José State). He also found time to win a Golden Gloves championship as an intercollegiate boxer. Like many aspiring coaches before him, Walsh interned under Paul Brown in Cincinnati. It was there that he learned a harsh lesson.

In 1970, when Cincinnati's strong-armed passer Greg Cook was lost for the season due to injury, Brown asked Walsh to create plays better suited for Cook's replacement: Virgil Carter. Although he was a smart man and a capable passer, Carter lacked the raw arm strength of his predecessor, so Walsh developed pass drops and quick-release throws to allow Carter to spread passes "horizontally" to receivers running free into open areas outside the hash marks rather than downfield. After a 1–5 start to their season, Carter mastered Walsh's scheme, then led the Bengals to seven consecutive wins and a playoff berth. And the "West Coast Offense" (WCO) was born.

In 1972, Ken Anderson replaced Carter as the Bengals' starting quarterback. Anderson's superior arm strength allowed Walsh to expand and perfect his offensive designs. Bengals pass catchers always seemed wide open, and Anderson's accuracy was uncanny. But Pittsburgh stood in the way of Cincinnati's ultimate success. So, when Brown announced his retirement following the 1975 season, Walsh believed that he'd earned the head-coaching job and the chance to challenge the Steelers' divisional dominance. However, in a calculated moment of short-sightedness, Brown (also the Bengals' owner) appointed Bill "Tiger" Johnson to succeed him. Walsh left the team. Years later, in a 2006 interview, Walsh said that Brown "worked against [his] candidacy" to be an NFL head coach. Despite Walsh's college boxing success, Brown said that he wasn't "tough enough" and "couldn't handle the highs and lows of the position."

Fortunately, Eddie DeBartolo Jr. hired Walsh to resurrect the floundering San Francisco 49ers. It didn't take long. In the third round of the 1979 draft, Walsh selected Notre Dame quarterback Joe Montana. In 1980, Walsh demoted starter Steve DeBerg, saying, "He plays just well enough to get you beat." By 1981, Montana was flourishing in Walsh's system, and San Francisco had earned a spot in the NFC Championship Game opposite Dallas. Just prior to the 49ers' game-winning play, an NFL Films soundman captured Walsh telling Montana, "If you don't get what you want, you just simply throw the ball away. . . . Not there, away it goes." Instead, Montana rolled right, then tossed up a historic touchdown pass to Dwight Clark that only Clark could reach, now known simply as "the Catch." An NFL dynasty was born. Fittingly, Walsh's team beat Brown's Bengals in Super Bowl XVI (16), 26–21. In Super Bowl XXIII (23), the 49ers beat the Bengals again, this time on a 91-yard, last-minute drive. By now, the man Brown had described as "not tough enough" was being hailed as a *football genius*, a term Walsh thoroughly disliked.

In 1995, I interviewed Walsh for an NBC segment detailing that historic drive. I walked Walsh through every play call and result, a possession that started on the 49ers' 9-yard line with just 3:18 left in the game and San Francisco trailing, 16–13. In a prelude, Walsh reminded me several times (paraphrasing), "We only needed a field goal to tie the score, so not until Jerry Rice's big 27-yard catch and run into their red zone did

I start thinking about winning the game." By the time he described Montana's 10-yard game-winning pass to John Taylor, Bill and I had bonded.

In the 49ers' postgame locker room, Brent Musburger asked Walsh whether he'd coached his final NFL game. Walsh fell into his son Craig's arms and broke into tears. One of my NFL Films colleagues captured the moment for posterity. Could he have won more Lombardi Trophies? His successor, George Seifert, won two with the team Walsh left behind. Not a bad legacy for "an offensive system born out of necessity in Cincinnati," as Walsh remarked to me when we finished our interview.

Two years later, in 1997, Green Bay Packers quarterback Brett Favre won his third-consecutive NFL Most Valuable Player award. But on September 28, on the road in Detroit, Favre threw three interceptions in a 26–15 Packers loss to the Lions. On one of them, Favre threw the ball while *kneeling* on the turf. That one riled the architect of the WCO to no end.

The next morning, my NFL Films office phone rang. At first, I thought that somebody was pranking me, but Walsh's voice was unmistakable, and his mission soon became quite clear. He described Favre's botched pass attempt, lamented the sad state of NFL quarterbacking, then told me about a project he wanted to do to teach young players "the right way to play the position." Finally, he asked *me* as an ex–high school quarterback whether I wanted to be involved. Are you kidding me, Coach? So, I walked down the hall to Steve Sabol's office.

"Why did Bill Walsh call *you*?" Steve wanted to know. I could tell that my boss was confused and a little bit offended. "Because we're football friends, Steve!" I answered succinctly and politely.

In retirement, I discovered a seven-part series on YouTube titled *Quarterbacking by Bill Walsh*. It features Walsh working with Montana and former 49ers teammates to demonstrate proper passing-game technique. I was not part of the production process, nor do I know who paid for it all. But I know how and why the idea was hatched, and I've screened all the episodes. They contain everything an aspiring quarterback needs to know to be successful at any level of the game. They speak volumes about Walsh's football knowledge and his undying attention to the time-honored craft of coaching. It still amazes me that Brown let him walk away.

For those of you who want to learn about offensive football and coaching but don't want to read an ancient graduate thesis or Walsh's five-hundred-page book, check out these videos. My kudos to whoever produced them. They capture an amazing mentor and his colleagues at their professorial best.

He hated this term, but the late Bill Walsh was truly a one-of-a-kind *football genius*—and a pretty damned tough guy to boot.

David Wilcox *(born 1942)*

Left Outside Linebacker

- San Francisco 49ers (1964–74)

On July 29, 2000, San Francisco 49ers all-time great Dave Wilcox was inducted into the Pro Football Hall of Fame. I don't recall which project I was working on, but I was there, and I must have had a press credential, because I was standing next to the main podium for the ceremony. When Wilcox rose to make his speech, he saw me and smiled broadly. His recognition reminded me of what really matters. I never felt more gratified in my professional life.

In the 1960s, NFL game telecasts weren't as readily available as today. The NFL and the AFL had yet to merge. By the mid-1960s, CBS Sports was paying the NFL $18.8 million for the rights to its schedule of games. NBC Sports paid a totally different number for its AFL package. To extend its football day, CBS began televising home games of the NFL's two California teams (Rams and 49ers) beginning at 4:00 P.M. Eastern (1:00 P.M. Pacific)—*nationally*! Their location crews were already in place, so why not? Pro football was becoming America's new national pastime—and CBS was cashing in.

Thus began the CBS doubleheader, giving East Coast viewers weekly exposure to West Coast teams and players. That's when I started to notice a truly dominant outside linebacker on some very mediocre San Francisco teams by the name of Dave Wilcox. He was a defensive diamond in the rough, playing for a franchise that produced four winning seasons over the entire decade. A seven-time Pro Bowl selection known to his teammates as "the Intimidator," Wilcox was lighting it up every week for an also-ran.

Years later, NFL Films producers needed 49ers segment ideas for their weekly ESPN Monday night pregame package. So, I set myself up to visit Wilcox's Oregon farm. Why not? I'd watched him derail Vince Lombardi's power sweep, toss aside tight ends who tried to block him, and stuff the toughest ball carriers of his generation. Eager to make certain that I was remembering these events correctly, I did exhaustive research of Wilcox in our film vault. My study confirmed my suspicions:

He played outside linebacker as well as anybody ever did, with Lawrence Taylor and Bobby Bell being the only two possible exceptions.

On a summer day in the late 1990s, I took a crew to Willamette, Oregon. Wilcox met me with a firm handshake and a cool drink. His log cabin, which he built himself, stood on a huge working farm where he harvested seeds for planting crops and sod for residential lawns. He and his wife, Merle, were living the post-NFL good life. I interviewed him outside on his deck and asked about specific plays from specific games: a one-on-one hit on fullback Larry Csonka on opening day in 1973, his literal ass-kicking of Chiefs wide receiver Otis Taylor on *Monday Night Football* in 1971. "It was our first Monday night game, and we didn't know how to act," he interjected. Wilcox quickly realized that I knew his body of work. Finally, I asked him the big question: "Do you think you belong in the Pro Football Hall of Fame?"

Wilcox composed his thoughts carefully before he spoke: "I did everything anybody ever asked me to do on a football field. And so far as I can tell, I did it pretty well. So, yes. I do!" That's all I needed to hear. Over the next few months, I questioned Wilcox's contemporaries:

Hall of Fame tight end Mike Ditka: "If he got his hands on you, he was unblockable."

Hall of Fame Cowboys head coach Tom Landry: "We knew we just couldn't operate our offense on his side of the field."

But the most telling testimony came from Wilcox's teammate Jimmy Johnson, the cornerback who played behind him on the left side of San Francisco's defense: "Even when the Packers ran their power sweep, I knew I could stay in coverage because nobody could turn Dave's corner."

I packaged these sound bites and more into the segment I produced for ESPN's *Monday Night Football* pregame show. But then, I went one step further: I made VHS copies of my Wilcox career retrospective and sent them to members of the Hall of Fame's voting committee. Some objected to my obvious motives. One called me to complain that NFL Films had no right to campaign for player nominations. I told him that the segment had aired nationally, so it was already public information. When he kept complaining, I hung up on him. Most digested the material for future reference.

Two writers, *Sports Illustrated*'s Paul Zimmerman and Peter King, took me quite seriously. Not coincidentally, Zimmerman had championed Johnson's candidacy for the hall, thus exposing him to Johnson's high regard for his teammate. Johnson, quite arguably the best cover corner of all time, was inducted in 1994. King had endured my "Wilcox-belongs-in-the-hall" arguments for years.

I've heard from people privy to the backroom discussions on how the Hall of Fame's "Senior Nominations" process works (for players who've been inactive for at least twenty years). Naturally, politics plays a big part, including such tactics as "I voted for your guy last year, so now I'm calling in the marker." I have it from reliable sources that an old-school AFL writer who wanted Buffalo Bills offensive guard Billy Shaw in the hall is the reason Wilcox didn't make it in 1999. Shaw holds the distinction of being the only player with no actual NFL experience to be inducted (he retired before the league merger). He was a great player, so more power to him.

My guy was elected one year later.

The late Steve Sabol was present at a 2000 Hall of Fame function where members screen NFL Films segments on new inductees. He told me the next day that Wilcox's segment generated the most response in the room *by far*—and Joe Montana was part of this class!

On induction day, I was just happy to be there, standing near the podium, watching Wilcox join an elite fraternity. I thought back to those CBS doubleheaders and Wilcox kicking ass. Almost on cue, Wilcox turned to smile at me. In his final acknowledgments, he thanked Zimmerman and King from *Sports Illustrated* "and Bob Angelo from NFL Films." I felt honored. He would have made the hall without my campaigning eventually. I just helped speed up the process—one of my proudest professional moments!

Sam Wyche *(1945–2020)*

Quarterback

- Cincinnati Bengals (1968-70) · Washington Commanders (1971-73)
- Detroit Lions (1974) · St. Louis Cardinals and Buffalo Bills (1976)

Head Coach

- Cincinnati Bengals (1984-91) · Tampa Bay Buccaneers (1992-95)

On a Sunday morning in the late 1980s, I met Coach Sam Wyche in the bowels of Cincinnati's Riverfront Stadium. He smiled when he saw me approaching. I said, "Sam, would it be OK if we . . . ?" I don't remember what Steve Sabol told me to ask him. Wyche pondered my question for a few moments, then said, "Sure, tell Steve that'll be fine." Then, he headed toward his locker room.

"So, you're on a first-name basis now?" my runner asked. I suddenly realized that I'd called Coach Wyche "Sam." In pro football circles, *Coach* is the default term of respect, but Wyche seemed not the least bit offended. Perhaps informality was his greatest innovation.

His history with NFL Films dated back to his playing days. During the 1972 NFC Championship Game (Dallas Cowboys at Washington, December 31, 1972), an NFL Films sound crew captured Wyche on the Washington sideline, hollering, "Die you dogs, die! . . . Die you yellow dogs!" After a Dallas receiver got flipped by a Washington defender, Wyche seemed delighted: "YEAH, he died! Wooo!" Washington went on to defeat Dallas, 26–3, to advance to Super Bowl VII (7). Billy Kilmer quarterbacked the "Over the Hill Gang" that day. Wyche was strictly a backup. In his first four NFL seasons, Wyche threw 220 passes. In his final four seasons, he threw just 2! As Wyche noted in one of his entertaining interviews, "I was the highest-paid player per minute of playing time in the history of the league . . . mainly because I never played."

But former Bengals assistant coach Bill Walsh admired Wyche's grasp of the quarterback position. (Walsh coached the Bengals' offense, while Wyche was a backup quarterback.) In 1979, Walsh hired Wyche to direct the 49ers' passing game and help develop rookie quarterback Joe Montana. By 1981, Montana had mastered the "West Coast Offense." History will remember the system as Walsh's creation, but Wyche was a major contributor. In Super Bowl XVI (16), the 49ers defeated the Cincinnati Bengals, 26–21, the first of four Lombardi Trophies they would win in the 1980s. In 1984, however, Wyche left Walsh to go coach the Bengals.

In his debut season, Wyche continued innovating. To limit defensive substitutions, Wyche assembled his entire offense around him on the sidelines before dispatching eleven of them directly to the line of scrimmage. The NFL objected. So, Wyche invented the "Sugar Huddle": eleven players or more assembled near the line of scrimmage. Bengals quarterbacks would call plays and then dismiss their extra personnel. When defensive teams got caught substituting, flags would fly, and referees would announce, "Defense, too many men on the field." Again, the league intervened.

By then, somebody in Pittsburgh had dubbed the coach "Wicky Wacky Wyche." But gridiron genius is not easily deterred. By 1985, Boomer Esiason had taken over as Cincy's quarterback. Esiason's poise at the line of scrimmage allowed Wyche to implement his trademark innovation: the "No-Huddle Offense." Before Wyche, teams abandoned huddles only during two-minute drills. By 1986, Cincinnati was lining up without huddling half the time. The Bengals won ten games that season. In 1987, a players' strike nearly cost Wyche his job. The Bengals' replacements floundered to a 4–11 finish, and Wyche offered NFL Films this candid confession: "I thought there was a pretty good chance they'd fire me. . . . I made jokes early on . . . [that] I was on one of those seven-day renewable contracts. . . . If we didn't make enough first downs, they would make a change."

But in 1988, Wyche's "No-Huddle Offense" reached full bloom. With Bruce Coslet calling plays, Esiason won the NFL's Most Valuable Player Award, and the Bengals finished the season 12–4. For their Week 2 game in Philadelphia—in an unprecedented display of cooperation and trust—Wyche allowed NFL Films to document his entire offensive operation. We wired Coslet upstairs and Wyche on the Bengals' sideline. During a fourth-quarter, game-clinching drive, Coslet checked his chart, then announced, "Regular in the game. . . . Drift left, Z swing." Wyche repeated the play call verbatim to Esiason, who took the snap, rolled left, then threw to Tim McGee, his Z receiver, in the end zone. When Esiason was roughed up after the pass, Wyche complained to the nearest official, "Hey, our quarterback was clubbed in the face and the neck right there. . . . He's gonna live, but that is a penalty." This NFL Films moment was TV sports magic!

But with each Bengals victory came new complaints about Wyche's "No-Huddle Offense." Opponents argued that it gave Cincinnati an unfair advantage to substitute skill players before defenses could counter. Nobody made the case more forcibly than Buffalo Bills head coach Marv Levy, Cincinnati's eventual opponent in the AFC Championship. Levy threatened to have his defenders fake injuries to slow down the game. Eventually, the NFL caved. Two hours before kickoff, the league office notified Wyche that the Bengals would be penalized 15 yards every time they operated the "No-Huddle Offense." So, Cincy huddled up, then ran Buffalo off the field, 21–10, advancing to Super Bowl XXIII (23).

There, Wyche would face Walsh, Montana, and the San Francisco 49ers. With time running out, Wyche's former student drove the 49ers 91 yards in 11 plays, hitting John Taylor with a game-winning 10-yard touchdown pass. Wyche looked at the game clock one final time before lowering his head in defeat. As usual, he was wearing a microphone for NFL Films: "Thirty-four seconds away from it." So close, so very, very close. At game's end, Wyche met his former boss Walsh at midfield. They hugged and then walked off the field arm in arm.

Walsh: "Love ya!"

Wyche: "I love you. . . . I am happy for you like I've never been. Congratulations, it's yours, you deserve it."

Then, a long pause before Wyche concluded, "That was a good game, huh?" Imagine this kind of exchange today with any number of win-at-all-costs NFL head coaches.

Wyche recorded just one more winning season in Cincinnati before enduring four losing seasons in Tampa Bay. As for Wyche's "No-Huddle Offense," Levy adapted it for quarterback Jim Kelly. In Buffalo, it became known as the "K-Gun," and the Bills rode it to four consecutive Super Bowl appearances. As Wyche once observed, "At the time, everybody was saying this won't work, this is crazy . . . but now everybody's doing it!" Wicky Wacky Wyche was way ahead of his time!

X-Factors
(Game-Changing Impact Players)

Dick Butkus *(born 1942)*

Middle Linebacker

- Chicago Bears (1965–73)

Dick Butkus was Steve Sabol's absolute favorite NFL player of all time. When NFL Films sent out ballots to NFL pundits and football writers to determine *The Top 100: NFL's Greatest Players*, Steve remarked, "If Butkus doesn't finish in the top ten, I'm going to put him there." No need—Butkus finished at number ten. Lawrence Taylor and Reggie White were the only two defensive players who tallied more votes.

A classic NFL Films shot that begins on a close-up of Butkus's wrapped, blood-stained hands, then slowly widens to reveal Butkus sitting on the Bears' bench ranked among Steve's all-time favorite images. I had always assumed that Sabol shot it. Turns out, a freelancer captured the moment. The shot speaks volumes about Butkus's career.

The Chicago Bears selected Butkus with the third overall pick in the 1965 NFL Draft. They used the fourth overall pick on Gale Sayers—two future Hall of Famers with back-to-back choices in a single draft. But Chicago's 9–5 finish in 1965 was the best season these Bears could muster during Butkus's and Sayers's combined tenures. Only twice did the Bears win more games than they lost. Needless to say, Butkus never played in an NFL championship.

A bad knee limited his playing time to just nine seasons. But while he was active, *nobody* made more of an impact. As Deacon Jones once remarked, "He was a well-conditioned animal, and every time he hit you, he tried to put you in the cemetery, not the hospital."

Or, as Butkus once observed, "I wouldn't ever go out to hurt anybody deliberately, unless it was important—like a league game or something."

So, when I traveled to Florida around 1978 or 1979 to produce an interview with Butkus, I was glad NBC's Mike Adamle was part of the crew. Adamle had played for the Bears, lived in Chicago, and was familiar to Butkus. The Hall of Fame linebacker agreed to meet us on a Saturday morning at his rural Florida home. But when we arrived at the given address at the appointed hour, then studied the average-looking, isolated residence to which we'd been directed, we all agreed that this could not be Butkus's retirement home. Eventually, I started knocking on the glass screen door—lightly at first, then with all the gusto I could muster. The place seemed deserted, and I felt somewhat relieved.

Suddenly, Butkus appeared. All signs indicated that I'd roused him from a sound sleep. I'd forgotten how imposing and intimidating he was, at six feet three inches and 245 pounds. He unlocked the screen door and sized us up. Then, in his deep, gravelly voice, he said bluntly, "We're gonna have to do this outside. . . . I'll be out in a few minutes." We settled around a picnic table located nearby, where Adamle did his work. I don't remember a moment of content from that interview.

Several years later, in the early 1980s, I met Butkus at a private home in Chicago for a "Legends of the Game" piece. This time, CBS's Irv Cross traveled with me.

I recall Butkus saying, "I looked up to Ray Nitschke [the Packers' Hall of Fame middle linebacker] and later Bill George [the Bears' Hall of Fame middle linebacker and Butkus's immediate predecessor]." Even back then, Butkus lambasted contemporary players who "do these celebratory dance things after making a play. . . . For Christ's sake, that's your job."

Finally, he touched on his famous "little yellow streak down their back" theme, a notion he still mentions when doing interviews today. I immediately remembered a game between the Bears and my Steelers I had watched while growing up in Pittsburgh. I remembered a particular Pittsburgh running back whom Butkus "intimidated from the get-go," in his own words. "And when you do that, you *got* him."

After the interview, I asked Butkus about that game and named the running back. Butkus smiled broadly, then replied, "You know your football, don't you?" Although I was proud that I remembered the game, I still felt sorry for the Steelers runner whom Butkus mauled that day nearly two decades earlier, and I was amazed at how vivid my recollections still were after all those years—Butkus's, too!

Those memories are why Steve Sabol and everybody else who ever watched Dick Butkus play held him in such high regard: his "X-Factor" impact on the game.

David "Deacon" Jones *(1938–2013)*

Defensive End

- Los Angeles Rams (1961-71) · San Diego Chargers (1972-73)
- Washington Commanders (1974)

In my story about NFL Films original narrator John Facenda (see Q-Ratings), I detail an indelible experience regarding a film I watched as a high school freshman while attending my first football camp in August 1966. Facenda's voice made Rams defensive end David "Deacon" Jones appear larger than life. My personal encounters confirmed the validity of that teenaged impression.

Jones was an innovator. A fourteenth-round selection of the Los Angeles Rams in the 1961 NFL Draft, he noticed that the LA telephone directory listed dozens of David and D. Joneses. So, he added the nickname "Deacon" to his own handle to distinguish himself from anonymous others. After watching Muhammad Ali set up his full arsenal with his left jab, Jones developed his own version of Ali's punch: the "head slap," a quick off-the-ball technique that he explained in amusing detail in his famous NFL Films interview, arguably the single-most-entertaining and enlightening conversation with a pro football player in my company's long and storied history: "The head slap was to do two purposes. . . . One was to give myself an initial head start on the pass rush . . . in other words, an extra step. Because anytime you go upside a man's head—or a woman—they have a tendency to blink they eyes . . . and that was all I needed."

Yes, he actually said that on camera. After Jones retired, the NFL outlawed the head slap. There's little the league can do about suggesting random misogyny.

Regarding his skill set, Jones confided, "I would safely say at this time that I was the fastest [pass rusher] in the history of the game. My lateral movement along with my initial speed was fantastic. . . . I could outrun daylight."

How can you not admire his word economy and candor? Because Jones talked the talk and walked the walk. His 173.5 career sacks would rank third of all time, except the NFL didn't recognize sacks as an official statistic until 1982, more than a decade *after* his pass-rush assaults helped popularize the term: "Sacking a quarterback is just like . . . you devastate a city or you cream a multitude of people. It's just like . . . you put all the offensive players in one big bag, and I just take a baseball bat and beat on the bag."

I got to work around Deacon at charity events and NFL celebrity golf tournaments. People gravitated toward the guy just to hear what might come out of his mouth. Even when surrounded by other Hall of Famers, Jones stood out. At six feet five and 275 pounds, he often was the largest player on the premises. He *always* brought the biggest personality. And he absolutely *never* went "upside a woman's head."

Hall of Fame Rams coach George Allen called Jones "the greatest defensive end of modern football." Allen's daughter Jennifer named her second son Deacon. Like most players and coaches who are "X-Factors," Jones was elected to the Pro Football Hall of Fame in his first year of eligibility, 1980. NFL Films's *The Top 100: NFL's Greatest Players* ranked him fifteenth of all time.

As he so eloquently stated in that interview, "I wasn't gonna be a lawyer. I wasn't gonna be a doctor. I wasn't gonna be president of the United States. I was destined, just like Ray Charles was born to sing the blues . . . Deacon was born to rush the quarterback."

Indeed, David "Deacon" Jones certainly did make a name for himself.

Ronnie Lott (*born 1959*)

Defensive Back

- San Francisco 49ers (1981–90)
- Los Angeles Raiders (1991–92)
- New York Jets (1993–94)

Back around 1989, a fellow producer and I collaborated on a home video project called *NFL Kids: A Field of Dreams* that became known simply as *The Kids Show*. Of the four active players who participated (Michael Irvin, Boomer Esiason, Christian Okoye, and Ronnie Lott) alongside four child actors, only one had chosen, after his left pinkie finger was crushed in a tackle, to have the finger amputated so he could continue his pro football career without pain or interruption. That took conviction and courage, the essence of "mind over matter."

But even before sacrificing his pinkie to expedite his NFL career, Lott was just plain scary: a brainy defensive back who could blast ball carriers. A student of the game with a potent knockout punch. A man of "mind" and "matter." I told him so in NFL Films's old green room as we prepped to shoot his portion of *The Kids Show*, a fantasized dream world through which to teach kids "All-Pro Lessons in Life"—or so the video jacket ultimately would say.

He laughed at my assessment of him and wanted to know more. So, I described my impression of being in his presence before games, saying, "You looked so damned focused inside that helmet." He took that as a compliment.

"I *was*! I *am*," Lott said. He told me that mental preparation was key and that distractions could ruin outcomes. Such distractions included NFL Films cameramen looking for pregame sound bites, but he did promise to be friendlier and more accessible in the future—and he kept that promise.

As a player, Lott epitomized "mind over matter." In Super Bowl XXIII (23), Bengals fullback Ickey Woods was finding his stride against San Francisco's defense. On Woods's fifth carry of the contest, Lott recognized the play design, accelerated to the point of attack, then launched his left shoulder into Woods, propelling him backward. Sound from the impact was audible on both sidelines as well as on the game telecast. No, that moment didn't clinch a 49ers' victory, but it did notify the Bengals that Woods would not be controlling the game's tempo by running the ball.

Over a fourteen-year career, Lott lowered the boom on any number of NFL pass catchers and runners. His style reminded me of a line from "'Twas the Night before Christmas": "He spoke not a word but went straight to his work." Lott's 63 career interceptions rank eighth of all time. His big hits inspired fear—or at least wariness among pass catchers. In Lott's ten seasons with the 49ers, the team won eight division titles and four Super Bowls. His role in that run of success was substantial. Whether he lined up at cornerback (1981–84) or safety (1985–94), Lott made an impact.

Perhaps not coincidentally, Lott's autobiography is titled *Total Impact*. The Lott IMPACT Trophy is awarded annually to college football's Defensive IMPACT Player of the Year (where IMPACT is an acronym for Integrity, Maturity, Performance, Academics, Community, and Tenacity). And Lott's impact extended beyond football. My son, Daniel, watched the *NFL Kids: A Field of Dreams* VHS so many times, he could quote the "All-Pro Lessons in Life" that Lott delivered to his child actor counterpart. Dan's favorite: "Remember, Tommy, the *mind* is what really matters."

Lott: a first-ballot Hall of Famer, the eleventh-best player of all time according to NFL Films's *The Top 100: NFL's Greatest Players*, and the ultimate "X-Factor" defensive back.

Randy Moss *(born 1977)*

Wide Receiver

- Minnesota Vikings (1998-2004, 2010) · Oakland Raiders (2005-06)
- New England Patriots (2007-10) · Tennessee Titans (2010)
- San Francisco 49ers (2012)

When Randy Moss was still available after twenty first-round selections in the 1998 NFL Draft, the Minnesota Vikings couldn't get to the podium quickly enough. He did not disappoint.

Randy's 17 touchdown receptions in one season (1998) remain an NFL rookie record. His ability to outjump double coverage and make acrobatic catches resulted in a ripple effect. When defenses schemed to stop Moss, wide receivers Cris Carter and Jake Reed and tight end Andrew Glover often each had only one defender to beat, which they did 162 times that season. Minnesota's big pass-play potential meant fewer defenders around the line of scrimmage and fewer obstacles for running backs Robert Smith and Leroy Hoard. Together, they combined for more than 1,500 rushing yards. Finally, two years after sitting out a season to supervise his granite business, veteran quarterback Randall Cunningham returned and put up his best career passing numbers.

The 1998 Vikings scored a then-single-season NFL record 556 points while winning fifteen regular season games. They missed a perfect season by 3 points, a 27–24 Week 9 loss in Tampa Bay. A missed 37-yard field goal against Atlanta in the NFC Championship Game cost them a berth in Super Bowl XXXIII (33), in which they likely would have been favored to beat John Elway and the Denver Broncos.

Would all these things have happened if Moss had not become a Minnesota Viking? Absolutely *not*.

NFL Films befriended Moss early on. I made a point of planting myself in Moss's face during pregame warm-ups every chance I got. Eventually, he started saying things. During an extremely difficult, walking-backward, hand-held tracking shot in the early 2000s, I caught up with Moss as he was heading toward the Vikings' tunnel. Immediately, he started in with "Hey, NFL Films, another big day here in the Metrodome. . . ." I kept walking, and he kept talking, until I started running out of room and had to stop and pan as he walked away. Moss finished his soliloquy right on cue. The whole thing looked staged. After seeing it the next day, Steve Sabol asked me whether Moss actually knew who I was—or what NFL Films did. "Beats me, Steve," I replied.

I did know that Moss had a dark side. His reputation preceded him to the NFL: a misdemeanor battery charge in high school, a probation violation that led to a sixty-day jail sentence, some minor recreational drug use, a driving incident involving a traffic control officer. He could be nasty. When things weren't going well on game day, he didn't just ignore my camera—he'd tell me where to shove it. But I knew my on-field rights and refused to be deterred, if for no other reason than Moss was just *so damned good* at football. His deeds needed to be documented.

He rolled up six consecutive 1,000-yard receiving seasons to start his Hall of Fame career. Five games into 2004, he'd already scored eight touchdowns and was on his way to his best season ever. Then, he pulled a hamstring against the New Orleans Saints. By season's end, he'd scored 13 touchdowns and then 2 more against Green Bay in the playoffs. After the second, he stepped behind the goal post and pretended to "moon" Packers fans in their end-zone seats. Joe Buck called it "a disgusting act." That off-season, the Vikings traded Moss to the Oakland Raiders. He suffered there through two painful seasons. Then, in 2007, New England acquired Moss to catch passes for Tom Brady. It cost the Patriots a fourth-round draft pick—a steal!

Together, Brady and Moss made magic. New England won all sixteen regular-season games. In their final win at the Meadowlands, on December 23, 2007, Brady launched a 65-yard TD pass to Moss to take a third-quarter lead they would not relinquish. For Brady, it was his fiftieth touchdown toss of the year, a new NFL single-season record. For Moss, it was his twenty-third touchdown reception of the season, also a new NFL record. The Patriots' 589 offensive points bested the Vikings' NFL single-season mark of 556. It was Moss's rookie year all over again—only this time, he would get to play in a Super Bowl.

There, he caught the go-ahead touchdown with 2:42 left in the game. But an unknown receiver named David Tyree made a circus catch of an Eli Manning desperation toss, and the New York Giants rallied to win Super Bowl XLII (42), 17–14. Four years later, in Super Bowl XLVI (46), Manning did it again, beating the Pats, 21–17. By then, Moss was a Tennessee Titan.

I love Moss as an analyst. I love watching defensive players get "Mossed," a term that actually dates to his early years with the Vikings. I've forgiven him for all his "bad days." Fact is, one day, while walking through the Vikings' locker room with a team executive, I was told to help myself to anything I wanted from any of the lockers (personal items excluded). I pulled one of Randy's game jerseys off a hook and tucked it in my briefcase. I wear it when the Eagles play the Vikings to infuriate my friends. And why not? When all was said and done, Moss retired fourth of all time in total receiving yards and touchdowns scored. He played football as well as any wide receiver ever. He made good quarterbacks better—even Brady.

That's what "X-Factor" players do. Like them or not, we *must* acknowledge their impact.

Walter Payton *(1954–99)*

Running Back

- Chicago Bears (1975-87)

Only two running backs finished among the elite in *The Top 100: NFL's Greatest Players*. Jim Brown tallied the second-most votes of all time. And the inimitable Walter Payton came in fifth.

Why "inimitable"? Because no running back Payton's size ever played the way he did for so long or so successfully. At just five feet ten inches tall and barely 200 pounds, he almost never ran out of bounds to avoid a tackler. By his own admission, Payton preferred "to be the hitter rather than the hit-ee." He added, "If I'm gonna get hit, why let the guy who's going to hit me . . . get the best shot? I explode into the guy who's trying to tackle me." The NFL Films library is full of such examples. Payton's collisions together with his stiff arm, a low center of gravity, and his signature stutter step made him very tough to slow down—let alone bring to the ground.

His third NFL season, in 1977, ranked as his individual best. But when CBS Sports requested that Payton do an interview with Phyllis George for *The NFL Today*, he said, "Why don't you interview my offensive linemen? They do most of the work." So, we did an elaborate two-camera shoot that I directed with Phyllis and all five starting linemen. Near the end, Payton snuck into the room and listened. His gentle voice and soft-spoken manner belied the ferocity of his running style. I suddenly understood why associates called him "Sweetness."

Over the years, I captured some famous images of Payton. The slow zoom into his half sunlit face during the national anthem that's often used as an establishing shot came from my camera in 1984. So did his leaping touchdown against the Minnesota Vikings sometime in the late 1970s. Magnavox's advertising agency later used it in one of the TV maker's *own* commercials.

Sadly, nobody ever shot a Payton touchdown in a Super Bowl—because he never scored one. In Super Bowl XX (20), Payton watched three Bears teammates cross the goal line before him, including rookie defensive tackle William "Refrigerator" Perry. By the time Chicago head coach Mike Ditka got around to calling Payton's number, the Patriots had little left to play for other than to deny him his Super Bowl moment. Ditka later listed that small gap in Payton's many career achievements as one of the "biggest regrets" of his coaching career.

By 1987, Payton's thirteenth and final season, Sweetness was splitting time with his successor, second-year running back Neal Anderson. In his final NFL game, a divisional playoff loss to Washington, Payton handled the ball 21 times for 105 total yards. At game's end, I finally located him sitting alone on the Bears' bench. I dropped to my knees, set and checked my focus, then did a slow zoom into a close-up. Almost on cue, he buried his facemask in his hands and started to weep. So did I. Steve Sabol called it my "best shot ever!"

In 1995, I was standing in the top-floor meeting room of the Chicago Airport Marriott, waiting to interview NFL commissioner Paul Tagliabue. I had no idea Payton would be joining us. As usual, he entered the space surreptitiously and waited his turn to talk.

On this occasion, Sweetness was there representing a delegation of investors trying to secure an NFL franchise for St. Louis. One of Payton's ambitions after his playing career was to become the first minority owner of an NFL team. He sat with Tags for a good half hour and pled his case. Ultimately, his efforts would fail. I engaged him briefly before he left and mentioned my shot of his career-ending realization moment on the bench.

"I remember it like it was yesterday," he told me. "Thanks for being there." I couldn't possibly have known that I would never see the forty-one-year-old Hall of Famer alive again.

Four years later, the inimitable Walter Payton succumbed to a rare liver disease that resulted in cholangiocarcinoma (bile-duct cancer). He died on November 1, 1999, at age forty-five. Only after his death did I learn of the numerous and varying charitable causes Payton had quietly supported during his lifetime and beyond, most notably, the Walter and Connie Payton Foundation, which helps the needy children of Chicago—and of the foundation's ongoing efforts to raise awareness regarding the need for organ donations. No wonder folks called him "Sweetness."

His legacy lives on with the Walter Payton Man of the Year Award, presented annually to an NFL player for excellence on and off the field. Payton won it in 1977. The NFL renamed it to honor him posthumously. Since 2017, previous winners of the award still active in the NFL are authorized to wear a "Man of the Year" patch on their playing jerseys for life. Like Payton, we celebrate their positive impact on pro football in particular—and humanity as a whole.

Jerry Rice *(born 1962)*

Wide Receiver

- San Francisco 49ers (1985-2000)
- Oakland Raiders (2001-04)
- Seattle Seahawks (2004)

When NFL Films sent out its ballots to determine *The Top 100: NFL's Greatest Players*, I would have bet my inheritance that Cleveland great Jim Brown would garner the most votes. Or Joe Montana. Or Walter Payton. Guess what, football fans? Jerry Rice won it all, fair and square.

I know this because I've seen the final tallies. Voters rated each player on a scale of 0–10. Nobody received a score of 10 from every selector, including Rice, who fell just one vote shy. During an interview in Dallas, former Giants great and CBS commentator Pat Summerall admitted to me that he was the guy who kept Rice from getting all 10s, saying simply, "Nobody's perfect." I wish a few other folks felt the same.

Rice perplexed me. Early in his career, he did an interview with NFL Films and discussed doing household chores—I'm talking laundry and vacuuming here. He also spoke fondly of his father, a mason in Crawford, Mississippi, for whom Rice carried mortar and bricks when his dad needed an extra pair of hands. He seemed charming and humble.

Flash forward a decade. A former NFL Films producer and executive named Jim Jorden, whose college football career statistics at Illinois's Wheaton College actually rivaled Rice's numbers at Mississippi Valley State University—albeit in different contexts—befriended Rice. Rice respected Jorden's small college background, and Jorden delighted in having access to the Super Bowl champion pass catcher . . . until one day, after Jim had flown across the country to interview him. Rice became so agitated at Jim's first question that he walked out of the interview. Gone. Not coming back. See you later. Nice guy, huh?

But Jorden persevered. Several years later, he convinced Rice to allow NFL Films to shoot him running up "the Hill," a 2.5-mile trail run in Edgewood County Park and Natural Preserve in San Mateo County, California. I shot one of the second cameras that day while Jim directed. After Rice arrived at the top of the trail, Jorden convinced him to do dozens of additional B-roll running shots for editing purposes. Incredibly, Rice never flinched. He even did some weight-lifting for our benefit. He could not have been more accommodating and cooperative.

Several years later, Rice (now an Oakland Raider) agreed to wear a wireless microphone during Super Bowl XXXVII (37). Tampa Bay jumped out to a 20–3 halftime lead. When the Raiders took the field for the second half, our audio people could not detect Rice's audio signal—with good reason. His wireless package was floating in a Raiders' locker-room toilet. Rice eventually scored a 48-yard touchdown in a 48–21 Oakland defeat.

Again, perplexing!

Rice's body of work speaks for itself. Over nineteen seasons, he caught more passes for more yardage than anybody else in history—by wide margins. He's the only person to score more than 200 career touchdowns (208). He led the league in receiving yards and scoring catches six times, was named the NFL Offensive Player of the Year twice (1987–88), and earned MVP honors in Super Bowl XXIII (23). As a pass catcher, he had no equal. He was pure "X-Factor."

I'm glad that when all the ballots were counted, Rice wasn't perfect. That said, no wide receiver played the professional game longer and more productively, and nobody worked harder to be successful. So, if he's *not* the greatest pro player of all time, then who is?

Lawrence Taylor (aka L. T.) *(born 1959)*

Outside Linebacker

- New York Giants (1981-93)

Every year, NFL teams draft collegiate edge rushers, hoping to land "the next Lawrence Taylor."

On November 11, 1990, Kansas City's Derrick Thomas recorded 7 sacks in a single game versus Seattle, still an NFL record. In 2002, Derrick Brooks won the Defensive Player of the Year Award. Denver's Von Miller earned MVP honors in Super Bowl 50. His Broncos teammate and longtime Dallas Cowboy DeMarcus Ware retired with 138.5 sacks, ninth on the all-time list.

But the next Lawrence Taylor has yet to arrive.

In 1981, the New York Giants used the second overall selection in the NFL Draft on Taylor (aka L. T.), a pass-rushing phenom from the University of North Carolina. Giants general manager and Hall of Fame executive George Young said confidently, "Taylor is the best college linebacker I've ever seen. . . . He's bigger and stronger than Butkus. . . . On the blitz, he's devastating."

After his early exposure to Taylor, Giants Hall of Fame head coach Bill Parcells added, "I like L. T. . . . That motherf***er's got a mean streak." In that first season, 1981, Taylor unofficially recorded 9.5 sacks, upset offensive game plans with overpowering blitzes, and earned recognition as the NFL Defensive Player of the Year, the first rookie ever to be so honored.

The next season, 1982, despite New York's 6–10, fourth-place divisional finish, Taylor won the award again. It was unprecedented. At some point during these formative years, NFL Films wired him for a preseason game at the Meadowlands. Prior to an early defensive series, Taylor stalked the sideline as he bellowed the sound bite that's become his calling-card moment:

"Hey, baby, let's go out there like a bunch of crazed dogs and have some fun!"

Remember the movie *This Is Spinal Tap*? The scene in which Rob Reiner is questioning Christopher Guest's character about the band's amplifiers? And Guest insists that Spinal Tap's amplifiers go beyond 10 to 11? Taylor's amp went to *12*. He had several additional gears that most players can't access and a game speed that most players never reach. He played like a "crazed dog," spawning fear and trampling whoever stood in his path. And he thoroughly enjoyed the process.

In 1986, Taylor's 20.5 sacks led the NFL and earned him his third Defensive Player of the Year Award as well as NFL MVP honors, the only linebacker ever to capture both of these ultimate individual accolades. In the divisional round of the playoffs, Taylor intercepted a pass from Hall of Fame quarterback Joe Montana and returned it for a touchdown.

In Super Bowl XXI (21), with the outcome still in doubt, Taylor stopped Hall of Fame quarterback John Elway short of the end zone with a crucial open-field tackle. Denver lost all its momentum, and the Giants rolled to a 39–20 victory, their first Super Bowl championship and the team's first NFL title in three decades.

Four years later, in the NFC Championship Game in San Francisco, Taylor fell on a 49ers fumble late in the fourth quarter, setting up a late Giants possession that resulted in Chris Bahr's game-winning field goal. In Super Bowl XXV (25), Buffalos kicker Scott Norwood sent his potential game winner wide right, as Taylor's Giants won their second Super Bowl in five seasons, 20–19, over the Buffalo Bills.

Soon thereafter, Giants head coach Parcells retired. Taylor pushed on, but his amp no longer went to 12. He suffered a torn Achilles tendon in 1992, then endured a devastating 44–3 defeat at the hands of the San Francisco 49ers in the 1993 playoffs. At game's end, TV cameras captured Taylor sobbing on the Giants' bench. During a postgame press conference, the greatest defensive player in NFL history announced, "I think it's time for me to retire."

"The greatest?" you ask. Consider these legacies. Parcells once told NFL Films, "He changed the way the game was played on offense. They had to do something different. Joe Gibbs started to use the one back offense to deal with [pass blocking] Lawrence Taylor."

After Taylor's arrival, more teams converted to three-man defensive fronts. Coaches and general managers reasoned that it would be easier to find *four* good edge rushers if one of them was smaller in stature than four larger, less mobile defensive ends and tackles. L. T. served as the prototype of this new hybrid. Certainly newer, more refined models will be forthcoming—right?

So, NFL scouts and player personnel have focused their efforts on finding "the next Lawrence Taylor": the third-highest vote getter in *The Top 100: NFL's Greatest Players*. An explosive edge rusher with game-changing impact, Taylor was defensive football's ultimate "X-Factor."

The search continues.

Mike Webster *(1952–2002)*

Center

- Pittsburgh Steelers (1974–88) · Kansas City Chiefs (1989–90)

Many pro football watchers rank Mike Webster as the greatest offensive center in NFL history. With all due respect to Oakland's Jim Otto, I concur.

Webster took over as the starter for Ray Mansfield in 1976, then anchored the Steelers' offensive front for the next 150 consecutive games. In the 1979 Pittsburgh Steelers highlight film, I described Webster and his colleagues as "an offensive line whose short-sleeved jerseys leave nothing to the imagination." These guys were unusually muscular. One winter day in 1981, I learned why.

The 1980 Steelers finished 9–7 and missed the playoffs for the first time since 1972. I needed some positives for that year's highlight film, and I'd heard that the Steelers' offensive linemen worked out as a group in the basement of a popular bar-restaurant south of the city: the Red Bull Inn, located in McMurray, Pennsylvania. I asked the team's public relations people about it. They approved my request to shoot there for the 1980 Steelers' highlights.

The day I took a crew there, Webster was one of five Steelers offensive linemen working out. Webster and his teammates knew that we were there and offered no objections. Their collective efforts made for an intriguing section in the highlight film.

Ultimately, one of the players present, offensive guard Steve Courson, later detailed his *own* use of steroids. In his 1991 book, *False Glory: Steelers and Steroids: The Steve Courson Story*, Courson confesses that he used steroids to build muscle mass while playing with the Pittsburgh Steelers. When Courson developed a heart condition requiring a transplant, doctors blamed his illness on steroid use. In a tragic irony, he died when a tree he was chopping down fell on him as he tried to protect his dog. His black Labrador was discovered alive and well beneath Courson's crushed body.

Webster's untimely demise at age fifty was far more complicated. After his retirement, "Iron Mike" was suddenly brittle. He suffered from acute muscular pain and body aches. He developed amnesia, then dementia, worsened by full-scale depression. He slept in his pickup truck or in train stations. The Rooney family and former teammates paid Webster's family's bills and offered him temporary lodging, but he routinely fell off the face of the earth for weeks at a time.

When he died of a heart attack, his body was cremated, but not before a Pittsburgh doctor named Bennet Omalu studied slides of Webster's brain tissue and then diagnosed him with chronic traumatic encephalopathy (CTE), the first confirmed case of the disease in a former player. Webster's symptoms resembled those of Alzheimer's disease and resulted in the kind of severely reduced cognitive function that heretofore had been observed mainly in boxers described as "punch-drunk."

Junior Seau's much-publicized death by suicide underscored the need for more concerted efforts. After thousands of hours of investigation, testimony, depositions, claims, litigation, attacks, and counterattacks, league owners finally introduced concussion protocols. The NFL settled its CTE lawsuit with 4,500 former players to the tune of $765 million.

So, what do steroids have to do with CTE or the premature demise of NFL players? Nobody truly knows the whole story. They certainly make for increased muscle mass and a clear competitive advantage as opposed to long-term well-being. In Courson's case, his heart deteriorated, not his mental faculties. And, ultimately, he was standing in the wrong place at the wrong time.

As for "Iron" Mike Webster, he denied ever using anabolic steroids. So, if those sculpted biceps came naturally, they allowed him to butt heads with larger nose tackles and defensive linemen for seventeen Hall of Fame seasons. They helped him become the greatest center of all time.

The 2015 film *Concussion* starring Will Smith as Dr. Omalu and featuring David Morse as Webster begins with his dead body being found in his pickup truck. As a longtime fan of Webster and employee of the NFL, I found it hard to watch. I can't imagine how Webster's family and Steelers' teammates must have felt.

But Webster's premature passing advanced NFL concussion-protocol procedures and prioritized genuine player safety over old-school machismo, making things better for future generations. He helped the Steelers win Super Bowls, then gave his life for a greater cause. For this reason alone, his Hall of Fame career was not in vain, nor will his "X-Factor" impact ever be taken lightly.

Larry Wilson (1938–2020)

Safety

- St. Louis Cardinals (1960-72)

On a Sunday afternoon in November 1965, I sat down to watch my Pittsburgh Steelers take on the St. Louis Cardinals from old Busch Stadium. Our trusty Magnavox black and white was in good form that day, and my Halloween candy sat in a big bowl next to me. I was twelve years old at the time.

Just when it appeared that the lowly Steelers might record a rare road victory, Steelers quarterback Bill Nelsen threw a strike to Cardinals safety Larry Wilson. Because both of Wilson's hands were broken and he was wearing wrapped bandages on each, I expected the pass to fall incomplete. Nope—Wilson pinned the ball to his chest with his right elbow, cradled it against his ribcage, then ran it back to the Steelers' 3-yard line. On the very next play, Bill Triplett scored, and the die was cast. Later, Wilson's second interception of the day secured a 21–17 Cardinals victory.

So, when Wilson's name showed up on my "Legends of the Game" subject list for CBS Sports's *The NFL Today* (1982–83), I couldn't wait to take Irv Cross and an NFL Films crew to St. Louis. Irv and Wilson were Pro Bowl teammates in 1965. The two former All-Stars sat opposite each other on wooden bleachers for their interview. At the time, Wilson was working as the Cardinals' personnel director. He eventually was elevated to general manager.

During Irv's interview, the conversation turned to Chuck Drulis, a long-time Cardinals defensive coach and coordinator. I'd never heard his name before. Listening to Wilson extol Drulis's virtues inspired me to do some extensive film and written research. I remembered enjoying the Cardinals' aggressive, blitzing defenses of the 1960s. I appreciated the pressure schemes the team employed weekly to harass opposing passers. I was certain that no NFL team of the era blitzed more. Now, I knew why: Mr. Drulis.

What I didn't know was Drulis's role in the development of the "Safety Blitz," the now-famous pass-rush scheme that features a safety running through a gap or circling the line of scrimmage on a last-minute beeline toward a passer. I always assumed that Wilson had invented it on his own out of pure desperation. Turns out, Drulis had it on his drawing board prior to Wilson's 1960 arrival. Wilson was the guy Drulis needed to make his scheme a reality.

Film research confirmed the story. On September 17, 1961, opening day, the St. Louis Cardinals played on the road in Yankee Stadium against the New York Giants. On that day, Wilson debuted Drulis's "Safety Blitz." At the time, Drulis called the maneuver "the Wildcat." Wilson sacked Giants quarterback Charlie Conerly twice, forced a fumble, and created havoc for New York's passing game. The Cardinals upset the Giants, 21–10. In a rematch three weeks later, Wilson recorded three more sacks against the Giants. The Giants won ten games and played for the NFL Championship. Wilson went on to pro football immortality.

In thirteen seasons with the Cardinals, Wilson played on just six teams with winning records. As a scout and team executive (1973–2002), Wilson's teams posted only six winning seasons. But individually, as an All-Pro safety, Wilson excelled. In 1966, he equaled an NFL record by intercepting passes in seven consecutive games. His 52 career picks make him the Cardinals' all-time leader. All this from a guy listed at 192 pounds, but who more likely weighed in at 180 or less.

As I wrote for Irv Cross's narration, "The smartest quarterbacks in football couldn't fool him. The fastest wide receivers couldn't beat him deep. And in the end, nobody could deny this most courageous of defensive backs his rightful place in the Pro Football Hall of Fame."

Said Wilson to NFL Films, "I always felt if I contributed my best . . . we had a chance to win. That's why I played so hard out there. . . . I wanted to make sure I wasn't the problem."

Following Wilson's retirement as a player in 1972, St. Louis fans raised more than $80,000 to erect a statue of Larry alongside the statue of Cardinals baseball great Stan Musial outside Busch Stadium. Wilson declined the honor and advised fans to donate all the money to the Children's Hospital of St. Louis.

Like all my "X-Factor" players, Wilson was elected to the Pro Football Hall of Fame in his very first year of eligibility, 1978. He remains one of only four Hall of Famers *never* to appear in a postseason NFL game. The Cardinals' team website calls Wilson "the Greatest Cardinal Ever." Somehow, Wilson didn't make the NFL Films *The Top 100*, but nobody who ever played against him has ever questioned his abilities, his courage, or his accomplishments.

Thanks to Wilson's skill set and Drulis's ahead-of-its-time design,

"Safety Blitzes" occur weekly and remain a permanent part of defensive game plans and pro football vernacular. And among the dozen or so pure safeties in the Hall of Fame, none ever recorded a pair of picks while wearing casts and elastic bandages on both hands except Wilson. Now that's pure "X-Factor."

Yelberton Abraham Tittle

(aka Y. A. Tittle) *(1926–2017)*

Quarterback

- Baltimore Colts (1948-50) · San Francisco 49ers (1951-60)
- New York Giants (1961-64)

Among the many famous old black-and-white photos hanging in the Pro Football Hall of Fame, one shows an NFL quarterback kneeling in pain in Pittsburgh. The Steelers have knocked his helmet off, intercepted his pass, then returned it for a touchdown. Adding literal injury to insult, the quarterback is bleeding from a pair of abrasions on his face and forehead.

The man in the photo is Y. A. Tittle. (Because nobody I ever worked with possessed a surname beginning with Y, I chose Yelberton for this story.) Back near the arrival of the new millennium, I produced and directed weekly segments for HBO Sports's *Inside the NFL* called simply "NFL Storybooks." One week, Tittle, a Steelers defensive end, and a Pittsburgh photographer were my subjects—joined for football eternity by that one famous photograph hanging in the hall.

Tittle never quarterbacked a team to an NFL championship, but he retired from football as the NFL's all-time leader in passing yards, attempted passes, completed passes, and touchdowns. He belonged to San Francisco's "Million Dollar Backfield," the only quarterback and three running-back quartet with all four of its members in the Hall of Fame (Tittle, halfbacks Hugh McElhenny and John Henry Johnson, and fullback Joe "the Jet" Perry). On November 22, 1954, Tittle became the first professional football player to appear on the cover of *Sports Illustrated.*

But, like far too many football pioneers, Tittle chose not to work with NFL Films for much of his retirement. He answered queries by stating bluntly that he should be paid for the use of his images. No argument from me. Fortunately, he truly wanted to tell the story of his "Bloody Sunday in the Steel City." So, I took a crew to his home in Atherton, California, for an interview.

Tittle and I got along famously. At one point, I described a favorite 49ers running play from the 1950s that I had discovered while doing film research. It included a play fake followed by a "hand back" to fullback Perry. As I described it, Tittle's eyes lit up. Before I knew it, he was explaining the blocking upfront while demonstrating the necessary quarterback pivot, ball handling, and nifty play action in his California rec room. I played the role of Perry.

As for "Bloody Sunday" and the iconic photo, Tittle remembered them both vividly. In the final week of the 1963 season, the Giants beat the Steelers in a winner-take-all game to claim the NFL Eastern Division title. The September 1964 game during which the photo was taken offered Pittsburgh a chance at revenge. In the second quarter, Tittle was steamrolled by defensive end John Baker. Defensive tackle Chuck Hinton ran under the fluttering football and returned it 8 yards for a touchdown. Tittle sat battered and bleeding where he fell, his helmet off, his career over. He'd suffered a concussion and a cracked sternum. Pittsburgh won, 27–24.

"I hadn't really thought about retirement until that moment," he told me. Tittle finished the season with twice as many interceptions as touchdown passes. The Giants won just two games: "That was the end of the road, the end of my dream. A whole lifetime was over." He retired at age thirty-eight.

I recall reading the story and seeing pictures in Monday morning's *Pittsburgh Post-Gazette*, but *not* the one hanging in Canton. Not until years later did I discover it in a magazine. I always wondered why. So, I tracked down the photographer, Morris Berman, and asked whether he would do an interview for my segment.

As Berman explained, the *Pittsburgh Post-Gazette* sports editor didn't recognize what he had in the now-famous image. He'd sent Berman to the game to find "human-interest" stories. Berman had focused on the veteran quarterback. The editor selected a collage of Berman's photos showing fans and nonfootball images that told a broader story for his Monday edition. But the veteran photographer preserved his iconic photo, knowing that he'd witnessed a special moment.

"I was fascinated by the old quarterback. I had his football card," Berman told me. "So, I entered the picture in some photo competitions."

Berman was no slouch with a camera. During World War II, he sent home images of the bullet-riddled bodies of Mussolini and his mistress. Unlike today's photographers, who can scroll through their digital images without breaking stride, Berman's individual film rolls had to be processed, then printed—first to be seen, then to make the morning edition.

"I knew I'd captured a moment in sports history out there that day." He was right.

Berman's "Fallen Giant" subsequently won a National Headliner Award for sports photography. For many years, it was one of only three pictures displayed in the lobby of the National Press Photographers Association. The other two: "Raising the Flag on Iwo Jima," by Joe Rosenthal, and "The Hindenburg Disaster," by anonymous photographer. That's pretty damned good company!

The perpetrator of the deed, the man who clobbered Tittle, was Steelers defensive end John Baker. He retired from football in 1968, then returned home, where he became the first African American sheriff of Wake County, North Carolina. Guess who helped him get elected?

"He actually used that photo during his campaign," Tittle told me laughingly. "Something like . . . this is what happens to people who don't support Big John Baker."

In 1989, Tittle even held a fundraiser to bolster one of Baker's reelection campaigns. Baker wound up serving for twenty-four years. "Couldn't buy better publicity," Tittle recalled.

As for Y. A. Tittle's legacy after football, he fathered four children who in turn produced nine grandchildren and great grandchildren. He lived for ninety-one years and suffered mixed emotions every autumn.

"Fall is the saddest part of the year," he told me. "You played—you know what I mean?" I truly did.

Tittle was inducted into the Pro Football Hall of Fame in 1971. Nobody who walks into the photo gallery at the hall can walk away from Berman's award-winning photo without a thorough study. No moment says, "My playing days might be over . . . ?" more poignantly.

Jim Zorn *(born 1953)*

Quarterback

- Dallas Cowboys (1975) · Seattle Seahawks (1976–84) · Green Bay Packers (1985)
- Winnipeg Blue Bombers (1986) · Tampa Bay Buccaneers (1987)

Assistant Coach or Quarterbacks Coach

- Seattle Seahawks (1997, 2001–07) · Detroit Lions (1998–2000)
- Baltimore Ravens (2010) · Kansas City Chiefs (2011–12)

Head Coach

- Washington Commanders (2008–09) · Seattle Dragons (XFL, 2020)

Steve Largent *(born 1954)*

Wide Receiver

- Seattle Seahawks (1976–89)

In 1979, NFL Films dispatched me to Seattle to produce a *The NFL Today* segment for CBS. Jayne Kennedy was my talent. Her subjects were the Seahawks' young, dynamic pass-and-catch combination: Jim Zorn and Steve Largent. "Get Jayne involved" was CBS's advice to me. Because I'd gotten to know both young players fairly well, confidence was high.

On my cross-country flight, I developed some ambitious stand-up ideas, including one in which both players would need to do some play-acting. We shot on a Tuesday, the players' day off. Sure enough, Kennedy's beauty-pageant charm and my game plan made good things happen.

In the longer, more complicated version of the setup, Kennedy spoke to the audience about "the only way to stop these guys. . . ." While she spoke, she manhandled Largent to the ground, then blitzed and sacked Zorn to complete the play. We needed four separate setups and shots to capture it all.

In the simpler one, Kennedy stood in the foreground, saying, "The NFL is loaded with a whole lot of dynamite passing combinations." ZOOM into a two-shot of Zorn and Largent kneeling as Zorn drew a play in the dirt. "But if I were an NFL defensive back, this is *one* combination I would not want to mess with." This version is the one we used, although I liked the longer one much better.

Before the main interview, I reminded Jayne that we were all about the same age, so have fun with it. Once she started, I realized that my advice was totally unnecessary. As I expected, Zorn and Largent had fun on their own, all the time, everywhere. Jayne and I were along for the ride. A sampling:

ZORN: Steve's just kinda in his own little world. . . . He's out there. . . . Earth to Steve.

LARGENT: Jim's left-handed, and left-handed people are different . . . they're *weird*!

ZORN: He's got an ability to adjust to the ball that makes me look good.

LARGENT: Right, Jim, but you forgot to tell her about my hands.

ZORN: He's got great hands. [Everybody laughs.] Don't take that to your head, son.

Exact quotations. Look them up online.

Zorn grew up in California, Largent in Oklahoma. Both failed their initial NFL trials, with Zorn leaving Dallas and Largent departing Houston. They found each other in Seattle, an expansion team where opportunity abounded. Zorn won the starting quarterback job during a solid preseason. Largent barely made the team. Fortunately, Seahawks assistant coach Jerry Rhome had worked with Largent at the University of Tulsa; otherwise, Largent might have never played an NFL down. As things turned out, Zorn and Largent became best friends (as did their wives): road-game roommates and passengers in Zorn's vintage yellow Volkswagen Bug at all Seahawks home games. Locals often didn't recognize them without a program.

Zorn was a mobile quarterback who could scramble with the best of his era. Seattle's offensive designs allowed him to play fake his way outside containment, then either unload short on the run or pull up, plant his feet, and launch the ball deep. He was proficient at both. "His competitive desire will make him the best quarterback in the NFL," Largent once told me.

In 1981, I shot a Seahawks–Jets game at old Shea Stadium. During pregame, Zorn seemed more preoccupied and serious than normal, so I called him on it. "My wife's about to have a baby, and I'm gonna have a *game* today," he predicted boldly. Seattle won decisively, 19–3.

Largent ran precise routes and almost never dropped a pass he could touch. As the greatest receiver of all time Jerry Rice observed, "I learned how precise[ly] he [Steve] ran his routes. . . . It's amazing how he could snatch the ball out of the air. . . . I idolized him for that. . . . I still do."

By 1983, Largent was well on his way to the Hall of Fame. Zorn, sadly, was not. Right around midseason, head coach Chuck Knox replaced the struggling Zorn with Dave Krieg. Largent caught 11 touchdown passes as the Seahawks made the NFL playoffs for the first time in their eight-year history. They lost to the Raiders in the AFC Championship Game.

Zorn played four more years with four different teams before transitioning into coaching. I shot him while working the sidelines dozens of times. Never once did he chase my soundman's microphone. He exuded enthusiasm and always conducted himself with quiet confidence. Our working bond endured wherever Zorn happened to be mentoring passers.

Twice, he coached Seattle's quarterbacks (1997 and 2001–07). He helped Mike Holmgren mold Matt Hasselbeck into an All-Pro and Super Bowl participant. In 2008, he succeeded Joe Gibbs as the head coach in Washington. It was not a good fit. In 2010, John Harbaugh hired Zorn to coach the Ravens' passers. That year, Baltimore quarterback Joe Flacco posted some of his best career numbers. At season's end, for whatever reasons, Harbaugh summarily fired Zorn. Flacco went public with his dissatisfaction.

Largent retired with more catches for more yards and touchdowns than any receiver in history. As his motorcade rolled past me on its way to his 1995 Hall of Fame induction, he called me over to the car, shook my hand, and wished me well. By then, he was a member of the U.S. House of Representatives for Oklahoma's first congressional district. He served eight years in Washington, then ran for governor in his home state. A heavy favorite, his stance against cockfighting—that's right, *cockfighting*—cost him the election. Sorry, but that's Oklahoma's loss.

Zorn refuses to walk away from what he knows best. In 2020, he acted as head coach and general manager for the newest football team in his adopted city, the XFL's Seattle Dragons. Tragically, COVID-19 wiped out their 2020 season.

Most encouraging are the things I learned while watching my old company's *A Football Life* episode on Largent. Seems that the guy living "in his own little world" with those great hands (Largent) and his "left-handed, weird" quarterback (Zorn) have stayed in close contact. So have their wives. All sounds too wholesome to be true—right? The bottom line: Two young studs who cultivated opportunity in Seattle, then fortified each other's nascent careers while having fun doing it . . . still enjoy each other's company. I call that a happy ending.

Acknowledgments

Paul and Mathilda Angelo, my mother and father, preached higher education and college to me long before I knew what any of it meant. When the time came, they paid for it all in full. And they didn't object when I majored in philosophy and journalism rather than engineering. Thank you, Mom and Dad.

And a special thanks to my Aunt Ann, who believed in me even when my own parents did not. The same for my cousin Betty.

My sixth-grade teacher Mrs. Goodrich was the first person to acknowledge my writing. In junior high school, Mrs. Bull encouraged me to express myself with short stories and oratory rather than profanity. And Mrs. Shelton (Crane) learned me up good about grammar—courtesy of the forgotten art of sentence diagramming.

At Penn State, my initial college English professor was a graduate student named Gordon Park, who persuaded me to write more like a modern young man and less like Ralph Waldo Emerson. Anthony Curtis taught me the basics of inverted-pyramid newspaper writing. Bob Farson did the same with broadcast copy and writing to picture.

At Northwestern, Jack Williams eliminated the flowery BS from my stories and made me speak my truth *first* before I wrote it. Ben Baldwin tutored me in professional sportswriting standards and practices. The lessons learned from these two men still live with me.

By the time I started dumping my football stories and college radio NFL postgame show scripts on Ed and Steve Sabol at NFL Films, I'd learned some basics. After they hired me, I survived a crash course in professionalism from my first boss, John Hentz. My sincerest thanks to all three of these departed souls for tolerating my excesses, forgiving my sins—and allowing me to thrive at one of the best production companies ever created.

My gratitude to my childhood friend and neighbor Wallis Withrow for stimulating my imagination, and to La Salle University professor Dr. Jim Mancinelli, whose words "Robert, these stories have *value*!" inspired me to finish the book. To the late Rick Kolodziej, a friend and freelance photographer from Minnesota, whose candid photograph appears on the cover. To his son Rick, who gave us permission to use it. And to my good friend Chad Ostlund, who pulled the entire enterprise together.

More recently, my sincerest thanks to Temple University Press editor Ryan Mulligan, whose patience and perseverance helped me streamline a hefty pile of words, observations, and self-serving autobiographical ramblings into a readable manuscript. Without his contributions, this book wouldn't have happened.

Finally, thank you, Barb Doll, my wife and soulmate, for finally liking something I wrote. And you, Danny, my favorite and only son, for challenging me to become a better father and man.

Bob Angelo is a retired producer, director, writer, editor, and cameraman for NFL Films, where he worked from 1975 to 2018. He developed and then directed the first two seasons of NFL Films's groundbreaking training camp documentary show, *Hard Knocks*, for HBO Sports and filmed forty Super Bowls and more than 850 NFL games. He has won twenty-one Emmy Awards for his work. Visit him online at bobangelo.com.